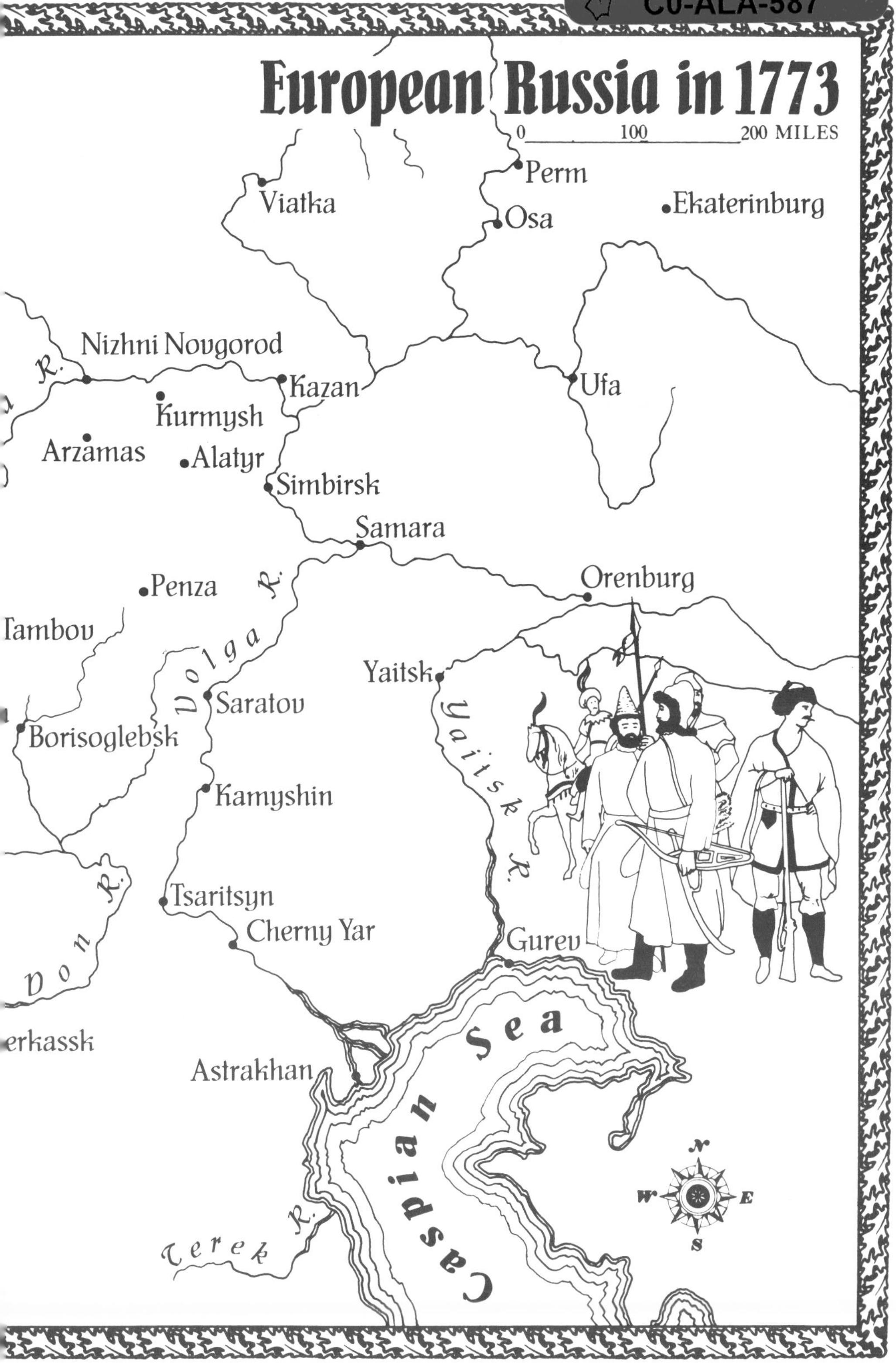
European Russia in 1773
0
100
200 MILES
Perm
Viatka
Osa
Ekaterinburg
Nizhni Novgorod
Kazan
Kurmysh
Ufa
Arzamas
Alatyr
Simbirsk
Samara
Penza
Orenburg
Tambov
Volga R.
Yaitsk
Saratov
Borisoglebsk
Yaitsk R.
Kamyshin
Don R.
Tsaritsyn
Cherny Yar
Gurev
erkassk
Caspian Sea
Astrakhan
N
W
E
S
Terek R.

THE CZAR'S GERMANS

Courtesy of the Nebraska State Historical Society, Lincoln, Nebraska.

Hattie Plum Williams. Photograph presumably taken in 1902.

The Czar's Germans

With Particular Reference to the Volga Germans

By

HATTIE PLUM WILLIAMS

Edited by

Emma S. Haynes

Phillip B. Legler

Gerda S. Walker

Published under the auspices of the
American Historical Society of Germans from Russia
615 D Street, Lincoln, Nebraska 68502

American Historical Society
Germans from Russia
615 D Street
Lincoln, Nebraska 68502

Published 1975

International Standard Book Number: 0-914222-01-5
Library of Congress Catalog Card Number: 75-32862

Printed by

World Press, Inc.
Denver, Colorado

Dedicated to

OUR PARENTS

all of whom were Volga Germans:

The Reverend and Mrs. J. C. Schwabenland,
from the colonies of Straub and Norka;

Mr. and Mrs. Jacob Legler,
from Doennhof;

Mr. and Mrs. John Stroh,
from Frank.

CONTENTS

ILLUSTRATIONS

INTRODUCTION

The American Historical Society of Germans from Russia is proud to underwrite the publication of *The Czar's Germans* by Hattie Plum Williams. The manuscript upon which this book is based was written between the years 1909 and 1915, and constitutes the first serious study of the Volga Germans in the English language.

Although Dr. Williams died in December 1963, biographical material about her is scarce. The University of Nebraska *Senior Class Book of 1902* tells that she was born in Iowa in 1878 and was the only girl in a large family of boys. She attended the University of Iowa for one year and then transferred to the University of Nebraska. During her undergraduate days, she married Thomas Frederick Arthur Williams who was seven years her senior and already practicing law in Lincoln. The *Class Book* facetiously refers to Mr. Williams as "Taffy" and mentions that he sees to it that his wife is brought to the University gate every morning.

Even as a young university student, Mrs. Williams became aware that Lincoln, Nebraska, had become a gathering center for thousands of Protestant Volga Germans who began immigrating to the United States after the special privileges which had been promised to them by Catherine the Great were withdrawn in 1871. With her keen mind and sympathetic heart, Hattie Plum Williams soon became very interested in this immigrant group. Her Master's thesis in 1909, entitled "The History of the German-Russian Colony in Lincoln," begins with these paragraphs:

> Standing at the corner of Tenth and O Streets in the city of Lincoln, Nebraska, any weekday morning between 7:30 and 8 o'clock, you may see pass by you from ten to twenty women with little black woolen shawls on their heads. Ask any citizen who they are and ninety-nine times in one hundred he will tell you they are "Russians".... As a matter of fact... his information is incorrect....
>
> These people, of whom there are about 4,000 in the city (including "beetfielders") are Germans, not Russians; they are Teutons, not Slavs; they are Lutheran and Reformed, not Greek Catholics. To be sure they and their ancestors lived in Russia for over one hundred years and they came here directly from the realm of the czar whose bona fide citizens they were – but they never spoke the Russian language, never

embraced the Greek religion, never intermarried with the Russians, and many of their children never saw a Russian until they left their native village for a new home in America.

Mrs. Williams was able to make these comments from personal experience. In the bibliography at the end of her M.A. thesis, she states that in June 1908 she took a school census of the Russian German colony in Lincoln; and that from December 1907 until May 1908, she had taught Russian German "beetfield children" in a Lincoln elementary school.

It is obvious that the writing of her Master's thesis merely stimulated Mrs. Williams' interest in the subject of Germans from Russia. She now planned a monumental study which would be divided into two sections. The first part, consisting of five chapters, was to be a complete history of the Russian Germans (a term which Mrs. Williams used from 1913 on). The second part, with seven chapters, would be a sociological study ending with a discussion of the integration of the group into American life. Unfortunately, the outbreak of World War I prevented Mrs. Williams from accomplishing her objective. In 1915 the first two chapters of her sociological study were accepted by the University of Nebraska as a dissertation for a Doctor of Philosophy degree. These chapters were published in *University Studies,* Vol. XVI, No. 3, Lincoln, Nebraska, July 1916, under the title, "A Social Study of the Russian German." The rest of her work was never completed.

From 1915 until 1945 Dr. Williams served as chairman of the sociology department of the University of Nebraska. She was a leading figure in the field of social legislation throughout the 1930's and 1940's and was often called upon to read papers on this subject. One of her lectures, "The School as an Assimilative Agent," was frequently repeated before churches and social clubs. Another paper, "The Road to Citizenship — A Study of Naturalization in a Nebraska County," appeared in Vol. XXVII of the *Political Science Quarterly.* In this article Dr. Williams described naturalization proceedings in Nebraska before World War I and mentioned how the votes of newly arrived immigrants were often used by liquor and other special interest groups for selfish ends.

Throughout her lifetime Mrs. Williams retained an avid interest in the history of the Germans from Russia. She was always the first person to come to their defense whenever misunderstandings over their background or political loyalties arose. And in her function as a teacher, she gave advice and guidance to many students who came to her for help.

Testimony of the role which Mr. and Mrs. Williams played in the lives of Volga German students is given on page seventy-three of William F. Urbach's book, *Our Parents Were Russian German* (privately published, 1963). Mr. Urbach relates that in 1910:

> Mr. and Mrs. Williams had me at their home very often, sometimes alone, but often with other students whom they chose to entertain. I never left an occasion at their home without an uplift. Their understanding of human problems, their interest in young people, the books and magazines which they made available to me for reading, and above all the very atmosphere of their pleasant, comfortable home inspired ambitions within me for educational advancement. I wanted very much to go to college, and both of them encouraged me, pointing out how it would open up opportunities for greater enjoyment of life.

In the summer of 1960 Mr. and Mrs. Urbach came back to Lincoln, Nebraska, to discuss with Mr. and Mrs. Williams the writing of the Urbach family history mentioned above. Dr. Williams took advantage of the visit to ask the Urbachs to help classify the Russian German material which she had collected and to turn it over to the archives of the Nebraska State Historical Society. She was, at the time, eighty-two years old and in poor health, but her enthusiasm and interest in Russian German history had remained undiminished. She urged the Urbachs to do their utmost to gather such things as letters, photographs, church records, visas, jewelry, trinkets, and china, which would be of value in a Russian German collection that could be placed in some appropriate historical museum.

During the ensuing years, Mrs. Williams' health continued to fail. Death came for her on December 29, 1963, and for her husband in 1970.

After the organization of the American Historical Society of Germans from Russia (AHSGR) in 1968, Mrs. Gerda Stroh Walker, genealogy chairman, was the first person to come to Lincoln and examine the manuscript material which had been given by Mr. and Mrs. Williams to the Nebraska State Historical Society. Mrs. Walker returned to Colorado wih the exciting news that the first three chapters of the unpublished *Czar's Germans* had been included in the bequest, and that other handwritten material constituted additional chapters. The bequest also included the original cards which had been used for a private census of the Volga German settlements of Lincoln, Nebraska, taken between March 15 and April 15, 1914, in which Dr. Williams was assisted by Mr. Jacob J. Stroh. The cards contain information on such subjects as: place and date of birth, date of arrival in Lincoln, and name and age of children in each family. Needless to say, such information is very important today for purposes of genealogical research.

In addition to this material, Mrs. Williams donated to the Nebraska State Historical Society her very valuable library of Russian German books. These included such extremely rare volumes as *Unsere Kolonien* by Alexander Klaus, published in Odessa, Russia, in 1887; *Volkslieder und Kinderreime aus den Wolgakolonien,* a collection of Volga German folksongs and children's rhymes, by Johannes Erbes and Peter Sinner (Saratov, 1914); two volumes on the history of the Evangelical Lutheran churches of Russia by E. H. Busch (St. Petersburg, 1862 and 1867); Friedrich Matthaei's description of the German settlements in Russia (Leipzig, 1866); and most important of all, Grigorii Pisarevskii's three volumes of archival material on the arrival and early history of foreign colonists in Russia, published between the years 1909 and 1916 in the Russian language. There are also copies of the Saratow *Volkszeitung* from March 25, 1912, to December 25, 1914. No issues of this newspaper have been preserved in the Library of Congress or in the Institute fuer Auslandsbeziehungen in Stuttgart, Germany. These may be the only copies in the western world.

In 1972 a second member of AHSGR, Mr. Phillip B. Legler, came to Lincoln on four different occasions, spending more than two months classifying and re-typing the historical section of *The Czar's Germans*. Finally, in August of the same year, the board of AHSGR appointed Mrs. Walker, Mr. Legler, and Mrs. Emma S. Haynes as a committee in charge of preparing the Williams' manuscript for publication. In the opinion of the board, this manuscript represented a major scholarly achievement.

One must always remember that in the years prior to World War I, practically nothing on the history of the Volga Germans had been written in the English language. Even such secondary sources as the histories in German by Gottlieb Beratz and Gerhard Bonwetsch did not, as yet, exist. In order to obtain material on the exodus of German colonists to the Volga, Mrs. Williams found it necessary to write to the directors of twenty-four state and city archives in Germany, asking that all available records of the 1760's be searched at her expense for information on this subject. She also corresponded with the Russian historian Grigorii Pisarevskii whose book on *Foreign Colonization in*

Russia in the 18th Century had been based upon hitherto unpublished archival information in Moscow and St. Petersburg. As a result, practically everything which she writes in the second chapter of her manuscript comes from direct primary sources. Unfortunately, the files in which Dr. Williams kept this extremely valuable correspondence have disappeared. One can only hope that they will come to light eventually.

The latter part of Chapter III deals with the Russification policies of the czars which played such an important role in causing immigration to the New World. It is interesting to note that repressive measures did not begin with the communists. Czar Nicholas I also attempted to prevent his subjects from leaving the country and introduced laws interfering with human rights. And in Chapter IV the objections that the Germans had toward assimilation into the Russian culture bear an interesting parallel with the reasons given by present-day Germans wishing to leave the Soviet Union.

Chapters II and III are being printed almost exactly as they were written except for necessary editing. However, much of Chapter I, which places the emigration of Germans to Russia within the general framework of German immigration to many countries of the world, has been re-written in abridged form by me. Chapter IV is based upon incomplete notes which had been typewritten by Mr. Legler.

In an explanatory note at the beginning of her thesis, Mrs. Williams wrote, "Some omissions of pages, given names, etc., in footnotes and in the bibliography are found because the books were used in eastern libraries and it seemed best not to have them sent to me until the final checking of references could be done." The editors have done their best to supply the missing references but in a few cases it was impossible to find the name of the company or the date of publication of a book which had been used.

This work is truly a cooperative effort of many members of the American Historical Society of Germans from Russia. Thanks should be expressed to Miss Ruth M. Amen, President, and Mr. David J. Miller, General Counsel, of AHSGR for their support of the project. Mrs. Clarence T. Olson, a patient and obliging researcher, undertook the time-consuming task of preparing the Index. We are especially grateful to Dr. Adam Giesinger for translating the French references within the text and for reading the manuscript prior to its publication. Dr. Giesinger sent important corrections, comments, and suggestions, as well as making numerous improvements in the translations from German to English. His unfailing kindness and courtesy were much appreciated.

Thanks should also be given to Mr. James E. Potter, Archivist of the Nebraska State Historical Society, for giving AHSGR permission to publish the Williams' manuscript, and to his staff, Mr. Donald Snoddy, Assistant State Archivist, and Mrs. Louise Small, Chief Librarian of the Nebraska State Historical Society, for their unfailing courtesy and help in making the Hattie Plum Williams' material available.

Here in Europe we are especially grateful to the archivist of the Hamburg City Archives for making accessible the letters of Hattie Plum Williams written in 1913 which are still being preserved there. The Institut fuer Auslandsbeziehungen and the Landsmannschaft der Deutschen aus Russland very graciously made their outstanding picture files available to us. Dr. Karl Scherer of the Heimatstelle Pfalz provided us with the painting for the dust jacket and many other archives, museums, and private individuals gave us copies of additional photographs.

Emma S. Haynes
Frankfurt, Germany
August 1, 1975

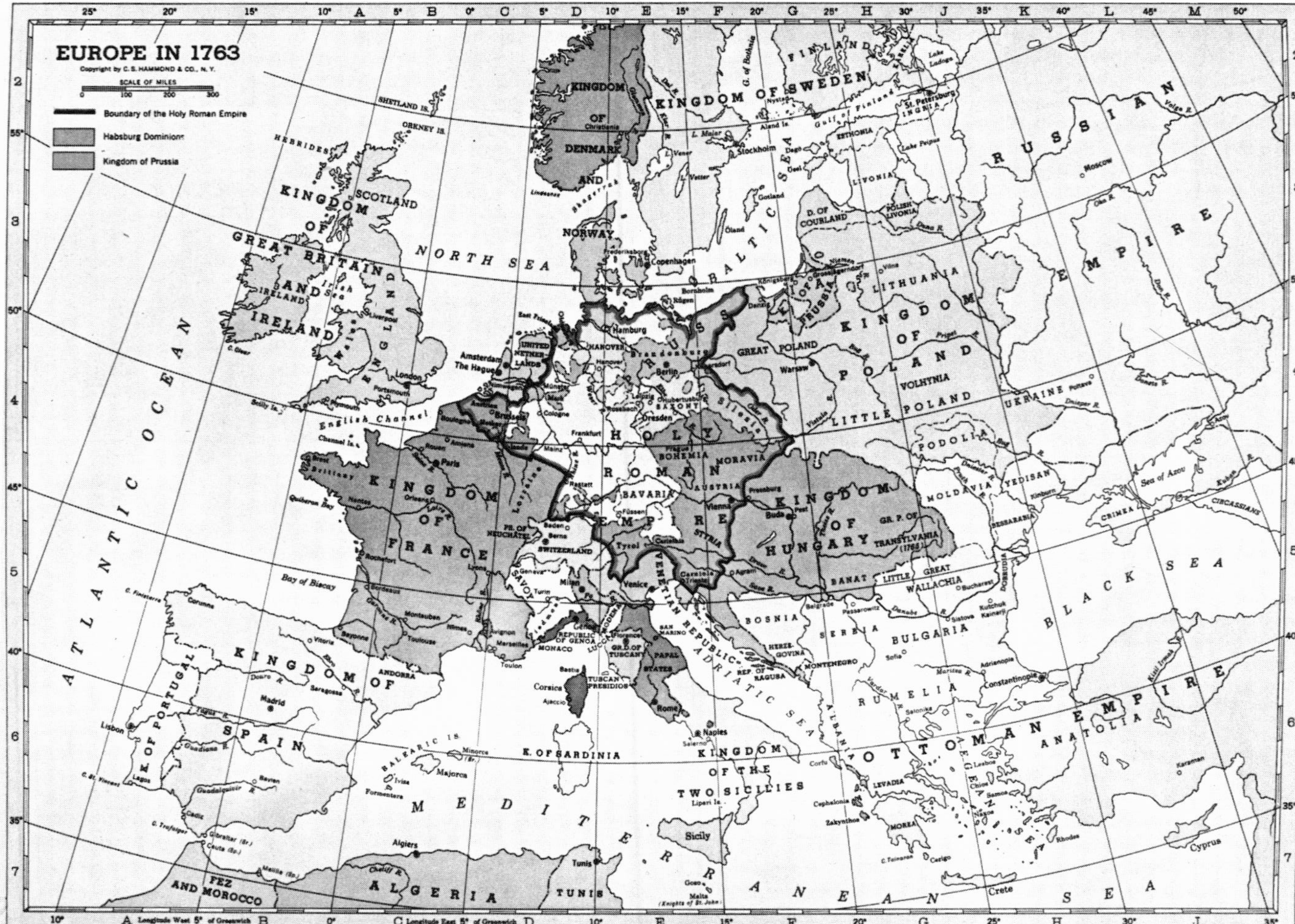
EUROPE IN 1763
Copyright by C. S. HAMMOND & CO., N. Y.
SCALE OF MILES
0 100 200 300
Boundary of the Holy Roman Empire
Habsburg Dominions
Kingdom of Prussia
KINGDOM OF GREAT BRITAIN AND IRELAND
SCOTLAND
ENGLAND
IRELAND
KINGDOM OF DENMARK AND NORWAY
KINGDOM OF SWEDEN
FINLAND
RUSSIAN EMPIRE
KINGDOM OF POLAND
LITHUANIA
GREAT POLAND
LITTLE POLAND
VOLHYNIA
PODOLIA
UKRAINE
PRUSSIA
HOLY ROMAN EMPIRE
KINGDOM OF FRANCE
KINGDOM OF HUNGARY
TRANSYLVANIA
WALLACHIA
MOLDAVIA
BOSNIA
SERBIA
BULGARIA
RUMELIA
ALBANIA
OTTOMAN EMPIRE
ANATOLIA
KINGDOM OF SPAIN
KINGDOM OF PORTUGAL
KINGDOM OF THE TWO SICILIES
K. OF SARDINIA
VENETIAN REPUBLIC
PAPAL STATES
SWITZERLAND
SAVOY
BAVARIA
BOHEMIA
MORAVIA
AUSTRIA
ALGERIA
TUNIS
FEZ AND MOROCCO
ATLANTIC OCEAN
NORTH SEA
BALTIC SEA
BLACK SEA
MEDITERRANEAN SEA
ADRIATIC SEA
AEGEAN SEA
Bay of Biscay
English Channel
Longitude West 5° of Greenwich
Longitude East 5° of Greenwich

chapter one

German Emigration In The Eighteenth Century

Today the average citizen of the United States thinks of Germany as a strong centralized power with high industrial efficiency. It is difficult for him to understand the political and economic conditions which formerly prevailed in the territory of what is now the German Empire.[1]

The Reformation (1521) had divided the German people into two irreconcilably hostile camps. A century later the country was plunged into the midst of a religious war which lasted for a generation and which, as armed conflict has so often done, bequeathed defeat to both combatants. The Treaty of Westphalia, which ended the war, left the German states nominally under the control of the emperor of the Holy Roman Empire. In reality he was shorn of his power and sovereignty was now vested in the princes of the various states. Germany thus became a confederation of the loosest sort with a state of anarchy such as the world had never before seen. For the next hundred and fifty years, her history is the separate record of 266 secular and 65

---

[1]The reader is reminded that Dr. Williams wrote these lines before 1915.
— The editors

ecclesiastical principalities.[2] Because of the widespread poverty which resulted from such disunion, German subjects were able to find relief only by wandering out into the wilderness of the world. They have done more to populate the frontiers of the earth with less advantage to their Fatherland than any other people of modern times.

When the western world was opened up to settlement, the German states contributed thousands of their children to help fill the empty land grants of the British Crown. During the second half of the 18th century, European countries, depopulated and impoverished by wars or possessed of vacant lands secured by conquest, drew other thousands under alluring promises. The German immigrants to the western world have been completely swallowed up in American life. On the other hand, the immigrants to European countries retained their German identity and to this day their "colonies" can be readily distinguished in any ethnographical survey, although all political and social connection with their respective German states were severed.

This dissertation proposes to tell the story of those 18th century Germans who immigrated eastward to the vast territories of Catherine the Great of Russia. In order to put their history within the general context of German emigration, it is necessary to recapitulate the motivating factors which caused an exodus, not only to Russia, but also to such diverse countries as the American colonies, Hungary, Spain, Denmark, and Prussia.

Causes of German Emigration

1. *Poverty Created by Devastating Wars.* The Thirty Years' War (1618-1648) had left Germany in a lamentable state. Some estimates of population put the losses as high as fifty per cent. Starvation and pestilence were everywhere. Commerce and industry were non-existent. Fields lay fallow, and towns which had once been prosperous were now charred collections of roofless houses. All restraint, moral and religious, was removed, and robbery, pillage, arson and torture were common.

Before the succeeding generation could restore normal conditions, Germany was again invaded. Louis XIV, desiring to extend his territory northeast, repeatedly attacked the Rhineland after 1674. In the Palatinate, in Baden and Wuerttemberg (before 1806, Wirtemberg), towns were burned, crops destroyed or requisitioned and peasants driven from their homes. Destruction was particularly savage in the

[2]This does not describe the full extent of the dismemberment of Germany. An additional 1400 noblemen were the sovereign rulers of their small estates. Germany thus consisted of over 1700 separate entities. Richard, *History of German Civilization,* 361. *Biedermann, Deutschland im 18. Jahrhundert,* I, 14, says that there were "almost 2000."

Courtesy of the Staatliche Kunsthalle, Karlsruhe.

Destruction of Heidelberg by the French under General Méloc in 1689. From a painting by Dietz.

year 1689 when the beautiful castle of Heidelberg and the cities of Mannheim, Worms, and Speyer were laid waste.[3] The Rhineland was to be turned into a desert so that it could not be used as a granary by the enemies of France.[4] During the War of the Spanish Succession (1701-1714), French armies were again quartered upon the Germans, and in 1707 the Palatinate suffered great destruction from French raids. To this day ruined castles and vineclad walls remind the traveler down the Rhine of the French vandalism of this period.

The most disastrous of 18th century conflicts – the Seven Years' War – was still to come. Although this was primarily a contest between Frederick the Great of Prussia and Maria Theresa of Austria for control of Silesia, all Europe soon became embroiled in the struggle. The combined armies of Prussia and England were opposed by almost the whole continent, with the majority of the German states joining in the coalition against them. Battles of the war were fought on German soil, and again, towns were burned, fields and crops destroyed and industries paralyzed. Saxony which Prussia disarmed shortly after the beginning of hostilities was heavily burdened with levies of troops and taxes during the entire period. The western provinces were the scenes of the campaign against the French, who, in 1757, made themselves masters of nearly all of North Germany west of the Elbe. At one time thirty thousand Russian troops marched through the Rhine provinces and were quartered upon the inhabitants. Various German provinces in the east, also, were overrun by the Russian armies whose Cossacks outdid the French in burning, wasting and killing everything in their path. The war ended with a final victory for Frederick the Great, but by this time conditions had become so desperate that widespread emigration resulted, not only to Russia but to many other countries of Europe.[5]

2. *The Stupid Vanity and Exactions of German Princes.* At the conclusion of the Seven Years' War, Prussia was the most devastated of all German kingdoms. Yet Prussia was the first of all German states to recuperate. It was only here that one could find a sovereign who considered himself the "servant of his people."[6] In most of the other German principalities petty rulers, puffed up with ideas of grandeur and self-importance, held to the principle that subjects ex-

---

[3]Erdmannsdoerffer, *Deutsche Geschichte. 1648-1740,* II, 11-17.

[4]Faust, *The German Element in the United States,* I, 57.

[5]Dr. Albert Pfeiffer, city archivist of Speyer, says in an abstract (1913) prepared for the writer, "Emigration played a prominent role in the 18th century in German lands. There were primarily three causes which enticed the people to seek their fortune far from their native homes. Either they fled from a land which was threatened or devastated by war, or they followed an uncontrollable desire for wandering and the enticing descriptions of strange splendors, or a too thickly settled land gave up its surplus people."

[6]Macaulay, *Life of Frederick the Great,* 116.

Courtesy of the City Archives, Stuttgart.

The Great Hunt at Bear Lake near Stuttgart in the month of October 1782 by V. Heideloff.

isted only for the good of their prince. As late as 1875 the following sentence could be found in a catechism used in the common schools of a South German principality: "Subjects should consider themselves as servants, because the prince is their master and has power over their property."[7]

Most of the minor princes regarded Louis XIV as their political ideal. Almost without exception they were vain, selfish, and extravagant. Educated at the courts of England, Italy and France, where they became accustomed to luxuries there prevailing, they did not seem to appreciate the absurdity of a small poverty-stricken state maintaining a retinue comparable to that of powerful empires and of building palaces as luxurious as those in which queens were housed.

More than one ruler filled an art gallery with famous paintings while his half-starved subjects left their homes and migrated into the wilds of America and eastern Europe. Private theatricals and the chase consumed much of the money which should have been spent in rehabilitating the destroyed lands and homes of the peasants. In *Gentleman's Magazine* (London) for 1764, we read on page 141:

> The 16th of February being the Duke of Wirtemberg's birthday, there was a grand hunting in the Duke's forests when His Highness, and the Lords of the Court, killed 304 deer, 290 foxes, 394 partridges, 141 pheasants and 27 woodcocks; in the evening the whole court appeared at the opera in their hunting dresses, and at night supp'd in high good humor.

This life of splendor and extravagance was only maintained by enormous taxes imposed upon the peasantry. Whenever money from taxes was not sufficient to support the pomp of a baroque court, subjects could be sold as soldiers to foreign powers. During the American Revolution nearly 30,000 Germans, primarily from Hesse-Kassel were brought to America to fight in the British army.[8]

The selfish attitude of the rulers toward their people, their heedlessness with regard to their subjects' welfare, and the absence of any bond of common interest between prince and people are reflected in the conduct of such rulers as Charles Philipp and Charles Theodore, the prince electors of the Palatinate. In 1720 Charles Philipp had moved his capital from Heidelberg to Mannheim. Forty years were then spent building one of the largest baroque palaces in Europe. Life

---

[7]Biedermann, *Deutschland im 18. Jahrhundert,* I, 80, footnote.

[8]von Bosse, *Das deutsche Element in den Vereinigten Staaten,* 17-18, and Faust, *The German Element in the United States,* I, 349 and 356.

in the realm of Charles Theodore (1742-1801) is thus described by the historian Bittinger:

> Bribery was open in the government; in the court avarice, extravagance and immorality . . . Karl Theodor's magnificent court, with innumerable fine rooms, stables with hundreds of horses, gardens and orangeries, was the resort of countless adventurers who were fed by scores at the monarch's table. Meanwhile every nineteenth inhabitant was a beggar; and the result of the census was concealed for it showed a progressive diminution of population."[9]

This "diminution of population" was to a great extent caused by the emigration of tens of thousands of Palatines to all corners of the world.

3. *The Lack of a Strong Central Government and of National Feeling.* The dismemberment of Germany was more pronounced in the south and west than in the north and east.[10] In the latter regions the principalities had been left by the earliest emperors large and more compact in order that they might serve as buffer states on the borders of their kingdoms. They were thereby enabled to protect themselves against the small powers which arose in their vicinity, and as time passed, to dominate over or to conquer them. These states were a unit, not alone geographically, but also religiously. Prussia in the north was the leader among the Protestant kingdoms while Bavaria in the southeast was uniformly Catholic and sympathized with Austria. It was this political unity, strengthened by its religious solidarity, which made Prussia one of the greatest states in Europe during the latter half of the eighteenth century.

In South and West Germany, on the other hand, a state of unbelievable chaos prevailed. Many independent principalities had as few as 1000 to 1500 inhabitants. These tiny enclaves were supplemented by numerous city states which had existed from remote times. The religious situation was also one of disunion. Some provinces were strongly Catholic; some strongly Protestant; others were torn with dissension between the two bodies or between the Reformed, the Lutheran and the Pietistic faiths.

Each of the princes had the sovereign right to declare war on his neighbors. Consequently the peace of the land was frequently broken by such trivial causes as the possession of a small town or of a forest, the location of a bridge, or the adjustment of tolls between provinces.

---

[9]Bittinger, *The Germans in Colonial Times,* 20.
[10]Biedermann, *Deutschland im 18. Jahrhundert,* I, 4-6.

Not even the danger of foreign invasions was able to act as a unifying force. The French kings were always able to play upon the vanity of the German princes in order to further French interests. They kept the courts of their German "cousins" swarming with their ambassadors, and received insignificant rulers at Versailles with the pomp and ceremony accorded great kings. The French rightly judged the effect of display upon the German princes; and their official retinues, gorgeously decked out, paraded the streets of German cities. What France could not gain through persuasion or threat, she did not hesitate to buy; and many a German prince, hard pressed for revenue for public or private ends, willingly exchanged his vote in the German Reichstag for subsidies furnished by the diplomats of the French government.

With such elements of disunion in both church and state, it is not strange that German citizens had no feeling of patriotism for a mother country. The author and playwright Gotthold Lessing, who did more than anyone else to create a German literary spirit, once said, "Of the love of country I have no conception; it appears to me at best a heroic weakness which I am glad to be without."[11]

4. *Religious Differences which led to Cruel Persecution.* The Treaty of Westphalia supposedly established religious toleration for members of the Catholic, Lutheran, and Reformed faiths.[12] Each ruler had the right to determine the religion of his realm and in many of the areas a state of confusion developed. A town might be transferred through inheritance or war to a ruler of the opposite faith; a Catholic archbishop might obtain territory in a predominately Protestant area; or a prince might decide to change his religion. The Rhenish Palatinate, for example, had been a Protestant stronghold since the time of Elector Frederick II (1544-1556) who had embraced the Reformed faith. In 1685 the line of Protestant princes died out and was succeeded by a collateral line of Catholic electors under whom religious persecution prevailed. During the French raids of this period, both Protestant and Catholic subjects suffered the destruction of their property, but when a peace treaty was signed in 1697, the Protestants were subjected to discrimination and efforts were made to force them to embrace the Catholic faith. [13]

Throughout the 17th and 18th centuries, established churches

---

[11]Bryce, *The Holy Roman Empire,* 401-402.

[12]Members of the pietistic sects were considered heretics and had no legal rights except in Prussia. The fact that the pietistic sects were persecuted is abundantly documented. — The editors.

[13]Erdmannsdoerffer, *Deutsche Geschichte,* II, 81-85 and 379-383; Haeusser, *Geschichte der rheinischen Pfalz,* II, 805 ff.

lapsed into a state of indifference and formalism, and a spirit of unrest, especially in the Evangelical sections of the country, became common. Sects were proclaiming the wrongfulness of war. They advocated simplicity of church ordinances and church government, and, carrying the same thought into their personal lives, opposed ornaments of dress. They repudiated the theological disputes into which the established churches had fallen and emphasized the "inner light," "feeling," and "works." Thousands of Germans fell under the sway of this pietistic movement and joined such sects as the Mennonites, Moravians, Schwenkfelders, and Dunkers. The doctrines in which they believed "separated them from the world" and made them the target for bitter persecution. Driven from one place to another, they finally despaired of ever finding peace at home and decided to seize the first opportunity to emigrate to foreign lands.

Between the years 1671 to 1677, William Penn, a member of the despised British sect of Quakers, made missionary journeys through southern Germany. In this manner he came in contact with German Mennonites who were much attracted to him because they and the Quakers held many principles in common. Consequently, when William Penn received a grant of land in the New World, he addressed a directive to his agent, Benjamin Furly in Rotterdam, inviting all persecuted sects to share his new home in Pennsylvania.[14]

The first response came from the Mennonites. Many of them had previously fled to Germany from Holland and Switzerland to escape persecution in those countries only to be subjected to renewed persecution from German princes. In 1683 thirteen families of linen weavers from Crefeld (near the border of Holland) arrived in Philadelphia on board the ship *Concord.*[15] Under the leadership of Francis Daniel Pastorius, who had preceded them by several months, they established Germantown, the first German settlement in America.[16] Soon other colonists arrived and located on land near the village. From this small beginning an increasing tide of immigration continued so that at the beginning of the Revolutionary War, approximately 225,000 German-speaking people were living in the American colonies.[17]

---

[14]This pamphlet was brought to light in the Royal Bavarian Privy State Archives at Munich and published by Learned in *German American Annals,* March-April, 1910.

[15]Most members of this group had actually joined the Quaker church. Historians usually refer to them as Mennonite-Quakers. — The editors.

[16]Pennypacker, "The Settlement of Germantown, Pennsylvania, and the Beginning of German Immigration to North America," Pennsylvania German Society, *Proceedings and Addresses,* IX, 1-300.

[17]Faust, *The German Element in the United States,* I, 285.

Eighteenth Century Emigration From Germany to America

The earliest emigrants from Germany to America came for religious reasons, but during the 18th century the most important motivating factors were economic. Among the various groups which arrived on the shores of the New World, none had a more dramatic story to tell than those who had participated in the "Massenauswanderung der Pfaelzer" (the massive emigration of the Palatines) which took place in 1709.

Shortly before this exodus, a French army had invaded the Palatinate and threatened to repeat the devastation of 1689. In their resulting despair, the Palatines turned eagerly to numerous pamphlets and books describing possibilities of immigration to Pennsylvania. Included among these was a detailed account written by Pastorius in 1700 in which he described the welcome which the German colonists had received from William Penn, the perfect freedom in religious matters which they enjoyed, and the fertility of the soil which promised abundant returns to all settlers. Two years later, another and more extensive account appeared, written by two Germantown colonists, Gabriel Thomas and Daniel Falckner.[18]

The hopes aroused by these reports were stimulated by an apparently insignificant event. In 1708 a small band of Lutherans under the leadership of their pastor, Kochertal, had started for America. After reaching London they suffered financial difficulties and appealed to the Board of Trade for help. In response to their plea, they were given liberal assistance for the completion of their journey. This circumstance aroused hopes in many poverty-stricken Germans that they also would receive financial assistance in London for the voyage to America.

The bitterly cold winter of 1708-1709 was the force which started the flood of emigration. Suffering was especially intense in the devastated and ruined Rhineland provinces where wild animals and birds froze in the woods, wine in its casks and fruit trees and vineyards were destroyed. As soon as spring would permit, approximately 15,000 destitute Germans left their homes and sailed down the Rhine to Rotterdam where they were given aid for the journey to London by various benevolent persons.[19] Thereupon they were kindly received

---

[18]Heuser, *Pennsylvanien im siebzehnten Jahrhundert, und die ausgewanderten Pfaelzer* in England, 55. Also *Sachse,* "Daniel Falckner's Curieuse Nachricht von Pennsylvanien," Pennsylvania German Society, *Proceedings and Addresses,* XIV, 17-256.

[19]Faust, *The German Element in the United States,* I, 77, says that 13,000 Germans came to England. Haeberle, *Auswanderung und Koloniegruendungen der Pfaelzer im 18. Jahrhundert,* 44, speaks of 13,000 to 15,000.

BIBLIA,

Das ist:

Die

Heilige Schrifft

Altes und Neues

Testaments,

Nach der Deutschen Uebersetzung

D. Martin Luthers,

Mit jedes Capitels kurtzen Summarien, auch
beygefügten vielen und richtigen Parllelen;

Nebst einem Anhang
Des dritten und vierten Buchs Esrä und des
dritten Buchs der Maccabäer.

Germantown:

Gedruckt bey Christoph Saur, 1743.

In Pennsylvanien.

Courtesy of the Frankfurt am Main Historical Museum.

Title page of Bible printed by Christopher Saur in 1743. This was the first Bible made available in a European language in the United States.

by Queen Anne who settled them in camps outside London. Financial support came from private charity and from appropriations of Parliament. However, the sheer size of the multitudes and their almost complete lack of income proved an embarrassment for the authorities.[20]

Pressure was soon exerted on Catholic colonists (who constituted 10% of the group) to either renounce their religion or to return to Germany. In response to this demand, several hundred Catholics did surrender their faith. The rest were shipped back to their native villages. Meanwhile conditions in the camps become more and more desperate and morale sank to new lows as the Germans became the "Hohn, Wunder und Schauspiel" (scorn, wonder and amusement) of the Englishmen.[21] Eventually 3,800 of the would-be colonists were settled in Ireland. Several hundred young men entered the British army and others found employment as servants in the London area. About five hundred were engaged by the merchants of Bedford and Barnstaple for Newfoundland fisheries. An unknown number returned to Germany or died in the overcrowded camps. Only two groups succeeded in reaching the New World, one of which settled in North Carolina and another, consisting of 3000 individuals was sent to New York, where it "made the largest body of emigrants coming at one time to this country in the colonial period."[22]

Meanwhile the rulers of the South German states had become so alarmed at the exodus of 1709 that they initiated severe measures to check it. In Coblenz an order was issued "that the property of those subjects who emigrate without permission shall be confiscated."[23] In Hesse-Nassau emigrants who did not secure proper passports were punishable both in person and in property. In Baden numerous measures were taken to induce the emigrants to settle under state aid in various parts of the Palatinate instead of going to Pennsylvania. In Wirtemberg an attempt was made to stop the emigration by forbidding subjects to sell their property, while in Mannheim they were specifically forbidden to emigrate.[24] But all of these orders were of little avail. The tide of emigration continued.

Pennsylvania now loomed larger than ever as the desired goal of

---

[20]In view of the size of the movement, there is very little material preserved in the State Archives. This is probably due to the fact that people left under circumstances such as to forbid the regular official formalities, or cause them to be omitted. Many of the emigrants fled before approaching armies, while others who had no property to dispose of slipped away in the night without waiting for permission to leave. Learned, in *German American Annals,* March-April, 1910.

[21]Haeberle, *Auswanderung und Koloniegruendungen der Pfaelzer im 18. Jahrhundert,* 46.

[22]Cobb, *Story of the Palatines,* 2.

[23]Learned, *German American Annals,* March-April, 1910, p. 84.

[24]Learned, *German American Annals,* March-April, 1910, Hesse-Nassau, 172; Baden, 234; Wuerttemberg, 203; Mannheim, 319.

Christopher Saur's home, Germantown, Pennsylvania.

the German emigrants. Throughout the colonial period approximately 50% of all Germans settled in this favored colony.[25] So many of them had come from the Palatinate that it became customary to refer to all Germans as Palatines regardless of their place of origin.

Germantown remained a cultural and religious center. It was here that the first public protest against slavery was issued in 1688; that the first paper mill of America was built in 1690; and that the first edition of a German Lutheran Bible was printed in 1743, many years before an English Bible was printed in America.[26] Farther west in the newly established settlement of Manheim, Baron Stiegel built the first iron foundary of Pennsylvania.

Throughout the 18th century, pietistic groups such as the Mennonites, Amish, Schwenkfelders, and Dunkers continued to cross the Atlantic. Mention should also be made of the Moravian Brethren who on Christmas Eve of 1741, under the leadership of Count Zinzendorf chose the name Bethlehem for their newly-founded settlement. However, in a short period of time the pietistic sects were vastly outnumbered by members of the Lutheran and Reformed faiths, who, in the 18th century, found two outstanding leaders in the pastors Heinrich Melchior Muehlenberg and Michael Schlatter, respectively. On the other hand, immigration of German Catholics remained limited during the colonial period.

So rapidly did the German settlers arrive in Pennsylvania that they aroused alarm on the part of the English, some of whom were suspicious of the Germans from the first. Various means were employed by local officials to check the immigration. In 1727 a law was passed requiring the oath of allegiance and the registration of all immigrants taking it.[27] In the same year a further check was attempted by placing a head tax of forty shillings upon each immigrant. All of this was done to prevent Pennsylvania from becoming "a German colony" as some feared.[28]

One factor that could not be overlooked in this mounting emigration was purely commercial. The financial profit accruing to the shipping interests was very great. Consequently, the simple advertising that had formerly been pursued by William Penn through his

[25]In the year 1775, 110,000 Germans were living in Pennsylvania; 25,000 in New York; 25,000 in Virginia and West Virginia; 23,000 in North and South Carolina; 20,500 in Maryland and Delaware; 15,000 in New Jersey; 5,000 in Georgia; and 1,500 in New England. Faust, *The German Element in the United States,* I, 285.

[26]von Bosse, *Das deutsche Element in den Vereinigten Staaten,* 43.

[27]As a result of this legislation a list of 30,000 German and other immigrants who came to Pennsylvania from 1727 to 1776 has been preserved. See Rupp, *A Collection of Thirty Thousand Names of German, Swiss, Dutch, French, Portuguese, and other Immigrants in Pennsylvania, chronologically arranged from 1727 to 1776.*

[28]Gordon, *History of Pennsylvania,* 187.

agent in Rotterdam was replaced in the German states by the so-called "Emissarii" or "Neulaenders." Against these agents the ruling princes and even the emperor issued order after order with little effect. These paid agents traveled among their countrymen in the German states spreading glowing accounts of a new paradise, gleaned either from their personal experience, from letters originating in the colonies, or drawn from their own imagination. Rich and poor alike were solicited and those who had property were encouraged to sell it in order to pay their way across the water.[29]

Transportation difficulties in the 18th century can hardly be imagined by people living today. The roads were so impossibly bad that rivers were used whenever possible. But even the trip down the Rhine was difficult. As late as 1804 one had to pass through thirty-six toll stations between Heilbronn (on the Neckar) and the Dutch border.[30] Such a journey took from four to six weeks. After their arrival in Rotterdam, passengers often waited another five to six weeks until the ships' captains were satisfied that their sailing boats were completely crowded with people.

Many emigrants who had taken with them well-filled chests of clothing and food, found after they had embarked that their baggage had been sent upon another vessel. The passengers were then forced to buy from the captain inferior food at exorbitant prices. This led to further abuse in prolonging the voyage until the food supply of the ship was gone. There is no doubt that often weeks were spent upon the water for no reason other than financial gain to the captain. Not infrequently an emigrant, usually a widow or other inexperienced person, would deposit money with the emigration agent for safekeeping. Sometimes this money would be embezzled before the emigrant had even left his home and he would arrive in the colonies in a penniless state.

Shipping companies permitted insufferable conditions of filth aboard the emigrant vessels. By the middle of the 18th century, the horrors of the traffic almost equaled those connected with the slave trade.[31] In good weather under normal conditions ten or twelve weeks sufficed for the crossing, but, in case of storms, ships would be driven far out of their course. The death rate was often high, especially among small children; hunger and thirst were always primary dangers, and diseases could run rampant. In 1752 a ship arrived in Philadelphia

[29]Cronau, *Drei Jahrhunderte deutschen Lebens in Amerika,* 116-117.

[30]Faust, *The German Element in the United States,* I, 68, footnote 2.

[31]However the stigma attached to negro slavery was never fastened upon these white "servants," who not infrequently intermarried with members of their masters' families. See *American History told by Contemporaries,* II, 310-311.

after having spent fully six months at sea. Of the 340 passengers who had left Holland, only 21 were still alive. A contemporary newspaper report of 1749 states that in that year over two thousand died during transportation, "mostly because they were not treated like human beings." In still another report we read, "Many a time parents are compelled to see their children die of hunger, thirst, or sickness, and then see them cast into the water. Few women in confinement escape with their lives; many a mother is cast into the water with her child."[32]

The poorer classes who could not pay for their transportation to America came under contract as redemptioners. According to this plan, they secured passage on credit and then agreed to serve the master of the vessel "or his assigns" for a certain number of years. Grown people bound themselves out for three to six years, and children to the age of twenty-one.[33] At the end of his service each was given a suit of clothing and, if it had been so stipulated, a woman received a cow and a man a horse.[34]

Some of the evils of the redemptioner system are apparent at first glance. Families were separated. Persons who were sick or too old to earn their living were left to beg or to become charity cases. The agents, who received so much per head for emigrants, were tempted into gross unscrupulousness in their solicitations because they often found that the unfit peasants were most easily persuaded.

The government of the Pennsylvania colony halfheartedly attempted to mitigate the evils of the emigration traffic by passing laws regulating the conditions under which passengers might be carried, and in 1764 the Germans of Philadelphia formed a society for the improvement of conditions. Printed attacks on the redemptioner system also began to appear. One of these was by Gottlieb Mittelberger, an organist and schoolteacher from Wuerttemberg, who spent four years in Pennsylvania. Upon his return to Germany he wrote a pamphlet entitled, "A Journey to Pennsylvania in 1750," in which he described the horrors of the voyage and the hardships endured by the redemptioners. He ended by advising his countrymen not to go to America. The testimony of Mittelberger was corroborated by Pastor Muehlenberg, one of the most prominent Germans in the colonies, who in 1768 wrote a letter for publication in which he warned his countrymen

---

[32]Quoted by Faust, *The German Element in the United States,* I, 70-71. See also Cronau, *Drei Jahrhunderte deutschen Lebens in Amerika,* 118-119.

[33]George Washington at one time considered importing Palatines for the purpose of settling and improving his lands in Ohio. See Hart, *American History told by Contemporaries,* II, 310-311.

[34]For further information, see Geiser, *Redemptioners and Indentured Servants;* Fisher, *The Making of Pennsylvania,* 98-109; Bittinger, *The Germans in Colonial Times,* 315-330.

against the "Neulaenders." Muehlenberg could speak from personal experience.[35] His voyage to Pennsylvania had lasted fourteen weeks and three days, during which the emigrants had experienced many hardships, the most serious being a lack of water.

Meanwhile the German princes were issuing frantic attacks on the companies bidding for German emigration. The archives in Wuerttemberg contain a document dated August 2, 1752, which castigates agents who "sell persons of all ages for three gulden to the merchants at Rotterdam who resell them for more money to New England and other places."[36] Even Prussia, which had always attracted emigrants to itself,[37] was not exempt from the work of the agents. A document dated June 1, 1753, "prescribes strict vigilance on the part of the police to keep out the emissaries who slip into the land in order to take away Germans to the English colonies in America and debauch them."[38] Prussia executed her orders with comparative success and few of her subjects were led away.

During the 1760's two other events occurred which had a discouraging effect on immigration to the New World. In 1763 the French Prime Minister Choiseul obtained from his government a large grant of land in the colony of Cayenne on the north coast of South America.[39] In accordance with the custom of the times, he advertised extensively in the South German states and in Alsace and Lorraine. Would-be colonists flocked in such crowds to the Emigrant Bureau in Strasbourg that it was necessary for French soldiers to be called in to control the mobs. Twelve thousand volunteer colonists were then sent to Cayenne, but the affair was so badly managed that it proved a complete failure. The settlers were landed at a point where no water could be secured; no provisions were made for the planting and care of crops; and no precautions were taken to protect the settlers against the climate. By 1765 only 918 colonists were left alive and these were starved and

---

[35]See Eddis, "The Wretchedness of White Servants," in Hart, *American History told by Contemporaries,* II, 308-310, in which the writer claims that of the four classes of persons in servitude in the colonies in 1770, the most "lamented were the redemptioners."

[36]Learned, *German American Annals,* March-April, 1910, 304.

[37]As early as 1685 thousands of Hugenots who were driven out of France for religious reasons were welcomed in Prussia. Similar tolerance was extended to other persecuted sects. Prussia's growth in population and prosperity was due in no small measure to this policy.

[38]Learned, *op. cit.,* 109.

[39]The colony of Cayenne had been founded by the French in 1635, and after a precarious existence under private initiative, it was taken over by the French government as a crown colony in 1764.

fever-ridden. The affair created such a stir in France that it was investigated and the leaders were imprisoned in Paris.[40]

A second incident, which occurred in London, was widely advertised in both the English and the German press. In 1764, six hundred German emigrants were stranded in London on their way to America. They were under the leadership of Colonel Stempel, a former army officer, who claimed he had secured a grant of land on the Island of St. John. With the usual glowing promises, he had succeeded in enlisting these Germans and in getting them across the channel into London. When his plans proved unsuccessful, he deserted the colonists and left them to the mercy of the public. This affair was indignantly denounced in the English magazines and copies of the articles were reproduced in the German press.[41]

Meanwhile English officials in Pennsylvania were becoming increasingly concerned over the presence of German immigrants who now constituted one-third of all inhabitants of the colony. Similar hostility also prevailed in England. The extent of this feeling is shown in a pamphlet which appeared in London in 1755. It demanded among other things that the right of naturalized Germans to vote for members of the assembly be suspended until they had familiarized themselves with the English language; that all legal documents be void until published in English; that all German publications be accompanied by an English translation; and finally that further importation of Germans to the British colonies cease.[42]

The outbreak of the Seven Years' War (or French and Indian War as it was called in America) succeeded in accomplishing what the decrees of the German princes and the hostility of English officials had failed to prevent. For all practical purposes emigration from Germany to America was completely suspended from 1756 to 1763. Shipping records reveal that only one small group of Germans numbering thirty individuals arrived in Pennsylvania during this period.[43] Immigration did revive at the close of the war, but it took many decades until it again reached the proportions of the first half of the 18th century.

This does not mean that emigration from the German states came

---

[40]Haeberle, *Auswanderung und Koloniegruendungen der Pfaelzer im 18. Jahrhundert,* 113-116; Learned, *German American Annals,* March-April, 1910, 217, 225, 235, 319; Pisarevskii*, *Foreign Colonization in Russia in the Eighteenth Century* (in Russian), 155. (*This spelling preferred by Dr. David G. Rempel. — The editors.)

[41]*Gentleman's Magazine* (September 1764), XXXIV, 446-447; *Annual Register,* VII, 145-147.

[42]Cronau, *Drei Jahrhunderte deutschen Lebens in Amerika,* 171-172.

[43]Rupp, *A Collection of Thirty Thousand Names of German, Swiss, Dutch, French, Portuguese, and other Immigrants in Pennsylvania., chronologically arranged from 1727 to 1776,* 276, footnote.

Courtesy of the Staedtisches Reiss-Museum, Mannheim.

View of Mannheim around 1730. Note the size of the palace on the right side of the picture. A copper plate by Y. Wolff.

to a halt in the 1760's. In actual numbers the movement even became greater, but the great bulk of German emigration now turned from America to European countries.

German Emigration to European Countries in the Last Half of the Eighteenth Century

During the second half of the 18th century the same underlying causes of emigration which have already been discussed continued to hold sway. In the Palatinate, Prince Elector Charles Theodore was doing everything in his power to spread the Catholic faith. To this end he discontinued the appointment of any Protestants to office, or dismissed those already in office in order to replace them with Catholics. At the same time he squandered "tons of gold" upon his little Versailles with its gardens, theaters, and galleries. In Wirtemberg, Duke Charles Eugene (1728-1793) who already possessed a baroque palace at Ludwigsburg consisting of 452 rooms, now began the construction of an imposing new residence in Stuttgart. To obtain money for his palaces and his mistresses, Charles Eugene sold a whole regiment of his soldiers to the "Honourable Dutch West India Company." In neighboring Baden, Margrave Charles Frederick was completing his own residence in Karlsruhe. All of this building went on in spite of the devastation and suffering of recurrent wars.

Meanwhile the Hessian provinces, which were divided among half a dozen rulers, also presented conditions most favorable for emigration. The two principal states, Hesse-Kassel and Hesse-Darmstadt, had been engaged for years in a quarrel over the division of minor Hessian possessions whose rulers had died without leaving successors. In addition, the ruinous effects of the Seven Years' War were everywhere evident. A state paper in the Darmstadt Archives, dated April 4, 1767, reports:

> The excessive burden of debt and the poverty prevailing at present among the prince's subjects originating partly in the last destructive war, partly in the cattle epidemic existing in many places, partly in the disastrous fluctuating of money values; the creditless and impoverished conditions of the royal subjects; and in addition to this, the present low price of grain, all taken together make the poor subjects unable to pay their present debts or to save themselves from those previously made.[44]

[44]"Bericht der Regierung zu Giessen an den Landgrafen," April 4, 1767, in the Grand-Ducal Hessian House and State Archives in Darmstadt, *Acten des Geheimen Staats-Archivs,* XI, Abtheilung, Convolut I. — Translated by editors.

Another state paper relates that the chief ground for emigration was the fact "that the subjects had reached such a degree of poverty that they could scarcely any longer support themselves and their families, still less pay the heavy feudal taxes." This condition, the writer continues, is due to the following causes:

"1) The subjects at present are overburdened with taxes, partly because of the large sums used for running the government, and partly on account of the debts necessarily contracted during the war.

2) The peasants are greatly oppressed, and often unnecessarily, through suits brought by the numerous money lenders.

3) They are further weakened by these law suits through the many and excessive fees levied by the various officers.

4) They are completely stripped (of their property) through the usurious trade of the circumcised and uncircumcised Jews.

5) Partly also their ruin is brought about by the quotas (of soldiers) that they must furnish.

6) Many are poor because a) new subjects have been admitted without adequate information about their property qualifications; b) too early marriages are permitted and too minute a division of property; and c) the communities are overburdened with too many 'Beisassen' (i.e., half citizens, who pay only small taxes).

7) Finally, many are to blame for their own misfortunes either through their laziness or their great extravagance."[45]

The local officials offered abundant and adequate remedies for the removal of these causes: an adjustment between creditors and debtors which would relieve the latter and yet secure justice to the former; a reduction in the taxes, and a levy of them in proportion to the property of the subject and to the time when it was most convenient for him to pay; the intervention of the government between the money lenders and the subjects, by means of granaries from which the peasant could draw in case of need; and by means of banks where money could be borrowed at reasonable rates of interest. Other remedies offered were by the enforcement of the marriage and inheritance laws, and by government aid whereby factories and mines might be provided for the employment of the worthy poor and workhouses for the beggars. To all of these suggestions the princes listened

[45]*Ibid,* April 29, 1767. "Bericht des Regierungs-Raths Frhr. Breidenbach an den Landgrafen das Emigrationswesen der fuerstlichen Unterthanen nach Russland betreffend."

and did nothing more, while their subjects wandered off or stole away by the hundreds.

A pitiful picture of the conditions of life among the German peasants of this period is drawn by an unknown author in a little book entitled "Briefe ueber die Auswanderung der Unterthanen besonders nach Russland," (Letters regarding the emigration of subjects especially to Russia) in which the writer accuses the princes themselves of being the chief cause of the loss of their subjects.[46]

> In our times, says the writer, agriculture is a most pitiable "creature"; the peasants are serfs; and their labor we can scarcely distinguish from that of the animals which they herd. If you happen to be in a village, you will see children running about half naked, insistently crying for food; the parents themselves have a few rags on their backs to cover their nakedness; two or three scrawny cows furnish them milk; their granaries are empty; their cottages threaten to tumble down every minute; and the people themselves present a most poverty-stricken appearance. Woe to those princes who by their lusts, tyranny, and mismanagement make so many people unhappy. The peasant is always threatened with feudal serfdom (that is, as a punishment, his entire time is given to this lord) and with running errands, fox hunting, and digging fortifications. From morning till night, he must till his fields over and over, no matter whether the sun scorches him or the cold freezes him. At night he remains in his fields in order to protect his growing crops from the wild beasts, and descends almost to the level of the animals against which he is forced to defend himself. That which he saves from the wild beasts is taken by the cruel officers for arrears of taxes.
>
> That this picture is especially applicable to our times, I hope you will not deny, nor that you will assert that the colors are spread on too thickly. Thousands of patriots tell exactly the same sad story but we cannot know the pitiful fate of the majority of the people from their words alone; we must actually see things for ourselves. When a subject once sees conditions for himself, he is convinced that the matter con-

[46]This pamphlet is cited in Pisarevskii, *Foreign Colonization in Russia in the Eighteenth Century* (in Russian), and the translation given above is made from an extract of a Russian translation of the original text. The pamphlet contains 110 pages, is composed of twenty letters written by an unknown author, and was published in Gotha (Saxony) in 1770.

> cerns him most vitally, and he actually feels that he is either already ruined, or else that, step by step, he must be brought down to direst poverty; that he must with his life and blood satisfy the lusts of his prince and his prince's undeserving friends. What is he to do? The most justifiable, the actually dutiful, thing for a man to do is to leave the country which does not deserve good subjects, and to seek another where such are respected and desired. Although he does so unwillingly, it is natural that (under such circumstances) he should leave his Fatherland, his friends, his acquaintances, his comfort of social life, etc. With a sorrowful heart, he chooses, as a wise man, the lesser of two evils; he prefers to risk his fortunes rather than remain in a country where his ruin is inevitable.

There were many countries nearer than the Americas where "good subjects were desired." One of the chief problems of all the west European governments was to cope with a scanty population, reduced by famine, epidemics, and war below the point necessary to carry out the commercial policy of the nations. Beyond their borders, in territories added by conquest or discovery, vacant lands demanded settlers before they could become an economic or political benefit to their owners. European governments everywhere resorted to solicited immigration, and the peasants of the South German states became the object of their interest and entreaties.[47]

One of the first bids for "colonists" came from Denmark.[48] Twice during the preceding generation she had tried without success to persuade her own people to settle in the uninhabited parts of Jutland; and in 1723, 1748, and 1751 edicts had been published inviting foreigners to come. But all these attempts proved unavailing until 1759 when a Danish Royal Commissioner undertook through his personal supervision the securing of settlers and turned for this purpose to the Palatinate.[49]

The terms offered are typical of the inducements held out by the European countries at that time. "Every colonist was to receive a

[47] Pisarevskii, *Foreign Colonization in Russia in the Eighteenth Century* (in Russian), 1-10.

[48] See Haeberle, *Auswanderung und Koloniegruendungen der Pfaelzer im 18. Jahrhundert,* 139-144, for an account of these Germans; also, Pisarevskii, *op. cit.,* 20-27. A decree found in the City Archives of Mannheim forbidding this emigration is cited in Learned, *German American Annals,* March-April, 1910, 319. Other documents at Karlsruhe are listed in *idem,* 235.

[49] Emigrants were solicited not only in the Palatinate but in other sections of southwestern Germany as well. In his booklet, *Auswanderung aus Hessen* (Bensheim, 1938), Ernst Wagner describes in detail how colonists from Hesse settled in Denmark, Poland, Hungary, Algeria, Brazil, the American colonies, and Russia. — The editors.

tract of land, situated as advantageously as possible, sufficient for a farm (Bauernstelle). He should be free from all tithes of stock and grain; and moreover, for the first twenty years should enjoy freedom from taxation, from military duty, and from every compulsory service (Spannleistungen), and from the boarding of royal travelers and the quartering of soldiers. There would be, of course, no free ownership in the land. The terms, or agreement, would mean only the right of use for a lifetime in exchange for a yearly tax."[50] Frankfurt am Main was designated as the rallying place from which the settlers were to be taken to Denmark by various routes. Upon arrival each man was to receive thirty Danish "reichsthaller"; each woman, twenty; and each child, from twelve to sixteen years old, ten to cover the expense of the journey. During the years 1759-1760, the Danish government succeeded in drawing 265 families, consisting of almost 1000 settlers, to Jutland where some of their colonies remain intact to this day.[51]

Another colonization scheme, limited but intensive, was carried out by Spain in 1767.[52] Over 6000 German and Flemish artisans and farmers – all Catholics – under the leadership of the Bavarian Johann Kaspar Thuerriegel, were led into the southern province of Andalusia which had been almost depopulated by the persecutions of the Jews and the Moors and by numerous foreign wars. Many of these colonists were from the Palatine where Thuerriegel conducted a lively campaign following the famine of 1766-1767.[53] The customary warning against being misled by these inducements and prohibitions against emigrating were issued by the princes with the usual fruitless result. In 1775 the number of German colonists in Spain was 10,420, settled in fifteen towns and twenty-six villages, where their descendants still live.

On a much larger scale, colonization at the expense of the South German states was carried on by Austria, Hungary, Prussia, and Russia all of which entered into close competition with each other at the close of the Seven Years' War. Each of these countries had profited from the addition of Germans to their population in times past. Russia had sent to Germany for individual artisans and soldiers as

---

[50]Haeberle, *Auswanderung und Koloniegruendungen der Pfaelzer im 18. Jahrhundert. 140.*

[51]*Ibid.*

[52]*Ibid.*, 153-161; Haeusser, *Geschichte der rheinischen Pfalz,* II, 938.

[53]An incidental reference showing that the Hessian provinces contributed their quota to Spain is found in a "Bericht eines Beamten (C. Allgeier) auf ein resolutum regiminale vom 5. Juni 1767, das Emigrationswesen der fuerstl. Unterthanen betreff," in the Grand-Ducal Hessian House and State Archives (Darmstadt), *Acten des Geheimen Staats*-Archivs, XI, Abtheilung, Bevoelkerungspolizei. I-er Abschnitt, Convolut 1. It is an indication of the prejudice of the times that the writer comforts himself with the loss of Hessian subjects by the fact that "only Roman Catholics were taken."

early as the sixteenth century, and German merchants had been encouraged in Russia as another means of introducing western culture. Austria and Hungary, on the other hand, as parts of the Holy Roman Empire had benefited from casual emigration from the neighboring German provinces. Prussia owed its rise largely to the wise colonization policy which was pursued by her rulers during the eighteenth century and her example was beginning to be appreciated by Austria, Hungary, and Russia.

As early as 1709, Hungary had received some of the stragglers from the exodus to America, and during the first half of the century not a few German settlers sought new opportunities here. In 1723, alluring promises by the government drew settlers into the Banat of Temesvár in southeast Hungary. The German princes were inclined to look upon this active solicitation with tolerance, for they reasoned that Hungary was a part of the Holy Roman Empire and it was better for their subjects to go there than to America, which had neither physical nor political connection with them. Hence, an order issued in Zweibruecken March 20, 1724, allowed its subjects to leave for Hungary without official permission, provided only that they pay an emigration tax of one tithe. In October of the same year, this privilege was withdrawn because it was felt desirable to retain in the land persons who had property. The interests of the emperor however were favorable to free emigration, and it was officially established again in 1730 and continued for fifteen years.[54]

In 1740 Maria Theresa succeeded to the throne of Hungary, and through the inauguration of various reforms sought to bring order out of a disorganized, exhausted, and partly rebellious empire. She set in motion a comprehensive plan for building up the waste places of her country through foreign colonization and wisely began by laying a strong economic foundation. She aimed at ameliorating the condition of her peasants by encouraging agriculture, and by decreasing the burdens of taxation through the building up of new industries which shared with agriculture in the support of the national revenue. Under these generally favorable conditions, she issued a patent at the close of the war (February 25, 1763) offering special inducements for settlement to discharged soldiers, and sent recruiting officers into the South German states to enlist the much wooed inhabitants as settlers in her realm. On the border of her kingdom, she established immigration stations with inspectors in charge who advised the colonists as they arrived, measured off the land for them, drained the swamps, and im-

[54]Cited by Dr. Albert Pfeiffer in an abstract of source material in the Royal Bavarian Provincial Archives at Speyer made for the writer.

proved sanitary conditions. Upon her death in 1765, her son, Joseph II, continued her policy and further promised that where possible, persons of the same speech and religion should be located in the same settlement and that under no circumstances should relatives and friends be separated. In the single year of 1770, 19,506 persons, not including children, emigrated to Hungary;[55] and by the close of the century, thousands upon thousands of South Germans had taken up their homes on lands belonging to the Austrian Crown.[56]

Prussia, a sharp competitor of Hungary in colonization as in all other matters, was a past master at the art of drawing foreign settlers.[57] It was in Prussia, as has been observed, that many of the persecuted sects – Huguenots, Schwenkfelders, Salzburgers, and Mennonites – had found an asylum. For a century the kings of Prussia had drawn settlers from the populous lands of South Germany, just as the western part of the United States has absorbed much of the population of its eastern commonwealths. In this work of colonization Frederick the Great was unexcelled. His policy was first to make inviting the place he had chosen to be colonized, then to offer strong inducements to settlers to come, and finally to see to it that all promises made to the newcomer by his agents were fulfilled. When a sufficient number had been attracted to a permanent settlement in one place, he withdrew his offers there and turned the incoming settlers toward another tract. It is said that during his reign (1740-1785) he enlisted no less than 300,000 colonists and established 900 villages and towns.[58] Immediately following the Seven Years' War, in order to recuperate the lost strength of his kingdom, Frederick extended most liberal terms to colonists. He offered to remit their taxes, to build houses for them, and to give them land, stock, tools, and money for their transportation. They came in droves, without regard to religion or dialect, and for ten years the archives of the South German states contain references to the extended emigration into Prussia.

But measured by the extent of the concessions tendered, it was from Russia that the most alluring call came to the distracted German peasant to leave the Fatherland and travel far over sea and land to seek his fortune under an alien flag. This call was voiced in the suc-

---

[55]Learned, *German American Annals,* March-April, 1910, 193.

[56]Haeberle, *Auswanderung und Koloniegruendungen der Pfaelzer im 18. Jahrhundert,* 161-181; Pisarevskii, *Foreign Colonization in Russia in the Eighteenth Century* (in Russian), 19-21; Barker, *Modern Germany,* 63.

[57]Haeberle, *Auswanderung und Koloniegruendungen der Pfaelzer im 18. Jahrhundert,* 126-139; Pisarevskii, *Foreign Colonization in Russia in the Eighteenth Century* (in Russian), 9-18.

[58]Henderson, *Short History of Germany,* II, 199; also quoted in Haeberle, *Auswanderung und Koloniegruendungen der Pfaelzer im 18. Jahrhundert,* 126; Barker, *Modern Germany,* 62.

Courtesy of the Denver Public Library, Denver, Colorado.

Portrait of Frederick the Great (Reigned 1740-1786).

cessive manifestoes of one of the most unique rulers of the century, Empress Catherine the Great, by birth a German princess. The Germans who responded to her invitation by the thousands are the ancestors of those immigrants to America who are erroneously known throughout the middle west as "Russians."

The reader has reviewed conditions in the Germany of the eighteenth century which gave rise to the remarkable emigration, largely from its southern states, during this period. He has followed these streams of emigrants into the British colonies of North America, chiefly Pennsylvania; into South America; into Ireland, Denmark, Spain, Hungary, Austria, and Prussia. Another of these streams now remains to be traced from its source in Germany into the most remote and least known of the European lands of that time – the interior of Russia.

chapter two

German Colonization In Russia

In 1762, Catherine the Great ascended the throne of Russia, then a realm of far-flung boundary lines and scanty population. At that time Russia was Europe's most backward child. The westward current of civilization, passing through Asia Minor into peninsular Europe, had left the great barren plains of the north and east untouched. The distribution of peoples in western Europe had been accomplished by the time that the movement of population in Russia had commenced; and in the centuries since the expansion of her empire had begun, her capacity for conquest had outrun her ability to people the lands which she conquered.

The nucleus of the Russian Empire was formed on the European side by the Slavs of what is now southwestern Russia. Until the fifteenth century, her history consists of the annals of a few small rival principalities struggling against each other, and succumbing to the Tartar invasions which, from the twelfth to the fifteenth century, reduced them to a state of dependence. The rule of the Golden Horde retarded the advancement of the Russian people, and the advent of the modern era found them far short of the best civilization of the time.

The history of Russia proper begins with the union of states into the Muscovite government during the reign of Ivan III (1462-1505), shortly before the discovery of America.

The geographical unity of eastern Europe invited — almost forced — a policy of indefinite expansion. This policy, once started upon, Russia has not abandoned to this day. Her rulers sought the natural boundaries of sea, ocean, and mountain range. By the close of the sixteenth century, they had acquired the territory north to the Arctic Ocean, and southeast to the Ural River, the Caucasus Mountains, and the Caspian Sea. This was the era of vast conquests throughout the world, when to secure clear title to a continent, a small group of men under a bold leader need only plant their country's flag upon a newly found land and lay claim to it in the name of God and of their sovereign. Spain, France, and England were thus taking possession of the continents beyond the sea. Russia too was taking possession of a new world — the continent which lay at Europe's back door. The acquisition of Siberia, which occurred during this period, forms an episode in history as interesting as Pizarro's conquest of Peru or the story of Cortez in Mexico.[1]

Territorial conquests in Russia proceeded far more rapidly than the natural increase of the population would support, for up to the eighteenth century all the lands added to the empire were practically uninhabited. From the region about the original seat of government at Moscow, the native Slavs had spread by the middle of the sixteenth century to the east and north of their capital, and along the Arctic rivers to the ocean. All the more fertile part of the country to the southeast, the famous black soil belt, was rendered unsafe by frequent incursions of Asiatic tribes, more terrible in their results than the Indian wars in America. During the century 1550-1650, the Muscovite government threw out a line of blockhouses and fortified posts on the Rivers Don and Oka, some distance beyond the border of its settled territory, and the intervening space was rapidly filled up by the native Slavs. As Forts Duquesne and William Henry on the Ohio, Vincennes on the Wabash, and Kaskaskia on the Mississippi represented an advancing frontier for American civilization. so Voronezh on the Don, Samara and Saratov on the Volga, and Orenburg on the Ural were constructed at various times as outposts to protect Muscovite settlers against the Tartar raids.[2] During the century 1650-1750, a second zone to the southeast had been partially settled, chiefly by military colonies under state aid, for the normal movement of the native pop-

[1]Rambaud, *History of Russia,* I. 206-7.

[2]Milyoukov, *Russia and Its Crisis,* 1-29, draws an interesting parallel between the colonization of Russia and of the United States.

ulation had reached its limit having been increasingly hampered by the growth of serfdom.[3] It was as if England had at that time tried to colonize the Mississippi Valley from her settlements along the Atlantic. In 1724 the most thickly populated section of Russia had only ten to thirty-five inhabitants per square kilometer while the average for the great rich plains west of the Volga was less than five inhabitants to the same area.[4]

Until the eighteenth century, Russia had turned her back upon western Europe. Separated from the aggressive powers of the continent by a large stretch of territory lying dormant in the hands of the western Slavs, isolated also by a hostile church which took its orders from an eastern capital, and occupied with conquests in Asia, Russia had been more an oriental than an occidental power. But in the eighteenth century, she was ruled by two monarchs whom history has endowed with the name "Great" – Peter I (1689-1725) and Catherine II (1762-1796) – both of whom sought to Europeanize their realm and to make it a factor in western politics. During the early years of the century, Peter the Great began putting into practice the ideas gained during his western tours. He introduced into Russia as sweeping and drastic physical reforms as have been seen in China in the present day. He determined to open a door into western Europe by way of the sea and for this purpose proceeded to the conquest of the Baltic provinces. Thus he laid the foundation for a new seat of government at a seaport, gave it a German name – St. Petersburg – and removed the capital thither from Moscow.[5] He advanced the naval prestige of Russia by establishing a port on the Sea of Azov, thus gaining access to commerce with South Europe.

Catherine's Colonization Policy

The circumstances under which Catherine the Great came to the throne forced her to give her undivided attention to internal affairs, and in the first years of her reign, she set herself primarily to the task

---

[3]Serfdom was instituted at the close of the sixteenth century when, after the union of Muscovite states under Ivan III, many persons dissatisfied with conditions began migrating into the steppes immediately beyond the Russian border. To stop this movement of the population, Czar Feodor forbade them to leave their homes. The institution thus begun, grew under various rulers who added other peasants to this class, until at the time of its abolition in 1861, twenty million inhabitants of Russia were bound to the soil.

[4]Milyoukov, *Essais sur l'Histoire de la Civilization Russe,* Diagramme following 295.

[5]The name of the capital became Petrograd in 1915 but was changed to Leningrad in 1924. — The editors.

Portrait of Catherine the Great by Lampi. From a print in the British Museum, London.

of building up her empire from within.[6] One of the first objects which engaged her attention was the colonization of the immense tracts of land in the southeastern part of the empire which for two hundred years had lain unoccupied under the rule of Russia. Peter the Great had tried to populate these steppes with Orthodox Slavs from Austria and Turkey, but the results of his efforts were inconsequential. When Catherine ascended the throne, she found an immigration program already worked out by one of her predecessors and she enthusiastically began putting it into practice.

Empress Elizabeth Petrovna (1741-1762) was the real originator of the plans for the colonization of Russia by foreigners; and, it is asserted, only the events of the Seven Years' War prevented her from realizing the fruits of her project.[7] Impressed with the need of peopling the frontier bordering on Turkey and with the futility of securing an expansion of the native population, she turned to her fellow Slavs and established a number of military colonies of Serbians near the Polish boundary. The pro-French attitude of her reign led her to look with favor upon the suggestion of a French immigration agent, De la Fonte, in 1752, that Russia enter the lists to secure French Protestants as settlers. Since 1689 they had been a considerable element in the populating of the British colonies in America, and in Switzerland, Holland, and Prussia. As a result of a new and oppressive edict in 1752, French Protestants were again preparing to flee in large numbers from the country. De la Fonte argued that by taking advantage of this fact, Russia would not only secure good subjects, but would injure her enemy, Prussia, by entering into competition with her, and offering better terms than the latter could give.

Active steps were taken to carry out the project, and a committee appointed to consider the matter recommended: 1) that De la Fonte be sent to Hamburg, Luebeck, and Danzig to find out in what places the French Protestants were located, and what privileges it would be necessary to offer them, and to inquire concerning means of temporary lodgment and transportation from these seaports; 2) that a College[8]

---

[6]Catherine was the daughter of the Prince of Anhalt-Zerbst, a general in the Prussian army. She was born in Stettin in 1729, and at the age of sixteen was married to Peter III, heir apparent to the Russian throne. In 1762, Peter became Czar and a few months later was deposed by his wife and probably killed by one of her accomplices. Catherine II ranks with the greatest rulers of modern times in the scope and value of her work. She abandoned everything German and turned to France for models upon which to build her empire anew. She had a passion for reform, particularly in the first years of her reign, and anticipated many of the changes of a century later, although her own work was often superficial.

[7]Pisarevskii, *Foreign Colonization in Russia in the Eighteenth Century* (in Russian), 28-45.

[8]A "College" in the Russia of Catherine II was the name given to a Department of Government. The term was introduced by Peter the Great who set up the first "Colleges" early in the 18th century. — The editors.

of Foreign Affairs be established to work out a plan for foreign colonization; and, 3) that engineers be sent to survey the Volga and the northwest part of the Caucasus. These recommendations were carried out and the newly established College of Foreign Affairs immediately set the Russian ministers in western Europe to work collecting information concerning the French Protestants. Information was also to be gathered regarding the edicts which various countries, especially Denmark, had published inviting foreigners for settlement. From the advice received, the College of Foreign Affairs worked out a plan and presented it to the Empress. After a delay of over a year and a half, she instructed them to present their plan to the Senate and ordered the latter to prepare a manifesto for publication in foreign newspapers and through their diplomatic agents abroad. The Senate also delayed a long time and the outbreak of the Seven Years' War put a check upon all of Elizabeth's colonization plans.

Near the beginning of this conflict, two suggestions for securing German immigrants, one especially at the expense of Prussia, were offered to Russian ministers abroad. The first came from a Saxon general who reported that in view of the enforced increase in taxation and recruiting by Frederick II, many of his subjects were being driven across the border into Poland; and that if Russia used the proper means, she could not only secure these refugees as colonists, but could also draw many others from Prussia itself. The other suggestion came as the result of a purchasing trip made through the German states by a Russian officer, who related that "thousands of German families," desiring to emigrate because of the hard conditions at home, had appealed to him for information concerning settlement in Russia. The Russian government was in no position at that time to follow up either of these suggestions and the whole colonization matter rested in abeyance until called into life by the accession of Catherine II to the throne.

Catherine had early become an enthusiastic advocate of foreign colonization at any cost; and while yet the wife of the Crown Prince of the Russian throne, wrote: "We need people. Make, if possible, the wilderness to swarm like a bee hive. I do not think that in the accomplishment of this it would be necessary to compel the foreigners to accept our faith . . . Polygamy would be of great use in increasing the population."[9] In her famous *nakaz*[10] in which she outlined her future policy, she repeated her belief in the necessity of colonizing Russia with

---

[9]Pisarevskii, *Foreign Colonization in Russia in the Eighteenth Century* (in Russian), 45.

[10]The *nakaz* expresses to the Senate the will of the monarch without detailing the plans for carrying it out; the *ukaz* is also addressed to the Senate but in a more particularized form; the *manifesto* expresses the will of the monarch to the people with more or less of detail.

foreign settlers and cited the beneficial results which had come to western European nations by following this course.[11]

October 14, 1762, less than three months after her ascension to the throne, she addressed to the Senate the *ukaz* in which she commanded them, from that time on, without any further formalities, except cooperation with the College of Foreign Affairs, to accept foreigners for settlement in Russia.[12] To avoid a probable delay such as Elizabeth had experienced, Catherine energetically took matters into her own hands, and on December 4, 1762, issued a manifesto which read as follows:

> By the grace of the Lord, We, Catherine II, Empress and Autocratic Ruler of all Russia, etc., etc., etc.
>
> Upon ascending the imperial throne of Russia, we have made it our main rule always to give our motherly attention and care to the peace and welfare of the entire vast empire entrusted to us by the Lord, and to the increase of its population. And since many foreign subjects, as well as our own who have been away from Russia, petition us to be allowed to settle in our Empire, we herewith announce that not only will we, with our usual imperial benevolence, receive all foreign nationals, with the exception of Jews, to settle Russia, and most solemnly proclaim that to all those coming to settle in Russia our imperial kindness and benevolence, will be shown, but we also permit our own subjects to return, who have in former times fled from Russia,[13] promising that although according to the law, they deserve punishment, we forgive them all their previous transgressions, hoping that, conscious of our maternal benevolence toward them, they will, after settling in Russia, try to live in peace and prosperity. Where and in what places of our vast empire the newcomers are to settle,

---

[11]Catherine early announced that "her chief aim would be to give attention to industry and to the increase of the population." *Idem,* 48.

[12]Pisarevskii, *ibid.,* 48; Waeschke, "Deutsche Familien in Russland," *Jubilaeumsschrift des Roland,* 68.

[13]These people were largely *Raskolniks,* the dissenters from the Greek church (usually called Old Believers), who from the time of the schism in 1667 to the reign of Catherine II were persecuted and exiled. December 14, 1762, she addressed a special invitation to these exiled subjects in the *ukaz* which began thus: "With what imperial grace and benevolence Her Royal Highness is ready to receive, for the purpose of settlement in Russia, not only foreigners from the various nations, except Jews, but also to allow those of her subjects to return who have fled from their country, forgiving them all their transgression—as is already known to everyone from the proclamation of December 4 of this year . . . " *Orders of the Most Illustrious, Most Powerful Great Empress Ekaterina Aleksieevna . . . from June 28, 1762, to 1763* (in Russian).

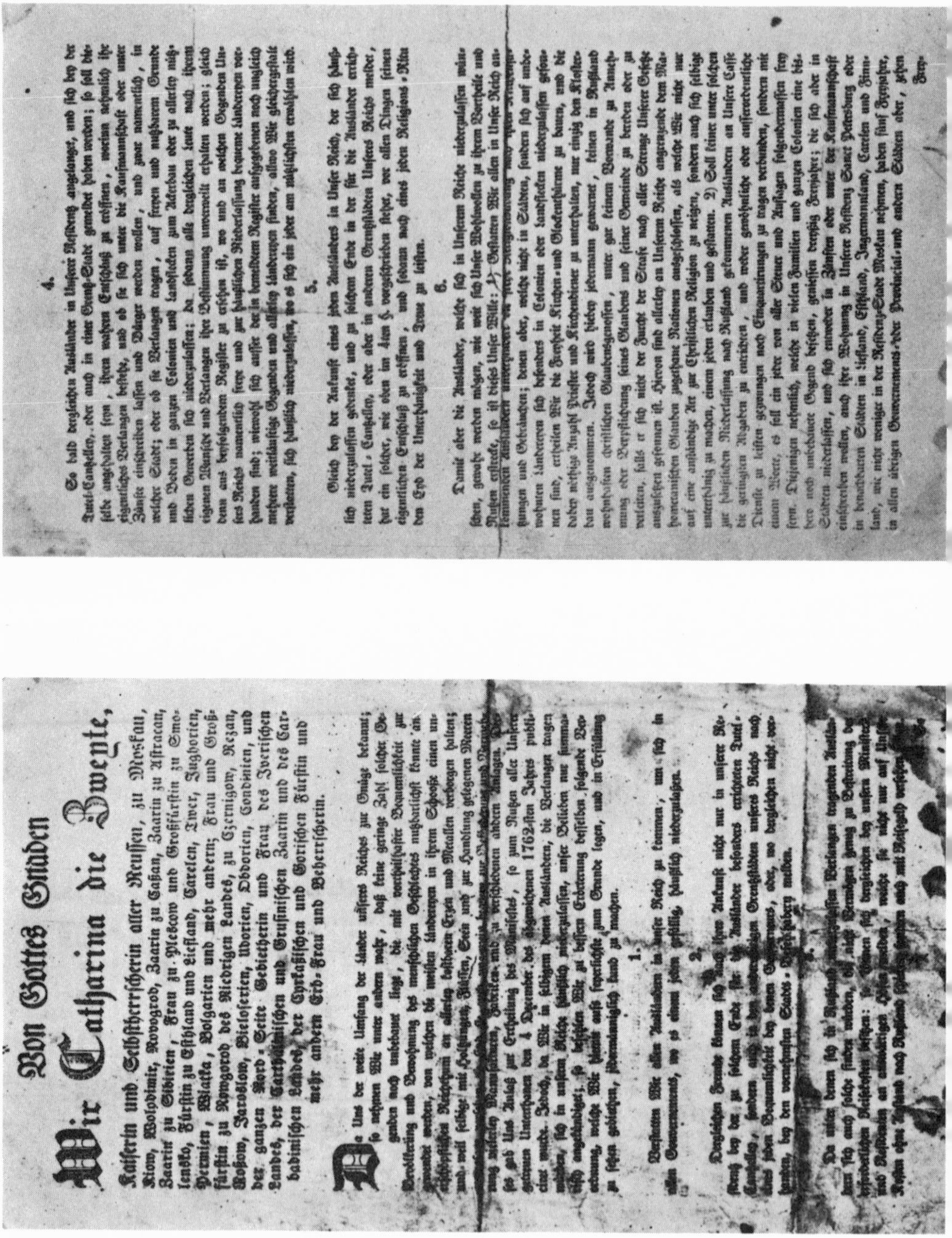

Von Gottes Gnaden
Wir Catharina die Zweyte,
Kaiserin und Selbstherrscherin aller Reussen

Courtesy of the Nebraska State Historical Society, Lincoln, Nebraska

Photographic reproduction of a copy of the Manifesto of July 22, 1763, reprinted by the government in 1856. This copy was loaned to Dr. Hattie Plum Williams by Mr. Henry Heinz of Sutton, Nebraska.

Freyjahre zu geniessen. Wonechst ein jeder, der nicht etwa nur auf einige kurze Zeit, sondern zur würklichen häußlichen Niederlassung, nach Rußland kommt, noch überdem ein halbes Jahr Quartier haben soll. 3) Allen zur häußlichen Niederlassung nach Rußland gekommenen Ausländern die entweder zum Kornbau oder anderer Handarbeit, oder aber Manufakturen, Fabriken und Anlagen zu errichten, geneigt sind, wird alle hülfliche Hand und Vorsorge dargeboten, und nicht allein hinlänglich und nach eines jeden Bedürfniß vortheilhaftes Land eingeräumet, sondern auch nach denen Umständen eines jeden, erforderlicher Vorschub gereichet werden, je nachdem es die Nothwendigkeit der künftige Nutzen von solchen zu errichtenden Fabriken und Anlagen erheischet, besonders aber von solchen, die bis jetzo in Rußland noch nicht errichtet gewesen. 4) Zum Häuserbau, zu Anschaffung verschiedener Gattung im Hauswesen benöthigten Viehes, und zu allerley wie beym Ackerbau, also auch bey Handwerken erforderlichen Instrumenten, Zubehör und Materialien, soll einem jeden aus Unserer Casse das nöthige Geld ohne allen Zinsen vorgeschossen, sondern lediglich das Capital, und zwar nicht eher als nach Verfliessung von zehen Jahren, in drey Jahren zu gleichen Theilen gerechnet, zurück gezahlet werden. 5) Wir überlassen denen sich etablirten ganzen Colonien oder Landflecken die innere Verfassung der Jurisdiktion ihrem eigenen Gutdünken, solchergestalt, daß die von Uns verordneten obrigkeitlichen Personen an ihren inneren Einrichtungen gar keinen Antheil nehmen werden; im übrigen sind solche Colonisten verpflichtet, sich Unserm Civilrechte zu unterwerfen. Falls sie aber selbst Verlangen trügen, eine besondere Person zu ihrem Vormunde oder Besorger ihrer Sicherheit und Vertheidigung von Uns zu erhalten, bis sie sich mit den benachbarten Einwohnern dereinst bekannt machen, der mit einer Salvegarde und Soldaten, die gute Mannzucht halten, versehen sey; so soll ihnen auch hierinnen gewillfahret werden. 6) Einem jeden Ausländer, der sich in Rußland häußlich niederlassen will, gestatten Wir die völlige zollfreye Einfuhr seines Vermögens, es bestehe dasselbe worinn es wolle, jedoch mit dem Vorbehalte, daß solches Vermögen zu seinem eigenen Gebrauche und Bedürfniß nicht aber zum Verkaufe bestimmt sey. Wer aber ausser seiner eigenen Nothdurft noch einige Waaren zum Verkauf mitbrächte, dem gestatten Wir freyen Zoll für jede Familie Dreyhundert Rubel am Werthe der Waaren, nur in solchem Falle, wenn sie wenigstens zehen Jahre in Rußland bleibet, widrigenfalls wird bey ihrer Zurückreise der Zoll sowohl für die eingekommene als ausgehende Waaren abgefordert werden. 7) Solche in Rußland sich niedergelassene Ausländer sollen währender ganzen Zeit ihres Hierseyns, ausser dem gewöhnlichen Landdienste wider Willen weder in Militair- noch Civildienste genommen werden; ja auch zur Leistung dieses Landdienstes soll keiner eher als nach Verfliessung obenangesetzter Freyjahre verbunden seyn: wer aber freywillig geneigt ist, unter die Soldaten in Militairdienste zu treten, dem wird man ausser dem gewöhnlichen Solde bey seiner Einrollirung beym Regimente Dreyßig Rubel Douceurgeld reichen. 8) Sobald sich Ausländer in der für sie errichteten Tutel-Canzelley, oder sonst in Unseren Grenzstädten gemeldet und ihren Entschluß eröffnet haben, in das Innerste des Reichs zu reisen, und sich daselbst häußlich niederzulassen, so bald werden selbige auch Kostgeld, nebst freyer Schiffe bis an den Ort ihrer Bestimmung bekommen. 9) Wer von solchen in Rußland sich etablirten Ausländern dergleichen Fabriken, Manufakturen oder Anlagen errichtet, und Waaren daselbst verfertiget, welche bis dato in Rußland noch nicht gewesen, dem gestatten Wir, dieselben zehen Jahre hindurch, ohne Erlegung irgend einigen inländischen See-oder Grenzzolles frey zu verkaufen, und aus Unserm Reiche zu verschicken. 10) Ausländische Capitalisten welche auf ihre eigene Kosten in Rußland Fabriken, Manufakturen und Anlagen errichten, erlauben Wir hiemit zu solchen ihren Manufakturen, Fabriken und Anlagen erforderliche leibeigene Leute und Bauern zu erkaufen. Wir gestatten auch 11) allen in Unserm Reiche sich in Colonien oder Landflecken niedergelassenen Ausländern, nach ih-

ren eigenen Gutdünken Marktäge und Jahrmärkte anzustellen, ohne an Unsere Casse die geringste Abgabe oder Zoll zu erlegen.

7.

Aller oben gezeigte Vortheile und Einrichtungen haben sich nicht nur diejenigen selbst zu erfreuen, die in Unser Reich gekommen sind, sich häußlich niederzulassen, sondern auch ihre hinterlassene Kinder und Nachkommenschaft, wenn sie auch gleich in Rußland gebohren; solchergestalt, daß ihre Freyjahre von dem Tage der Ankunft ihrer Vorfahren in Rußland zu berechnen sind.

8.

Nach Verfliessung obenangesetzter Freyjahre sind alle in Rußland sich niedergelassene Ausländer verpflichtet, die gewöhnlichen und mit gar keiner Beschwerlichkeit verknüpften Abgifften zu entrichten, und, gleich Unsern andern Unterthanen, Landesdienste zu leisten.

9.

Endlich und zuletzt, wer von denen sich niedergelassenen und Unserer Bothmäßigkeit unterworfenen Ausländern Sinnes würde, sich aus Unserm Reiche zu begeben, dem geben Wir zwar jederzeit dazu die Freyheit, jedoch mit dieser Erläuterung, daß selbige verpflichtet seyn sollen, von ihrem ganzen in Unserm Reiche wohlerworbenen Vermögen einen Theil an Unsere Casse zu entrichten; diejenigen nehmlich, die von Einem bis fünf Jahre hier gewohnet, erlegen den Fünften, die von fünf bis zehen Jahren aber, und weiter, sich in Unsern Landen aufgehalten, erlegen den zehenden Pfennig; nachhero ist jedem erlaubt ungehindert zu reisen, wohin es ihm gefällt.

10.

Wann übrigens einige zur häußlichen Niederlassung nach Rußland Verlangen tragende Ausländer aus einem oder andern besondern Bewegungs-Grunde, ausser obigen noch andere Conditiones und Privilegien zu gewinnen wünschen würden, solche haben sich deshalb an Unsere für die Ausländer errichtete Tutel-Canzelley, welche Uns alles umständlich vortragen wird, schriftlich oder persöhnlich zu wenden: worauf Wir alsdenn nach Befinden der Umstände nicht entstehen werden, um so viel mehr geneigte Allerhöchste Resolution zu ertheilen, als sich solches ein jeder von Unserer Gerechtigkeitsliebe zuversichtlich versprechen kann. Gegeben zu Peterhof im Jahr 1763. den 22sten Julii, im zweyten Jahre Unserer Regierung.

(L. S.)

Das Original haben Ihro Kaiserl. Majestät Allerhöchst eigenhändig folgendergestalt unterschrieben:

Gedruckt beym Senate den 25 Julii 1763.

Catharina II.

Wem noch unbekannt, daß Ihro Rußisch Kaiserl. Majestät Leute, so nehmlich Profeßion oder Ackerwerk verstehen, annehmen lassen; So wird dieses hiermit bekannt gemacht: Zu Roßlau bey Dessau im schwarzen Bäre werden sie Verpflegung erhalten, auch wird vor alles bestens gesorget werden. Nehmlich der Gastwirth Hoffmann bezahlet jeden Mann täglich vier Groschen, der Frau zwey Groschen sechs Pfennige, auf jedes Kind täglich ein Groschen sechs Pfennige, dabey frey Quartier und Transport, ingleichen werden ledige Frauenspersonen zur Verheurathung verlanget und angenommen, es muß sich aber ein jedes bald möglichst daselbst einfinden, weil der Commissarius binnen 4. Wochen nach Sankt Petersburg abgehet. Geschrieben den 12. April 1766.

Печатать позволяется. Москва. 21 Декабря. 1856 г. Цензоръ Н. Гиляровъ-Платоновъ.

and also everything pertaining to arrangements with reference thereto, we have ordered the Senate to make public.

Catherine.

Printed in Moscow, at the Senate, December 11, 1762.[14]

By her vigorous activity, Catherine then set in motion the machinery which Elizabeth had evolved during the preceding ten years. Within a week, the Senate had carried out her order to publish the manifesto in the various languages of western Europe; and by the close of the month the College of Foreign Affairs was in communication with the Russian diplomatic agents abroad who were ordered not only to circulate the manifesto, but to take steps toward seeing that it became effective. Immediately upon receipt of it, the foreign ministers expressed their opinion of its impotency because it did not detail the rights and privileges under which the settlements were to be made and hence little or no result could be expected from it. An appeal to the Senate to supply this lack which the manifesto itself recognized and correction of which it promised, would probably have been made in vain had not Catherine taken the initiative and appointed a chairman whose work promptly resulted in important measures. These were embodied in the two manifestoes of the Empress, July 22, 1763, and became the foundation or "cornerstone" of foreign colonization in Russia.

By the first of these manifestoes, there was organized an immigration bureau known as the Tutel-Kanzlei fuer Auslaender (Guardianship Council for Foreigners), whose duty it was, not only to receive and care for colonists according to the terms laid down in the other manifesto, but also to elaborate and set in motion a system for actively encouraging such settlement. As an indication of the importance attaching to this department, it was placed upon the same level as the other state colleges, being responsible to the Empress only. Catherine appointed as its president her favorite, Count Gregory Orlov, and the Senate voted 200,000 rubles annually for the purpose of inducing immigration.[15]

On the same date Catherine included in another manifesto the recommendations of the Senate regarding the terms upon which

---

[14]*Idem.*

[15]Schloezer, *Neuveraendertes Russland,* Pt. III, 107-140; Klaus, *Unsere Kolonien,* 34-35; Pisarevskii, *Foreign Colonization in Russia in the Eighteenth Century* (in Russian), 51-52.

foreigners should be admitted to the empire.[16] The most important provisions were as follows:

1) All foreigners, without exception, were allowed to come and to settle in any *gouvernement*[17] they pleased.

2) On arrival they could present themselves either at the Tutel-Kanzlei fuer Auslaender in St. Petersburg or to the governor in the border cities of the empire, or in his absence, to the chief authority or commander of the city.

3) Transportation and expense money for the trip were to be provided, beginning at the time of enrollment.

4) As soon as settlers presented themselves to the authorities in Russia, they must determine upon their destination and be assigned to it.

5) They must thereupon take the oath of allegiance in accordance with their own religious rites.

6) Further privileges were:

a) Entire freedom of religion; if colonies were formed, the building of churches and belfries[18] but not monasteries; and the maintenance of pastors and assistants, but not the proselyting of anyone except Mohammedans.

b) Immunity from the quartering of soldiers; from all "services" usual or extraordinary, and from taxation for thirty years if settled in colonies, or for five to ten years if settled in cities, besides free quarters for the space of half a year.

c) Grant of subsidies for factories or other new industries.

d) Advancement of money for ten years without interest for providing houses, stock, and tools.

16See facsimile of this manifesto published at Moscow in 1856. It is taken from a copy found at Sutton, Nebraska. Translations into German are found also in Bauer, *Geschichte der deutschen Ansiedler an der Wolga,* 10-15; Klaus, *Unsere Kolonien,* 22-26. Original translations are in the General-Landesarchiv at Karlsruhe (cf. Haeberle, *Auswanderung und Koloniegruendungen der Pfaelzer,* 145, footnote), in the Koenigliches Kreisarchiv at Amberg, in the Kreisarchiv fuer Unterfranken und Aschaffenburg at Wuerzburg, in the Koeniglich Bayerisches Kreisarchiv at Bamberg, in the Koeniglich Bayerisches Kreisarchiv der Pfalz at Speyer, and the Koeniglich Geheimes Staatsarchiv in Berlin. A summary in the Russian is given by Pisarevskii, *Foreign Colonization in Russia in the Eighteenth Century* (in Russian), 52-55.

17Throughout her dissertation, Hattie Plum Wililams had used the word *gouvernement* which is synonymous with the English word "province" and the Russian word *guberniia.* The editors decided to use the English word.

18The building of belfries was a sign of great liberty in worship. The English laws in 1741 forbade bells and belfries on any except Episcopalian and Lutheran churches. Jacobs, *History of the Lutherans,* 213.

Courtesy of the Nebraska State Historical Society, Lincoln, Nebraska.

Belfry in Walter Chutor. It was a great concession of Catherine II to allow Lutheran and Catholic colonists to construct such belfries.

e) Permission to bring in property to the amount of three hundred rubles free of duty.

f) Local autonomy if desired; otherwise, a manager or guardian provided at state expense.

g) Freedom from military and civil service during entire residence in Russia.

h) Freedom of trade within and without Russia for ten years to those establishing new factories.

i) To those establishing businesses at their own expense, the right to purchase serfs.

j) Right to colonies to institute market days and annual fairs free of duty.

7) These privileges were to be enjoyed not only by incoming settlers, but by their descendants.

8) After the period of immunity, the settlers were to pay the same taxes as other subjects of the empire.

9) Freedom to leave the empire was not to be denied, providing a certain proportion of property acquired in Russia was relinquished to the government.

10) Other privileges desired by the settlers might be requested of the government in writing.

Attached to this manifesto was a register of the lands which the Empress opened up to settlement.[19] It included vast regions in the province of Tobolsk in northwestern Siberia; and smaller and non-adjacent tracts in the province of Astrakhan, along the Volga River, above and below Saratov, in Orenburg, and in Belgorod. Later, in the year 1764, it was decided to confine the settlement to the Volga territory, although theoretically the colonists were permitted to establish themselves anywhere they expressed a choice, even outside the territories mentioned in the register. The Russian government had a distinct motive in choosing these distant frontiers when its southwestern lands still lay vacant. In the first place, there was the strong probability that nearness to the border of western Europe and a comparative facility of transportation might induce the settlers to return home if they did not find everything to their satisfaction; but more especially there was the apprehension that the liberties necessary to secure col-

[19]A list of these lands is appended to a copy of the manifesto found in the Koenigliches Kreisarchiv in Amberg; cf. also Pisarevskii, *Foreign Colonization in Russia in the Eighteenth Century* (in Russian), 55.

onists for Russia might at some future time be turned to her own disadvantage, since these foreigners might "teach our savages not only of their arts but also spread their political ideas among the subjects of your Imperial Majesty."[20]

The Work of the Ambassadors and the Professional Enrollers

The first plan of the Russian government was to work through its foreign ambassadors who were instructed to attend to the solicitation and transportation of colonists under the direction of the College of Foreign Affairs. In view of this, a number of rescripts giving details, chiefly concerning the transportation of the colonists and cautioning against unnecessary expenditures, were issued to the foreign ministers. They were enjoined openly to supervise colonization only in those countries which did not prohibit emigration "for it would not be fitting for an accredited minister publicly to solicit citizens of such a country, in which he is located or to encourage and transport the families in parties under his protection."[21] But in countries where emigration was forbidden, the ambassador was to work "secretly and with caution . . . that there might not be the least occasion for raising objections by the court"[22] to which the Russian minister was accredited. Hence he was to issue no passports to the subjects of these countries, but he might accept such people and send them individually so as to avoid comment; the foreigners in such lands he was to solicit openly. While manufacturers were to be given every attention and encouragement, the ministers were to bear in mind that "Russia needs farmers in particular,"[23] and these were to be accepted in unlimited numbers and with varying degrees of ability. In this respect only did Catherine's policy differ in theory from the plan of Elizabeth, who desired chiefly manufacturers.

The first results of these measures were negligible. The manifesto of December 4, 1762, had as the ministers anticipated, practically no results, chiefly because it lacked definite terms upon which the settlement was to be made. The issuance of it caused as much surprise in the western world as an invitation of Japan to open commercial relations would have caused before 1854. Moreover, Russia was looked upon by western Europe much as were the Scythians by Greece and

---

[20]"Report of Henry Gross, Ambassador at the Court of Holland, to the College of Foreign Affairs, December 5/16, 1763," in Pisarevskii, *Foreign Colonization in Russia in the Eighteenth Century* (in Russian), 58.

[21]*Ibid.*, 56.

[22]*Ibid.*, 56.

[23]*Ibid.*, 56.

Rome, and the term "barbarous Russia" called up visions of wild frontiers from which Asiatic peoples had but recently withdrawn and which they still overran at their pleasure. Life and property were insecure at the hands of the "terrible Turk" on the one hand and of the Tartars on the other, either of whom was more feared than the wild Indian tribes of America. Even the native Russian was not considered a fit associate for civilized people, and the experience of western Europe with the Cossack armies during the Seven Years' War had confirmed this belief.[24] Besides these constant elements of hindrance, there was the temporary obstacle caused by the unstable political conditions then prevailing in Russia. Until the beginning of 1764, there were repeated rumors of dethronement, assassination and revolution, assiduously spread by the enemies of the new government, and this of itself would prove a powerful deterrent to immigration.[25]

Aside from the apathy of western Europe toward the invitation of Catherine, the inexperience and misdirected zeal of her ministers served largely at first to neutralize any good results which might have come from her colonization policy.[26] Each representative abroad was anxious to show his devotion to his sovereign by sending immediately as large a contingent of settlers as possible, and often he paid little attention to the quality of the people. In this way many disreputable persons secured support for a time from the Russian government and then refused to emigrate and the ambassadors spent money with an alarmingly free hand.

The Russian minister in England, Vorontzov, collected a party of two to three hundred persons who received their daily expense money as soon as they enrolled, and for whom he chartered a special ship to take them to Libau.[27] While completing preparations for the voyage, some were lured away by the English government and others by private colonization companies for their colonies in America so that only

---

[24]"The horrible impressions of the Cossacks which I brought from Germany where we learned to know them during the Seven Years' War were very much changed when I sat among them." Zuege, *Der russische Kolonist,* I, 133-134.

[25]Gentleman's Magazine, XXXII (Sept., 1762), 443, report of unsettled conditions; XXXII (Oct., 1762), 497, denied; XXXII (Nov., 1762), 547, sympathetic reference to politics in Russia; XXXII (Dec., 1762), 595, reports of new revolution denied on undoubted authority; XXXIII (Jan., 1763), 41, precedence given English ambassador by Catherine; XXXIII (Aug., 1763), 409, rumors of conspiracy against Catherine but no particulars as yet; XXXIII (Sept., 1763), 460, report denied; XXXIII (Oct., 1763), 513: "The accounts from Russia continue still to forebode some fatal catastrophe to the reigning Empress. In several foreign countries her death has been declared, but upon what grounds does not appear. The latest accounts, however, to the Russian ambassador at the court of London give no such intimations; and the report seems rather to take its rise from the hope and expectations of her enemies, than from any real foundation."

[26]Pisarevskii, *Foreign Colonization in Russia in the Eighteenth Century* (in Russian), 58-65.

[27]In present-day Latvia. It is now called by its Lettish name, *Liepaja.* — The editors.

sixty-eight of the original number finally started on the journey. Shipwrecked on the coast of Holland, the colonists rebelled and all but fourteen of them left the vessel. These appealed to the Russian minister residing in Holland, refusing to go by boat but expressing their willingness to continue the journey by land. They were given permission to do so at their own initiative, but no escort was provided them and not one of them ever reached his destination. In addition to the total loss of these colonists and of the expense money given them, the Russian government was compelled to pay the ship's master the entire sum agreed to for carrying more than two hundred colonists.

More successful was the Russian ambassador, Rehbinder, at Danzig, who in April and May of 1763 sent to St. Petersburg several parties of ten people, among whom were some Poles; but he rewarded his colonists, who were chiefly artisans, with such comparatively extravagant sums that the government was obliged to put a stop to his negotiations.[28] Count Dolgorukov,[29] resident at the court of Prussia, in spite of that country's opposition to emigration, sent several colonists and even went so far as to pay the debts of two of these in addition to advancing them their expense money. Such conduct was not approved by the Russian government and he too was ordered to proceed on a more economical basis.

Quite different was the conduct of the Russian ambassador in Holland, Henry Gross, to whom large numbers came for enrollment. One group of 6,000 people, gathered by a French engineer from the provinces of the Netherlands, Belgium and adjacent places, was refused by Gross on the ground that they were not fitted for life as colonists. As a matter of fact, his racial antipathy played a great part in the matter, for being a native of Wuerttemberg, he did not desire to see Frenchmen settle in Russia; and he summarily dismissed the whole group on the basis of unfitness and questioned loyalty.

The efforts of the other ambassadors were similarly fruitless. Mussin-Puschkin in Hamburg, Simolin in Regensburg, and Golitzyn in Vienna, all sent colonists during the earliest period but few ever reached their destination. Those sent by land were lured away by other agents, notably Prussian, while many others who had enrolled and had received their expense money in advance, hid themselves at the last moment or refused to make the trip. Learning its lesson from these barren results, the government sought to systematize the campaign in two ways. In the first place, it appointed a central gathering

---

[28]To one single family Rehbinder paid 300 rubles while to several individuals or families he gave 100 to 200 rubles. Pisarevskii, *Foreign Colonization in the Eighteenth Century* (in Russian), 59.

[29]Compare spelling of Prince Dolgoruki on page 75. — The editors.

place to which all colonists, whether singly or in parties, were to be directed and from which they were to be shipped to St. Petersburg. Experience had shown the difficulties of transportation by land; hence Luebeck was chosen (December 15, 1763) as the port of departure and a special commissioner was selected (May, 1764) to manage the immigration at that point.[30] By securing the cooperation of the local authorities the colonists could be forced to keep their contracts with the Russian government, and the deception practiced could thus be reduced to its lowest point.

The second measure in the organization of the campaign was the employment of professional enrollers to supplement the efforts made by the ambassadors. The slow results of the latter's work came partly from the fact that they were restricted in their operations by their official positions. It was hazardous for them to work in countries where emigration was prohibited, for they had to proceed secretly, and could scarcely hope to avoid discovery which would lead to international complications. Since most of the lands of western Europe just at this time forbade emigration, the scope of the activities of the Russian government was greatly reduced. Again, the ambassadors were limited in the methods they might use, and since much of the colonization of that day was carried on under questionable procedure, the ministers found it difficult and often impossible to meet their competitors.

The methods of advertising which they were forced to use were also inadequate. The newspapers reached only the urban population and drew chiefly manufacturers when agriculturists were most greatly desired. The copies of the manifesto, scattered in every nook and corner, penetrated the rural communities, but many could not read them; others were so little inclined to emigrate that someone was needed to urge them to leave their "nests"; while still others had to be convinced that the offer of Russia exceeded in advantage the tender of any other country. On this account, it was not sufficient simply to spread written announcements of the plans of the Empress and depend upon the emigrants to present themselves to the ambassadors; it was necessary rather to send into these secluded districts experienced persons who would come into contact with the people individually,

[30]The man chosen for this task was a Luebeck merchant, Henry Schmidt, who was to receive the colonists brought to him by the enrollers, provide for their lodging, pay them their daily allowance, and secure the aid of the municipal authorities in forcing the colonists to obey their *Vorstehers* and fulfill their part of the contract. Of his first meeting with this man, Zuege wrote: "We found in him just the smooth sort of man needed for a business of this kind. He corroborated all that his subservient spirits had deceived us into believing yesterday, and congratulated us upon the much desired and brilliant establishment which we were to find in Russia." —*Der russische Colonist,* I, 19.

make friends with them, and by their personal influence secure their consent to emigrate.

In this plan the Russian government found both precedent for its task and professional workers ready to undertake it. Especially Holland and the southwest German states were overrun with agents who made a business of enrolling colonists and mercenaries for foreign countries. England[31] and France had made use of them for colonizing their American possessions, and Denmark and Prussia for settling their own unoccupied districts; while Prussia, Spain, and England had employed them for securing soldiers. Although the occupation was a dangerous one, the remuneration was sufficient to attract large numbers of a certain class who applied themselves energetically and successfully to the work. Since they were paid on a commission basis, they did not discriminate either in the class of people accepted or in the methods used to secure them. To them the people were "zhobogo Tovara" or human merchandise, while to the people the agents were "soul-sellers."[32]

These enrollers were, as a class, of doubtful character while some of them were plainly rascals, as will be seen from the conduct of those employed by the Russian government. In addition to the professional agents, at this particular time, due to the end of the war, a large number from almost every class in the community sought a like occupation. Superior and inferior officers left idle, clerks and merchants whose business had been ruined and who returned to find themsleves without means of making their livelihood, hereditary noblemen, and even ministers joined the ranks of the enrollers and sought employment under the Russian government. Some of these applicants presented their own plans for carrying out the campaign; one had in mind especially the small artisans whose living was becoming more and more precarious because of increasing specialization in their trades, while another looked to the retired soldiers as the source of the largest contingent. The latter were to be taken on pretense of forming a military regiment in Russia; but since it was contrary to the policy of the Russian government to employ foreign troops, they were to be discharged a few years later and settled in various parts of the empire.

Neither of these plans appealed to the Empress, who was intent

---

[31]England was cited as a successful example, which, "by the help of enrollers, gathered in the past year, 1762, 200 persons in the Palatinate, and, according to the newspapers, sent them, a few months ago, from Germany to Florida, and, according to the same report, they had sent to this American colony over 5,000 families." — Pisarevskii, *Foreign Colonization in the Eighteenth Century* (in Russian), 82. The probable inaccuracy of the report did not detract from its influence on the Russian government as to the value of immigration agents.

[32]*Ibid.* Also called "Emissarii," "Werber," "Neulaender," and "Enrolleur."

upon agricultural colonies, but another suggestion struck her fancy. It was the idea of the proprietary colony in accordance with which large grants of land were to be given to foreign noblemen who should form their own settlements upon the basis of the French feudal system which existed before the Revolution. Adopting this suggestion, three contracts were made by the Russian minister in Paris, two with French colonization companies and one with Baron Caneau de Beauregard who worked independently. Acording to the contract with the latter,[33] the Tutel-Kanzlei was to designate tracts of unsettled lands for colonies which he might distribute at his discretion, In case the grant was not settled within two years, it was to revert to the government. The proprietor was to receive 15,000 rubles for securing not fewer than three hundred families, besides an allowance of forty rubles per family for traveling expenses and 1,000 rubles per hundred families for board. The colonists were to be delivered either at Hamburg or Luebeck from which ports the government would superintend their voyage. These proprietary colonists were to have all the rights guaranteed in the manifesto and the director was not to promise them anything contrary to the Russian law, nor to allow them to return until their expense money had been repaid. Aside from these conditions, the director was at liberty to make such terms with his colonists as he saw fit. Although the land lay upon the east side of the Volga, the colonists were to be permitted to settle on the opposite side among the crown colonies if they desired. No colonist was to be deprived of any title which he had formerly possessed although military officers were not to be allowed to wear the Russian uniform. To preserve order in the colonies and to furnish protection against surrounding enemies — although this latter was not mentioned in the contract — the director was permitted to organize the colonists into military companies according to the plan of the Swiss infantry and to confer upon the worthy ones military titles, although these were to be of no significance outside the colony. Under such terms the entrepreneurs took their places on a level with the ambassadors, and proprietary and crown colonies were established side by side.

It is frequently asserted that, although addressed to all foreigners, Catherine had in mind Germans, chiefly Palatines, when she issued her manifesto. But the history of the steps leading up to this policy and of the measures which the Tutel-Kanzlei and the College of Foreign Affairs took to carry out her manifesto, do not warrant this conclusion. It has been shown that ministers in countries other than the German states were the first and most active agents of Her Majesty

[33]*Ibid.*, Appendix, 1-6.

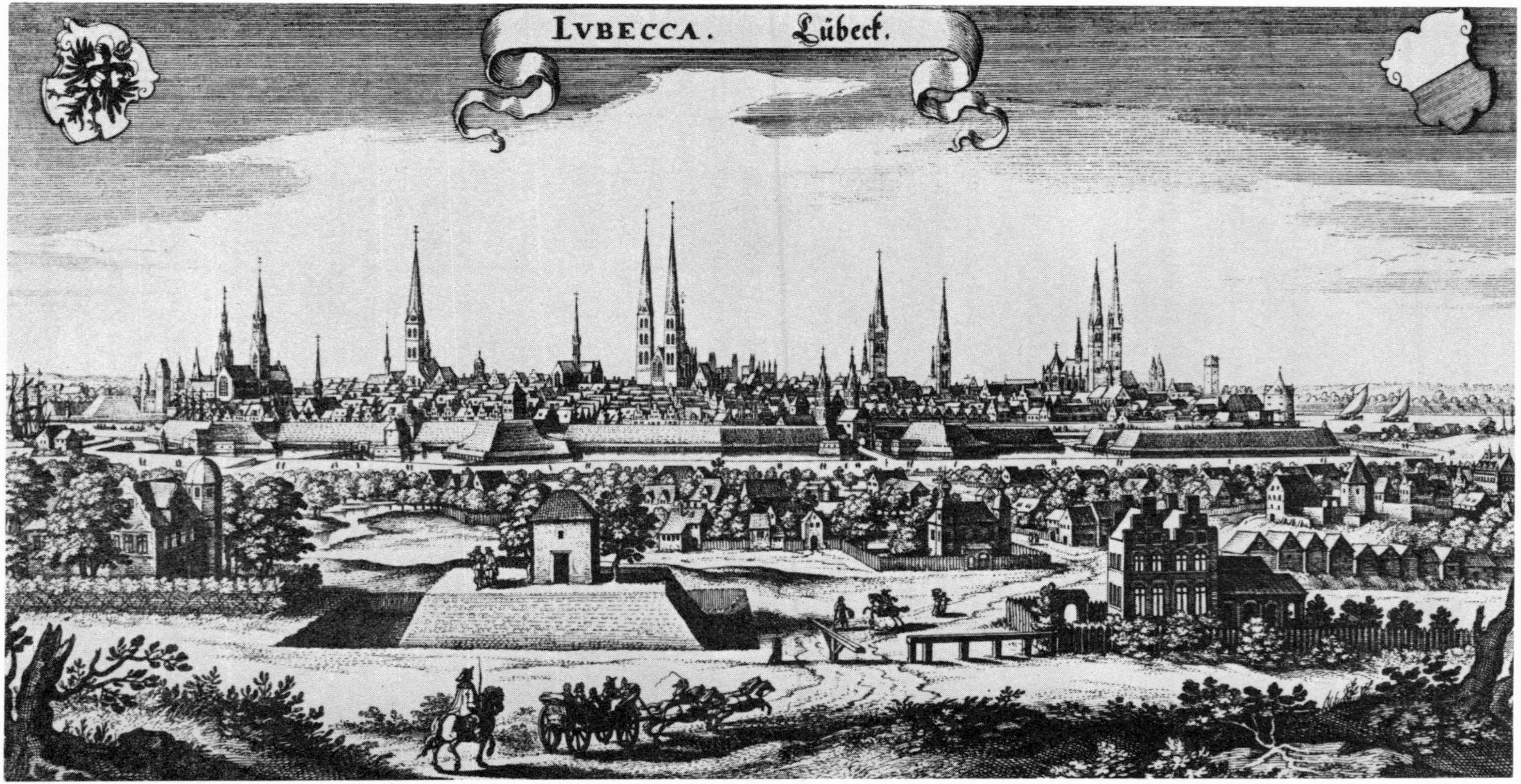

Courtesy of Mrs. Emma S. Haynes (Private Collection).

General view of Luebeck in the Eighteenth Century.

and rescripts and advertisements were addressed impartially to all. Every country in Europe was flooded with news of the Russian Empress's manifesto, and the fact that none except the German states were seriously affected only shows how prone the Germans of the eighteenth century were to follow the will-o'-the-wisps of fortune in foreign lands, and how well all other states but these succeeded in keeping at home their subjects who wished to leave.[34]

The advertising done by the government in the first stages of the project was extensive and impersonal; but when opposition from foreign powers developed, as it very soon did, the process became an intensive one, carried on by individual and personal agencies. As has been seen, the Russian government depended first upon newspapers in foreign lands. In one instance, however, the ambassador made use of the pulpit as an advertising medium; e.g., when he requested the clergymen of Courland to announce the manifestoes of Catherine, but in few countries were the political relations such that this course could be followed.[35]

In Denmark, England, Scotland, and Ireland the newspapers were utilized without restraint for advertising purposes, while in Holland and the free German cities only the German and French press respectively was used. In Swabia and Austria the first manifesto was printed in the newspapers, but opposition was so pronounced that the second was edited separately and sent as a supplement to the foreign journals printed there. Austria excused her hostile conduct on the ground that Russia's plan interfered with her own colonization policy. She recalled the mass emigration of Serbians at the invitation of Elizabeth Petrovna; and, since these colonists had kept in touch with their countrymen who always entertained the hope of some day joining their co-religionists in the empire to the east, she feared that the publication of such an alluring invitation just at this time would cause another mass movement of her subjects. Like Prussia's, Austria's population had been greatly reduced by the Seven Years' War; and Maria Theresa, in view of her plans for restoring her kingdom through foreign colonization, forbade the publication of Catherine's manifesto in the newspapers and issued a special manifesto, November 16, 1763, stating her reasons for prohibiting emigration.[36] It was because of this attitude that the Russian ambassador at Vienna avoided asking permission to publish the second manifesto in the Austrian press, but instead, utilized the foreign

---

[34]*Ibid.*, 65-78.

[35]The pulpits in some of the German lands were used as advertising agencies and the manifesto read from them: Haeberle, *Auswanderung und Koloniegruendungen der Pfaelzer*, 146.

[36]In 1762, Hungary revived her old emigration laws of 1609 and 1613 which forbade subjects to leave their country on pain of capital punishment.

newspapers published there. The Russian government also used great caution in communicating with him on the subject, addressing its orders to him in cipher and sending by special messenger, instead of by ordinary mail, the copies of the manifesto printed in the Greek, Serbian, and Rumanian languages for use among the orthodox population in Austria.

Sweden also was thoroughly aroused by the second manifesto of Catherine. Like Austria, she forbade its publication in the newspapers of that country on the ground that the prevailing poverty and high prices had already caused unrest among her people and they were showing a tendency to emigrate which Sweden felt forced to prevent. Spain and France, too, were hostile to the plan of Russia. They had lost many of their inhabitants in the colonization of the New World; and, to avoid further depopulation at this time, they revived former edicts prohibiting emigration. Hence, Russia did not attempt to advertise through their newspapers but printed separate copies of the manifesto and scattered them broadcast over the two countries. France, in particular, interposed a persistent and vehement opposition to the Russian campaign, which came at the crisis in French colonial affairs, just after she had lost her Indian possessions in 1761 and her American lands in 1763.[37] Therefore, she met this attack by a most active and thorough system of police espionage, inspecting all travelers who crossed the border and reporting all persons whose conduct led to the slightest suspicion that they were connected in any way with the Russian immigration project.[38] The Russian ambassador complained to his government that the only way to get out of France was by land through The Hague and that when emigrants applied to him, he was placed in the difficult position of trying to carry out the policy of his government and not get into trouble at the court where he was located.

In Prussia, the manifestoes of Catherine were published, but the second invitation was met with a polite supervision as prompt and effective as was established in France. In addition to inspection at the border, so careful that no one either on foot or otherwise left the kingdom uninvestigated, the local officials were made "responsible that not a single person left their county."[39] The Russian ambassador

[37]France expressed her attitude in these words. "We must conserve our population; the soldiers, for the army; the farmers, for the land; the artisans, for the factory; the actors, for the theater." — Pisareveskii, *Foreign Colonization in Russia in the Eighteenth Century* (in Russian), 136.

[38]The manifesto of Maria Theresa of November 16, 1763, was published in all the French newspapers as a justification of the antagonistic attitude of the French government.

[39]Pisarevskii, *Foreign Colonization in Russia in the Eighteenth Century* (in Russian).

considered it dangerous to send emigrants from Prussia, both because it might lead to international complications, and because the government ran too much risk in losing the expense money advanced to the colonists in case they were arrested and returned. However, he did not hesitate to accept secretly such persons as applied to him for emigration and to send them away unaccredited if he could do so.

A somewhat different opposition arose in Turkey where Catherine counted especially upon the Greek subjects as immigrants. It was based on the fear of the Turkish government that Russia, after populating her territory bordering on the Turkish empire, would attempt to enlarge her boundaries at the expense of her neighbor. Besides, the privilege of proselyting the Mohammedans which Catherine granted in the manifesto proved a source of offense to the Turkish government; hence, the Russian ambassador decided to conduct the whole enterprise secretly in Turkey and not to attempt broadcast publication.

Thus, the number of countries where Russia could pursue her policy unhindered was very limited; and even in England and Holland where no restrictions existed, internal conditions promised little success. British subjects were not likely to desert their own American colonies for the flattering but uncertain promises of Russia, and in Holland where "the people live in complete liberty, and the most of them in luxury,"[40] meager results were to be anticipated. Only foreigners living in these lands, or natives who were paupers, or criminals might be expected to accept the Empress's offer.

The chief source of supply, therefore, proved to be the free cities and the southwest states of Germany where prohibitions against emigration existed as severe as in other countries, but where the weakness of the princes and the distress of the people combined to defeat them. Although practically all the results of Russia's colonization policy put into effect by Catherine came from the German states and cities, such had not been her expectation; she desired "to establish all Europe in miniature in foreign colonies on the Russian soil, regardless of nationality and religion; Frenchmen and Greeks, Rumanians and Germans, Slavs and Swedes — all were expected guests of the Russian Empress."[41]

Results of Enrollment in Various Countries Outside the German States

The Russian colonization campaign shows the following meager results outside the German lands: In the Balkan states and Austria,

---

[40] *Ibid.*
[41] *Ibid.*, 74.

where the government had early sent special secret agents, over seven hundred Moldavians and other orthodox Christians had been induced to settle in Russia. They were located near Kiev and placed under the care of the President of the College for Little Russia. Being co-religionists, they were accepted fully into the empire and not considered *foreign colonists* as were the rest of the immigrants.[42]

From the agent sent by the government to Italy, no report came and the official correspondence shows no result whatever from his mission although an Italian (Peter Bianci) is found in one of the first parties of colonists sent to Russia (1764).[43] From England where great efforts were made by the ambassador to secure a large emigration, only a few individuals were induced to go to Russia. The *Vorsteher* of the colony Stahl in 1774 was an Englishman, "Nylson,"[44] probably Nelson. The presence in the colonies of such names as *Harres,* the probably Germanized form of *Harris,* indicates the English origin of those who bear them. Belgium,[45] Austria, and Hungary each contributed a few individual settlers, while Poland due to the efforts of the Russian ambassador at Danzig, sent a small group of emigrants.[46] Most of the colonists from these countries were either single men seeking adventure, or Germans who had settled in these countries and were dissatisfied with conditions there. Some of the former escaped from Russia and the others became so fully assimilated by the German colonists that usually there is no trace of their nationality except through the Teutonized form of the name.

Denmark, Holland, France, and Switzerland each furnished a contingent large enough to have exerted some influence upon the settlements. From Denmark came a few Danish subjects from the cities, but principally German colonists who had settled there a short time previously. It will be recalled that these people were not entirely satisfied with conditions in Denmark and claimed that the government was not fulfilling its contract with them. Aware of these facts, the Russian ambassador at Hamburg, Mussin-Puschkin, thought to profit at the expense of Denmark and he received not only the colonists who had been discharged by that government, but those who had left with-

---

[42]*Ibid.,* 85-86.

[43]*Volkszeitung,* III, No. 49 (June 22, 1914). "Verzeichnis der Kolonisten, die im Jahre 1764 unter dem Kommando des Kapitaens Paykul und des Kornetts Rehbinder nach Saratow befoerdert wurden."

[44]Bauer, *Geschichte der deutschen Ansiedler an der Wolga,* 31.

[45]In 1764, an immigration agent, formerly an officer in the German Imperial service, was arrested in the Austrian Netherlands and fined while threats were made of driving the Russian ambassador out of the country.

Appendage to Footnote [45]: In the 18th century Belgium was known as the Austrian Netherlands. — The editors.

[46]The Poles were settled with the French Catholics in their village, Franzosen.

out its permission. In addition to this, he actually sent into the Danish settlements (1764) a secret agent with letters purporting to have been written by their friends who had gone to Russia. This man was instructed to use every means possible to induce the Germans to leave and go with him to Russia. On learning that fact, the Danish government took immediate steps to prevent this by arresting the agent and sentencing him to six months' hard labor, but not before it lost a considerable contingent. For example, in March, 1764, there were colonists from Denmark (probably Germans) in the emigrant house near Hamburg;[47] and in one of the first parties sent to Russia (1764) there were Danes from Copenhagen and Kiel.[48] In 1766 a deserter was arrested at the emigrant house near Hamburg by the Danish authorities.[49] Of Danish colonists as such, we hear practically nothing, although the Swiss, French, and Hollanders were an element to be reckoned with.

The Russian government had at first expected to use Amsterdam as one of its ports of departure as did all the countries of western Europe which drew colonists from the Rhine and adjacent provinces. To this end, an emigrant house was built in Wessp, a few miles from Amsterdam.[50] But the immigration agents took advantage of the hospitality of Holland to enroll persons who were in debt and who took this means of escaping the authorities. When this practice continued in spite of the government's protest, the authorities confiscated the emigrant house and carried their complaints to the Russian Empress. Few Hollanders were secured even by the questionable tactics of the agents. Not enough of them emigrated to Russia to found a separate colony. They were scattered among several German colonies on the *Wiesenseite*, but their influence was felt in the introduction of the "Dutch windmill" and in the cultivation of tobacco which they successfully carried on.[51]

As has been stated, one of the most active struggles against the Russian enrollers was made by France. In addition to the police inspection of all travelers crossing the boundary, the most drastic measures were taken against the enrollers themselves. Detectives were put upon their trail and traps were set to catch them. The chief agent operating in France was decoyed in this way across the border and

[47]Staatsarchiv der freien und Hansestadt, Hamburg, *Extracts from II, No. 1756*, made by Dr. Hagedorn, Senatssekretaer, for the writer.

[48]*Volkszeitung*, III, No. 49 (June 22, 1914), 2.

[49]Staatsarchiv der freien und Hansestadt, Hamburg, *Extracts from II, No. 1756*, made by Dr. Hagedorn, Senatssekretaer, for the writer.

[50]Pisarevskii, *Foreign Colonization in Russia in the Eighteenth Century* (in Russian), 134.

[51]Bauer, *Geschichte der deutschen Ansiedler an der Wolga*, 27-28.

sentenced to life imprisonment. His co-laborer, fearing a similar fate, killed his guard and then committed suicide. International complications were avoided only because France concealed the matter and Russia was afraid to push an investigation. Other agents were arrested and imprisoned in the Bastille. One of them was kept for three years on the unproven charge of distributing copies of the manifesto in Alsace and released (in 1769) only after all solicitation of emigrants had been stopped by the Russian government. France further opposed Russia's colonial policy by assisting Frenchmen in Russia who wished to return. Thus, in 1764, and again in 1765, French subjects who had escaped from the proprietary colonies on the Volga appealed to the French ambassador in Russia who provided them with funds to return home. Russia protested against this practice, but France persisted and Russia finally agreed to release all French colonists for whom their government would pay the expenses.[52]

In spite of the frantic efforts of the French to prevent the loss of their subjects, a considerable element mostly from Alsace and Lorraine, joined the movement to Russia. Enough Catholics emigrated to form a colony of their own which retained its original name, Franzosen, although now inhabited entirely by Protestant Germans.[53] The French Protestants were scattered among the German colonies and have become entirely assimilated, leaving no trace of their presence except possibly in some of the numerous French words found in use among the German colonists.[54]

Aside from the Germans, the largest foreign element going to Russia in response to Catherine's call for colonists was the Swiss. These people had been especially called to the attention of the Russian government by one of its agents, who pointed out that in spite of the "incredible" emigration from Switzerland every year, the population did not seem to decrease because of the high birth rate; and that be-

---

[52]Pisarevskii, *Foreign Colonization in Russia in the Eighteenth Century* (in Russian), 136-40.

[53]Some of the French were invited to become tutors and governesses in Russian families and many of them left for this purpose. Others deserted to seek their fortunes elsewhere and the government filled their places with Germans. When the number of the latter exceeded that of the French, these moved to other Catholic villages and the character of the settlement became entirely changed. Cf. Muench, *Historical and Geographical Encyclopediae of Saratov* (in Russian), for a sketch of this colony; also Zuege, *Der russische Colonist,* I, 108 and 193, for mention of the French emigrants; and Pallas, *Bemerkungen aus einer Reise durch die suedlichen Staathalterschaften des russischen Reichs,* II, sec. 9, 625-26.

[54]Many French words are found in the various dialects of the Volga Germans. Some of these can be accounted for as survivals of the French element in the German language of the eighteenth century, but undoubtedly the French settlers left some evidence of their presence in the vocabulary of the German colonists. (Some French family names such as Chevalier, Masson, and Hagin remained in the Catholic colonies of the "Wiesenseite" until Stalin's deportation of all Volga Germans in 1941. — The editors.)

cause England refused to accept the Swiss Catholics as settlers, and as there was at that time great unrest in Switzerland, Russia had an exceptional opportunity to secure these people. Since the religious and political disunion of the Swiss Confederation apparently prevented any concerted or effective action against emigration, the agents had a comparatively free hand and secured quite a large number of colonists for Russia.

The first contingents show an astonishing variety of source of emigration. One of the first companies which sailed, arriving at St. Petersburg in July, 1764, contained the following number of colonists from the various places indicated.[55]

Hungary	3	Magdeburg	2
Denmark		Koenigsberg	1
Kiel	10	Breslau	1
Copenhagen	3	Oldenburg	7
Sweden	6	Braunschweig	1
Stockholm	5	Frankfurt	5
Pomerania	1	Leipzig	3
Baltic Provinces		Luebeck	4
Reval	2	Waldeck	
Courland	2	Winterberg	45
Narva	2	Hesse	
Poland	2	Nassau	6
Elbing	10	Baden	
Danzig	10	Durlach	6
Italy	1	Anspach (?)	6
German States		Saxony	16
Prussia		Mecklenberg	32
Berlin	12	No residence given	31
		Uncertain	105

Tactics of Agents in German States

After the employment of immigration agents by the Russian government, the source of supply became localized and practically all colonists came from the German states, chiefly the southwestern Rhine provinces. The character of these men, the methods they used to carry on their trade, and the measures taken to check their work by the governments of the countries in which they operated will be treated briefly.

[55]*Volkszeitung,* III, No. 49, p. 2, "Verzeichnis der Kolonisten, die im Jahre 1764 unter dem Kommando Kapitaens Paykul und des Kornetts Rehbinder nach Saratow befoerdert wurden."

The campaign was short and sharp. Competition with other countries, notably Prussia and Hungary; competition between the agents themselves; extravagant use of public money, marked with much dishonesty; and violent opposition on the part of governments where they succeeded in interesting the people, characterized the movement and led to its sudden and unexpected discontinuance.

One of the first difficulties encountered by the Russian ambassadors was in securing permission for a rendezvous for the colonists, preliminary to sailing for Russia. It will be recalled that at first each ambassador arranged for the transportation of the people who applied to him, but this proved expensive and impracticable and a central place was decided upon from which the people were to be shipped. This port was Luebeck, one of the free cities, and the one most conveniently located for passage to St. Petersburg. Tributary to Luebeck and second in importance was the city of Hamburg, which, due to its location, became the point through which many emigrants were transported. Those from the Upper Palatinate and Switzerland came down the Rhine and were shipped from Amsterdam to Hamburg, while those from the southern and central provinces were carried in small boats down the Elbe to the same destination.[56] Here they were sent overland, thirty-five or forty miles to Luebeck, the sole port of embarkation during the period from 1764 to 1768. In these two cities the people were quartered until a sufficient number had gathered to fill a vessel, when a ship's master from St. Petersburg would come and conduct them thither. The free cities had little to lose in the way of desirable population while the shipping and mercantile interests had much to gain in a financial way.[57] Hence, a minimum of opposition arose, and although a law against emigration existed, the authorities did not trouble themselves to enforce it, but met the protests of the princes with a nonchalance born of the business instinct.[58]

The attempts of the Russian ambassador in South Germany to secure rendezvous resulted quite differently. He appealed first to the authorities of Regensburg where he was stationed and was granted the use of a large public building as quarters for his colonists. Although

---

[56]There is no authority for the statement of Haeberle in his *Auswanderung und Koloniegruendungen der Pfaelzer,* 147, that the majority of the immigrants were shipped down the Rhine and then over sea by way of Gibraltar and the Black Sea.

[57]Bremen is included in the complaints of the princes against the northern seaports and a copy of Emperor Joseph's Edict of 1768, which was aimed very largely at the shipping interests, is found in the archives there. (Private letter from Dr. Ulrich of the Free Hanse City Archives at Bremen). But there is no other mention of the subject and this of itself, aside from the geographical position of the city, is good evidence that there was never any considerable traffic through this port.

[58]As will be seen later, the city authorities even lent their aid to the Russian enrollers in forcing the colonists who tried to escape to return and fulfill their contracts.

Regensburg was also a free city, this action was almost immediately annulled on the ground that since the Imperial Assembly had its seat there it was an improper place for the Russian colonists to gather, because the gathering of all sorts of people would cause the spread of disease. In reality, the authorities indirectly let it be known to Simolin that they did not desire to demand the withdrawal, but that it was requested by the German princes and Maria Theresa because the use of the city as an emigrant station interfered with Maria Theresa's colonization campaign. After this failure, Simolin tried in succession to secure quarters in Bavaria, Saxony, and Swabia, but in all these places he was refused. Finally he returned, "like a beggar," as he says, to Anhalt-Zerbst; and there in the principality of the Russian Empress's brother, he at last was given permission to use as a station Roslau on the Elbe, with the distinct understanding that the Russian agents were not to solicit colonists within the boundaries of Anhalt.[59] Because of its central location upon one of Germany's most important waterways, Roslau became the most noted of the inland rendezvous and during the summers of 1765, 1766, and 1767, thousands of colonists were assembled there and shipped down the Elbe to Luebeck via Hamburg.

Two other enrolling stations much desired by the Russian ambassador were Worms on the upper course of the Rhine and Ulm on the Danube. The former, most conveniently situated with reference to the German states subject to constant emigration, was used for a time; but the early opposition which developed in these provinces, and the difficult task of running the gauntlet down the Rhine of almost fifty cities, each with its tolls and various trade laws, made Worms an impracticable point. Moreover, the mouth of the German Rhine was controlled by Prussia which placed every conceivable barrier in the way of the Russian emigrants. Ulm also proved unavailable because of opposition, particularly from Hungary, although the transportation facilities for sending colonists from there to South Russia were excellent. But few people were secured, and those who promised were stopped by the German rulers or were lured away on their journey through Hungary by the agents of Maria Theresa.[60]

---

[59]In spite of the condition imposed, the excitement attendant upon the quartering of great crowds of emigrants could not help affecting the surrounding inhabitants. In a list of the colonists who were married in Roslau are several "daughters" of that city. Undoubtedly unattached men tried to slip away with the emigrants also, for in October, 1765, the prince issued an order to the government to see that none of his subjects were permitted to leave. A request from the Russian agent in that district that two Anhalt subjects be granted permission to join the colonists met with his prompt refusal on the ground that they were "noch bey guten Jahren und Kraeften und gut arbeiten koennen." Cf., Waeschke, "Deutsch Familien in Russland," in *Jubilaeumsschrift des Roland,* 80.

[60]However, six colonies (the Belowesh group) were established by Protestants and Catholics, and one colony by Hutterites, in Chernigov province of the northern Ukraine. — The editors.

Courtesy of Frankfurt am Main University Library.

View of the main square in Frankfurt am Main, an early recruiting station for Germans bound for Russia. (The largest building to the right is where the Holy Roman Emperors were crowned.) A painting by Kleiner, 1738.

Besides these emigrant stations used for the temporary quartering of colonists, there were numerous recruiting stations scattered over the German states, at each of which was located a Russian Royal Commissioner. From these centers, sub-agents scoured the country round about and ordered all persons desiring to emigrate to report for instructions to the officials there. Most of these recruiting stations were free cities since only the municipal authorities would have to be dealt with, and the matter could be made of financial benefit to the locality either from the sale of provisions or in subsidies paid to them by the Russian agents. Thus Frankfurt am Main, Friedberg, Fuerth, Regensburg, Deutz, Buedingen, and other towns were chosen as recruiting stations in their respective districts at one time or another and were used either until the work in that locality proved futile or until the agents were driven out by the authorities.

The German states where the most active work was carried on were slow to realize their position and only a few protests were made before the proprietary agents, in particular, had sowed the seed and begun to reap a tremendous harvest. Then, and then only, did the German princes, engrossed in petty international affairs or seeking personal pleasure, realize what was occurring to them and try too late to counteract the movement. But before noting these acts, let us look for a moment at the character and work of the immigration agents in the employ of Russia.

We have seen that, analagous with the British plan of settlements in America, the Russian government proposed to found two types of colonies, the crown and the proprietary. The details of conducting the former were turned over to commissioners, who received their credentials from and worked under the direction of the Russian ambassadors – von Simolin in Regensburg, Mussin-Puschkin in Hamburg, von Voronzov in The Hague, etc. The second type of colony was to be founded under charters granted to individual proprietors by the Tutel-Kanzlei to which alone they were responsible. This double system, which was occasioned by the desire of the government to push colonization more rapidly than the ambassadors had at first succeeded in doing, caused no end of trouble, first in Germany and later in the colonies in Russia.

The difference between the crown and the proprietary agents, so noticeable from the documents of that period, was less in character than in methods, since the manner of conducting the campaign was determined largely by the men under whom they worked. Some of the ambassadors used tactics as questionable as those of the proprietors, but they were forced to conceal them, or if discovered, to repudiate them. The agents themselves were practically all of one stripe. Most of the enrollers were Germans, judging by their names, and worked in localities in which they were familiar with the customs and conditions of the people.[61] Many of them did not claim any residence and, thus, the officials in the countries in which they worked could not trace them down. Those with French names claimed Switzerland, Netherlands, or Holland as their homes, while the Germans pretended to be subjects of Russia or openly defied the princes of their petty states. Some of these agents were escaped convicts or had served their time in prison and were forced to conceal their identity under assumed names; others were lured into the work by the chance of dishonest gain through mistreating the people or defrauding the government. Some of them were unreliable in their business relations, hiring out to furnish a certain quota of colonists to one proprietor and then selling them to another for a higher sum, or purchasing provisions from merchants in the recruiting stations and then leaving without paying their bills.

Being almost exclusively of this unreliable and disreputable character, the tactics used by these agents were as vicious as their employers would permit. Encouraged by the advice of one of the ambassadors that "in order to entice colonists (to Russia) the proprietors and their agents must use every sort of seduction,"[62] bills for beer and whiskey occupy a considerable place in the expense accounts of the agents. In certain of the cities, and especially by the agents of one of the proprietors, young girls were actually ravished and carried off while every sort of unprincipled means was used to lure or coax them away. In order to secure discharged soldiers, all kinds of impossible promises of fine titles and offices in the Russian army were made.

According to the Russian custom at that time of giving military titles to civil officers, these agents were all styled Lieutenant or Captain. Dressed in the Russian uniform of red and green and well supplied with ready money, their evident prosperity was a sign of the good fortune awaiting those who accepted their invitation to emigrate.[63] Suave, hopeful, enthusiastic, and usually careless about the truth of their statements or promises, they persuaded men often against their better judgment to take their chances on this new and untried

---

[61]For example, there were von Weymar, Meixner, von Kotzer, Seippel, Rollwagon, Facius, Wildstack, and Florentin.

[62]Pisarevskii, *Foreign Colonization in Russia in the Eighteenth Century* (in Russian), 112, footnote 3.

[63]Cf. Koenigliches Kreisarchiv, Bamberg, *Bamberger Stadthaltereiakten,* 1766, (Rep. 153, Bd. 32, Prod. 19); Koenigliches Kreisarchiv, Speyer, *Abtheilung: Oberrheinischer* Kreis, Akt. No. 1798, "Letter from Geheimrat von Wagner to the Churfuerst von Trier"; Pisarevskii, *ibid.,* Appendices; Zuege, *Der russische Colonist,* I, 18.

venture. These agents scoured the country places, watering the seed of discontent which war, poverty, and religious persecution had planted in the minds of the people. They devoted their attention first to persons who were planning to emigrate, and where possible, persuaded those who were starting to America, Hungary, or Prussia to change their destination and "go with them" to Russia. Further, they tried to induce those who had not thought of leaving, but who were temporarily embarrassed by the hard conditions then prevailing in the German states, to emigrate to Russia under promise of the wonderful opportunities described in the advertisements and copies of Catherine's manifesto.[64] Their assurances were vouched for by the official seal of the Russian ambassador upon these advertisements and also by letters purporting to have been written by colonists who had previously gone to Russia.

An interesting recital of the work of these agents is given in an account which one of the original colonists has left of how he chanced to go to Russia.[65] He was the son of a cloth manufacturer at Gera and had received a good education for one of his social standing. He had always had a desire to visit foreign lands and his study of geography had intensified that craving. His parents had succeeded in keeping him at home until he was eighteen, when a family quarrel brought matters to a crisis and they reluctantly gave their consent for him to see the world. After a year's stay in Berlin where he worked at his trade, he went on to Luebeck with two companions whom he had picked up. Here the lure of the sea decided him to start for foreign shores.[66]

> My plan was to go from Luebeck to Hamburg, ship from there to Amsterdam, and then to present myself at the West Indies House for a voyage to America. I had heard that in this way one could make the trip without cost; to be sure, of course, one had to be a soldier, but for that one received money in addition. As to this fact, it never once signified anything to me; I only wanted to satisfy, without expense, my curiosity to see the countries of the world far beyond my native land. This, I hoped, might be brought about in this way; but when, a short time later, someone pointed out another way to me, I struck into it; for it was all the same to me whether I went to America or some place else, if only the goal

[64]A bonus of 3 to 4 ducats was offered to anyone who would point out a prospective colonist family. Pisarevskii, *ibid.*, Appendix, 10.

[65]Zuege, *Der russische Colonist, oder Christian Gottlob Zueges Leben in Russland*, I, published in 1802, 214 pp.

[66]*Ibid.*, 14-18

of my journey was far from my home, offered me a quiet life and a peaceful abode, and the sight of much that was new and striking.

Once when I was about to lie down to rest with my two companions from Berlin, several well-dressed persons came into the traveler's room, and began such an animated conversation that we all gave up any hope of being able to sleep so long as they were present. We therefore joined in with them, half unwillingly at first; but after a short time I was glad to have chanced upon these people. The conversation was soon general; the new guests asked us where we came from and of what profession we were. We had no cause for concealing the one or the other, and I, who was already in America in spirit, explained to these people that I wanted to ship thither, and that my companions, partly won over by me, had similar intentions. In a tone which seemed to my inexperienced soul very sad and sincere, the strangers with one voice warned us to give up our plans if we did not want to be most painfully deceived in our hopes. One in particular took the floor, while he assured us that he had been in America himself several times, and from that experience gave us a description, in comparison with which that related by Herr von Buelow recently is still mild and alluring. He asserted that everyone who went to America without considerable means and without the best possible recommendations went to an unavoidable slavery in which he found himself little better than his brothers stolen from Africa. He volunteered to introduce us the next morning to some travelers who were here, and who would confirm everything that he had said. We thanked him for his kindness; but I could not refrain from expressing great regret that my hope of seeing distant lands should be frustrated by him at one stroke.

"Go with us to Russia," another now began; "Yonder, the great Catherine, herself a German, has opened a new paradise to all her countrymen who are not satisfied at home. Under the mildest climate in her broad kingdom, she wants to settle colonies of Germans, to whom she is not only giving passage money, but also whatever is necessary for their support, for several years to come; moreover, she has ordered paid to each one the sum of 150 rubles in order that he may with this amount settle down anywhere at his own pleasure. Thither you can go to a certain fortune, travel through no small part of the world on your way there, learn to know Cossacks, Kalmucks, Morwins, Tschuktsch, and a host of other unknown things of which people here have scarcely heard."

While this man was arousing my curiosity, he produced in me no slight desire to change my plan for a journey, and this desire ripened into a firm resolution when he showed us a royal manifesto printed in St. Petersburg, in which everything claimed by him was promised. Besides, he showed us several letters purported to be written by Germans already settled in Russia, but which were really a worthless compilation of the Russian commissioners and their helpers, for they represented everything so bright and inviting, in short, so utterly different from that which my experience on the spot taught me to know. Inclined by reason of my youth to rosy hopes, the manifesto and the letters produced upon me exactly the impression which was desired by the exhibitors, who were plainly recruiting officers for Russia, or, in other words, "Soul-sellers." We therefore asked our companions if they could provide us the opportunity of accompanying them to Russia; they said yes, and mentioned to us a certain Schmidt, a merchant in Luebeck who was a Russian commissioner, accepted colonists who applied, paid out the money to them, and provided for their transportation. They said he had likewise engaged them, and they finally left us with the promise of coming again in the morning to take us to him.

Between the agents of the crown and the proprietors there existed the keenest rivalry and often open conflict, and the ambassador, von Simolin, is one of the most virulent critics of the latter. Some of his own conduct in this matter, however, is not above reproach. For instance, in 1764 he sent a secret agent into the Frankish, Swabian, and Rhenish districts to whom he gave no passport for fear of identification and whom he instructed to act as if on private business, but to secure colonists by sending them individually to Luebeck and guaranteeing the return of their expense money. Nevertheless, he bitterly reproached the Kanzlei for the conduct of its proprietary agents and advanced the idea that the immigration campaign should be so conducted as to lay a broad foundation upon which to build a policy which should extend through the years. As the German states had furnished thousands of settlers through a long period of years to the British colonies in America, so they might, if properly handled, help

Russia to people her waste land, "if not now, then by and by."[67] To accomplish this, it was necessary to proceed slowly and to avoid arousing the enmity of the German princes, either through a superfluous number of agents or through an unwise display of zeal. The crown commissioners were ordered "to use all tact, thoughtfulness, and caution so that in the management of this business the city (in which they were located) as well as the officers of the province and even of the entire country, may have as little cause as possible for complaint, either actual or apparent, and thus avoid as far as possible any further limitation upon the freedom of emigration in Germany."[68] They were "expressly commanded to keep an eye open for the literature distributed in their territory, so as to check as much as they could the public and private distribution of all writings aiming directly or indirectly at the calumny or defamation of the (German) states by Russia".[69]

Owing to the character of the men employed to solicit immigrants for Russia, to the fact that the proprietary agents were paid according to the number of persons secured, and to the keen competition between the crown and the proprietary agents, no discrimination was made in the character and fitness of the immigrants. The proprietary agents solicited all persons alike and accepted everyone who applied to them without inquiring as to their morals, their health, their fitness for agriculture, or their properly authorized passports. As an indication of the work of these agents, the term "drummed up" was applied by the Russians to the colonists solicited.[70]

Von Simolin complains long and loudly about the abuses which the proprietary agents were allowed to practice and of the harm which resulted to the Russian campaign from their conduct. One of the first difficulties arising between them came from an order of the Tutel-Kanzlei that the commissioners should take a receipt from each colonist for the different items of expense paid out of government funds. This was necessitated by the dishonest conduct of two of the proprietors and the inability of the government to get a settlement with them. Von Simolin protests against the impracticability of this pro-

---

[67]Pisarevskii, *Foreign Colonization in Russia in the Eighteenth Century* (in Russian), "Letter from von Simolin to Empress Catherine, April 17/28, 1766," Appendix, 17.

[68]The crown commissioners received 500 rubles a year for their services, besides a bonus if they were able to save anything over a certain allowance for transportation expenses of the colonists. Their chief duty was to make known the terms of the manifesto of July 22, 1763, and of the printed advertisement concerning the transportation and maintenance of the colonists, and to attend to the printing and distribution of the same. Cf. *Ibid.*, "Instruction fuer den Russisch-Kaiserlichen Commissarium," Appendix, 11-14.

[69]*Ibid.*

[70]*Ibid.*, 102.

cedure and the "unnecessariness" of its being applied to the crown agents since "they can be trusted to handle the funds honestly."[71]

In the heat of the campaign of 1766, constant clashes occurred between the two factions. In March, von Simolin requested Count Orlov, the President of the Tutel-Kanzlei, to allow no proprietary agent in the territory where the crown agents were at work.[72] So many of the former were "swarming around in monstrous crowds" that their excessive number resulted in "the keenest competition which does the immigration business the greatest harm."[73] These agents were blamed for the opposition manifested in certain quarters against the crown commissioners and von Simolin served notice upon Orlov that he would not use his influence to protect the proprietary agents with whose methods he had no sympathy.

In contrast with this policy of the proprietary agents, the crown commissioners were instructed to search especially for well-to-do colonists who were able to pay their own expenses. Poor colonists were not to be refused, however, although they should be given to understand that the money advanced in accordance with the promises of the manifesto must be paid back before they would be permitted to leave Russia. In no case should people too old for manual labor or unfitted for agriculture be accepted.[74] Moreover, the commissioners were to take great pains to see that no secret solicitation was carried on, and that no colonists were accepted who could not show their regular dismissal by their landlord and by the government.[75] Other requirements such as the payment of an emigrant tax and the adjustment of all the colonist's debts were also investigated; and in one case cited, the crown commissioner had a provincial officer examine the applicant for emigration conjointly with him.

The proprietors on the other hand made a special appeal in their advertisements to those in economic distress, and though there were

---

71"Letter of Simolin to the Empress Catherine, Sept. 12/23, 1765," *idem*, Appendix, 8-11.

72Simolin repeated this complaint in a letter to the Empress April 17/28, 1766, in which he says, "Die uebertreibende Anzahl von Privatwerbern fuer die russischen Colonien, womit die vorliegenden deutschen Reichs-Kreysse, so zu sagen ueberschwemmt sind, thut dem diesseitigen Colonistengeschaefte im Grunde wirklich den groessten Schaden." Cf. *Ibid.*, Appendix, 17. Translation by the editors: "The excessive number of private recruiters for the Russian colonists, with which the leading German districts are flooded, so to speak, basically does truly the greatest harm to the present work of immigration recruitment."

73"Letter of Von Simolin to Orlov, February 20/March 3, 1766," *ibid.*, Appendix, 15.

74Instructions fuer den Russisch-Kaiserlichen Commisarium, *idem*, Appendix, 11-14.

75"Letter from von Simolin to Prince Golitzin, March 11/22, 1766, *idem*, Appendix, 29. Translation from the French to the English by Dr. Adam Giesinger: "All our commissioners in Germany are directed not to transport to Russia under any circumstances anyone who can not prove by a certificate from his territorial lord or the lord's law-officers that he is free to emigrate."

Avertissement.

Nachdem es ohnehin schon offenkündig ist, daß alle und jede Ausländer, welche sich vermöge des allerhöchsten Rußisch Kaiserlichen Manifests de dato Peterhof den 22sten Julii 1763. in dem Rußischen Reiche häuslich niederlassen, und insonderheit bey dem Anbau fruchtbarer, aber noch uncultivirten Ländereyen, eine gute und reichliche Nahrung suchen wollen, von den Rußisch Kayserlichen Gesandtschaften durchgängig die willfährigste Aufnahme und Förderung zu gewarten haben: So dienet hiermit weiter männiglich zur Nachricht, daß nunmehro auch die Anstalt ist getroffen worden, daß selbigen sofort nach ihrer Ankunft und Anmeldung in Hamburg oder in Lübeck bey den dortigen Rußisch Kaiserlichen Ministris und Commissarius, nachstehende Vortheile angedeihen sollen:

Erstens empfängt täglich eine erwachsene Manns-Person Acht Schilling, eine Weibs-Person Fünf Schilling, und ein Kind, ohne Unterschied des Geschlechts, Drey Schilling schwer Geld zum Unterhalt, welches in Reichs-Münze respective ohngefehr zwanzig Kreuzer, zwölf und einen halben Kreuzer, dann sieben und einen halben Kreuzer beträgt, mithin für eine ganze Familie etwas nahmhaftes ausmachet.

Zweytens wird in Hamburg für ihre gemächliche und wohlfeile Einquartierung, bis zur Zeit ihrer Abreise nach Lübeck, Sorge getragen, und allenfalls noch, zur Erleichterung der kurzen Reise von Hamburg nach Lübeck, für die Weiber und kleinen Kinder ein Fuhrwerk verschaffet.

Drittens wird in Lübeck gleichergestalt, nach aller Möglichkeit, für ihr Unterkommen gesorget, und zur Bestreitung des Quartiergeldes und ihrer übrigen Bedürfnisse, werden ihnen vorbemeldete Taggelder, bis zu ihrer Einschiffung nach Rußland, immer richtig abgereichet.

Viertens, ehe sie sich in Lübeck würklich zu Schiffe setzen, erhalten sie besagte Taggelder für vierzehn Tage mit einander auf einem Brete, damit sie sich die benöthigten Lebensmittel und andere Erfordernisse zu dieser Seefarth darvon anschaffen können. Endlich und

Fünftens, wann eine genügliche Anzahl solcher Colonisten in Lübeck beysammen ist, wird zu ihrer Ueberfarth nach Rußland ein eigenes Schiff, das sonsten keine andere Ladung bekömt, bedungen; und da sich für eine jede Familie nicht gleich ein besonderes Schiff befrachten läßet, so dörfen die in Lübeck ankommenden Colonisten daselbst nur so lang verziehen, bis sich ihrer so viele gesamlet haben, daß sie ein eigenes Schiff besetzen können.

Courtesy of Dr. Karl Stumpp of the Landsmannschaft der Deutschen aus Russland, Stuttgart.

Example of an "Avertisement" used to entice people to go to Russia.

many worthy people whom the war had reduced to poverty, the invitation drew many unworthy people whom the agents had not the courage to eliminate because they were paid so much per family. One such advertisement read: "There is offered to persons of both sexes, and particularly to those householders who find themselves in unfortunate circumstances, the advantages of fortune in a new colony, etc." After reciting the terms of settlement, it closes with these words:

> From all these advantages, it is to be seen that those householders who have nothing in their own land, can easily find themselves owners of houses, lands, perhaps fields or vineyards, even of a factory, if they have the industry for it; and in the course of time, just as is evident from those who have already gone into that country (and their number is very considerable) they may find themselves owners of an estate, which will put them in a position to live with much comfort, and then one day furnish to their heirs, who otherwise would have remained as wretched as their fathers, the hope of sharing an estate, which under other conditions these householders would never have been able to acquire.[76]

Such advertisements, emphasized by the personal work of enthusiastic agents, might be expected to draw many undesirable and unreleased people, none of whom were rejected. Von Simolin complains to the Empress: "In order to gain their private ends, the proprietary commissioners snatch up anybody and everybody, and very often use the most unpermissible means to do it. They do not bother to see whether the people are free and properly dismissed, or whether they are bound out; then their transport is stopped and searched by the soldiers and they lose their prey, besides raising a great hue and cry throughout the country."[77] Zuege notes the fact that one of his companions who had no proper passport was accepted without question or comment, just the same as he and his companion who had legal dismissals.[78] In the colony to which he was sent were people physically incapacitated for work, such as several cripples, but they were not rejected though their uselessness was apparent to everyone. Moral and industrial fitness were more difficult to determine, but the proprietors accepted those whom everyone knew were immoral and lazy or ignorant of the simplest kinds of work. This competition between the crown and proprietary agents, championed respectively by

---

[76]"Aussicht derjenigen Vortheile, so bey der im Russisschen Reich neu zu errichtenden Colonie anzutreffen sind, *idem*, Appendix, 6-8.

[77]"Letter of von Simolin to the Empress, April 17/28, 1766," *idem.*, Appendix, 17.

[78]Zuege, *Der russische Colonist,* I, 19-20.

the ambassadors, chiefly von Simolin, and by the Tutel-Kanzlei, was carried to an absurd extent. Thus, von Simolin complains to the College of Foreign Affairs that the colonists of Baron de Beauregard were especially degraded and the Kanzlei replied that this is a lie, concocted by jealous and unsuccessful rivals.[79]. The rivalry between the agents led to their coaxing or stealing away from their opponents groups of colonists, and to their spreading among the people false rumors intended to induce them to desert or to change their leaders.[80] For instance, a party of eight hundred colonists in the emigrant house in Wessp, Holland, were thrown into a panic by the report that they had been sold into serfdom in East India or Turkey, and not until they had received written assurances from the Russian minister at The Hague, brought by a committee of colonists who visited him, would they quiet down and proceed on their way. In Roslau a quarrel between two agents was taken up by the colonists, and on Easter Sunday, 1766, a riot broke out which was quelled by the soldiers only after the destruction of much property. In Luebeck a revolt against the enrollers who were accused of not providing sufficient traveling expenses to the colonists resulted in the injury of three agents and a suit in the municipal courts. All these troubles, brought the emigration business into disrepute in the countries where they occurred, disagreeably affected the better class of colonists and caused embarrassment and diplomatic complications to the Russian government.

In their methods of advertising there was less distinction between the crown and proprietary agents than there was in their personal conduct, because much of the immigration literature for both was put out by the government and sent to them from Russia. This material varied from a one-page broadside giving a mere outline of the terms of settlement to a pamphlet of ten to fifteen pages, detailing minutely not only the conditions of colonization, but the advantages to be gained, a description of the country, the price of produce, and directions for the colonists to follow in enrolling as emigrants.[81] As a rule, the crown

---

[79]Pisarevskii, *Foreign Colonization in Russia in the Eighteenth Century* (in Russian), 112, footnote 2. According to the list prepared by the Kanzlei in 1769, the crown colonists showed 6.7 per cent of their number unfitted for agriculture; Beauregard's colonists furnished 10.9 per cent, while the colonists of Pictet and Le Roi produced 18 per cent. These figures as a general basis must be accepted cautiously because of the difficulty of fixing a standard and the desire of the Kanzlei to make the best possible showing. However, this does not affect their value as a comparison of the two kinds of colonists.

[80]*Ibid.,* 114-118.

[81]A copy of one of the more conservative of these advertisements is found in the Kgl. Kreisarchiv at Amberg, accompanied by a copy of the manifesto of July 22, 1763, and a roster of the lands thrown open to settlement. After stating simply the general invitation, the document explains very distinctly in five short, concise paragraphs the amount of money each person is to receive for passage, the plans for the colonists' stay in Hamburg and Luebeck, and the arrangements made for their shipment.

commissioners used the more conservative and general of this literature while the proprietors enlivened and enriched it with comments and interpretations of their own and with phrases suited to catch the attention of people in certain localities.

The proprietors exploited certain colonies which they represented as having been started in the Saratov region where their land grants lay. Thus Catherinen-Lehen[82] was the Mecca for the emigrants of Baron de Beauregard while Katherinengab[83] and Katherinenburg[84] were the goal for the settlers of the two colonization companies. Although none of these places ever existed except as paper towns, this fact did not prevent the proprietors from advertising them. For instance, a circular distributed in the spring of 1766 represented the land for colonization as "near the new German city, Katherinenburg . . . where already more than 1,000 German families are to be found.[85] According to the locality in which the advertisement was to be distributed, the land for settlement was described as "a region which is in no respect inferior to France," or which "may be compared with the Upper Rhine."

The following is a translation of an advertisement distributed upon the streets and in the inns of Duesseldorf in 1765:[86]

ADVERTISEMENT.

> Her Royal Majesty, the present Most Liberal Reigning Empress of all Russia, and Self-Ruler of all the Russians, deigns hereby to make known to each and every person of either sex; to artisans, manufacturers and tradesmen; to agriculturists, vine-dressers, etc., that, out of a naturally kind disposition to alleviate poverty, she has been moved to set aside many millions of rubles as an advance payment for a ten years' tax-free period to such free people as may desire to settle down in Her Majesty's lands; particularly in her newly established colony, Catherinen-Lehen. It should be especially noted that anyone with a wife and children, or persons who,

[82]Mentioned in an advertisement found in the Kgl. Staatsarchiv in Duesseldorf, and in the Kgl. Kreisarchiv in Speyer, *Abtheilung: Oberrheinischer Kreis,* Akt. No. 1798.

[83]See in the Koenigliches Staats-Archiv in Muenster the reports of two Paderborn officers on Sept. 9, 1765, concerning a transport of colonists bound for this "city."

[84]Mentioned in an advertisement found in the Kgl. Geheimes Staatsarchiv in Berlin, *Rep. XI, Russland, Conv. 70;* and in one given in Pisarevskii, *Foreign Colonization in Russia in the Eighteenth Century* (in Russian), Appendix, 6-8, which is found in the Archives du Ministère de l'Agriculture et des Domaines de l'Étàt à St. Pétersbourg, No. 25.782.

[85]Haeberle, *Auswanderung und Koloniegruendungen der Pfaelzer,* 146; "Nachricht von denjenigen Vortheilen so bei der in Russischen Reich neu zu errichten Colonie anzutreffen sind," in Berlin Kgl. Geheimes Staatsarchiv, *Rep. XI, Russland, Conv. 70.*

[86]Kgl. Staatsarchiv in Duesseldorf, *Julich-Berg Geheimer Rat,* No. 39.

because of a lack of capital, are unable to advance in their trades, will be assisted not only with money for board from the date of their leaving home to their arrival at their destination, but also with all money necessary for fares and for expenses for an entire year; or at least until the next harvest. All necessary horses, cattle, sheep, goats, hogs, poultry, wagons, harness, tools, etc. will be provided, or cash for setting up factories. Winter and summer seeds will also be furnished, depending upon the amount of land assigned to each person for exclusive hereditary ownership.

INFORMATION

Therefore, whoever is free from serfdom and desires permission to enter this new colony and transportation thither, should address himself to the duly appointed Royal Russian Commissioner here at Deutz, Herr Colony-Captain von Weymar, staying with the proprietor of the "Golden Star" in the above place, within the next eight days, before the last transport for the year has been closed, which will be on the 21st or 22nd at the latest. The matter may then be discussed more at length and the applicant may satisfy himself as to its safety and reliability.

Another advertisement distributed by the proprietary agents was much more lengthy and in some respects not so accurate. It was dated August 23, 1765, but was being used as late as 1767. Vouched for by the seal of the Russian ambassador at The Hague, it represented its statements as being corroborated "by many delivered letters of both Protestant and Catholic clergymen, and by various other foreigners who, four years ago, settled down with several thousand (colonists) in the surrounding territory, and have been proven to be satisfied."[87] These "letters" are very suspicious documents as are the facts which they are intended to prove, but they doubtless allayed the fears of any who questioned whether their spiritual welfare would be provided for in the distant and religiously uncongenial land.

For cleverness of presentation, this advertisement was a gem of literature, and the bright colors in which it was arrayed could not fail to draw the moths to the light. According to the statements made therein, stock which compared most favorably with the black cattle of Holland and the horses of Arabia sold for only a few rubles. Luxuries

[87]"Beschreibung der Vorzuege der Russischen Colonie, Catherinen-Lehen, 1735," found in the Kgl. Kreisarchiv in Speyer, *Abtheilung, Oberrheinischer Kreis,* Akt. No. 1798.

such as asparagus and tobacco grew wild in abundance. The forests were full of animals useful for food and clothing; the streams were full of fish, and the meadows full of wonderfully beautiful tulips and other wild flowers. The establishment of a vast commerce with western Europe through the northern and southern seas (and hence constant communication with their old homes) only awaited the coming of new settlers. Even in winter, the trip to St. Petersburg was a mere "joy-ride." Following this radiant description, the advertisement outlines the contract to be made between the settlers and the entrepreneur in the terms of the Empress's *ukaz* and of the proprietary charter.[88]

The points emphasized in these advertisements furnish some interesting side lights upon the Russian immigration. The independence of the colonists from Russian officials was assured by the constant advertisement of the proprietors that the colonies were to be under the management of "directors from foreign countries," and thus the settlers were to be relieved from even temporary supervision by the Russian government. Religious freedom was continually dwelt upon. One advertisement enumerated the "Catholic, Lutheran, and Reformed" as being the beneficiaries of the Russian Empress; others said "Catholic and Protestant" alike; while all assured the colonists absolute freedom in ministry and in worship. The right to settle in colonies having the same language and religion was constantly mentioned. It is interesting to note that the question of military freedom, which became the bone of contention with the Russian Germans a century later and which led to their emigration, was seldom, if ever mentioned.

Action Taken by German Princes to Stop Emigration

In the German states the effect of the manifesto and of the work of the agents was first apparent about the cities, especially Regensburg in the south and Hamburg in the north. One of the first protests came from Elector Maximilian Joseph at Munich, February 28, 1764, in which the opinion of the prince concerning the Russian immigration campaign is expressed as follows:[89]

---

[88]Other advertisements used by one of the proprietary companies exploiting Katherinenburg are found in the Berlin Kgl. Geheimes Staatsarchiv, *Rep. XI, Russland, Conv. 70,* and in the Archives du Ministère de l'Agriculture et des Domaines de l'Etat à St. Pétersbourg, No. 25.782, quoted in Pisarevskii, *Foreign Colonization in Russia in the Eighteenth Century* (in Russian), 6-8.

[89]See also the protest of February 10, 1764, "Die Ausser-Land-Ziehung der Unterthanen betreffend" in *Sign. Sam. II, 518, Mar. VI of Wuerzburger Original-Verordnungen* im Kgl. Kreisarchiv, Wuerzburg.

> Not only has it been reported to us, but we are satisfied that the matter is in actual process of accomplishment whereby foreign emissaries have taken up their residence in our land and are seeking to deceive our peasants and subjects through false pretenses and to induce them to emigrate into a foreign country.
>
> Since now this bold undertaking aims at an entire depopulation of our lands, and hence may be regarded as not much better than treason against our country, we therefore command that all our police officers exercise careful watch for such emissaries; whenever they are found, have them arrested; and, after establishing their guilt, either through confession or other evidence, have them hanged by the executioner within twenty-four hours, at most.

A reward of fifty gulden and "silence" is offered to anyone who finds "such a villain"; on the other hand, anyone who assists an emissary in soliciting colonists will be punished "an Leib und Leben." Any subject who attempts to emigrate secretly will have his property confiscated; he himself will be arrested if found, and will be punished with hard labor and similar penalties, while any sale of property made for the purpose of emigrating will be declared null and void.[90]

Another German province to take early action against the enrollers was Saxony, which on August 21, 1764, issued an order "against seducing subjects and inhabitants to emigrate from the country."[91] The principal loss sustained by this province was a group of sectarians known as the Moravian Brethren who in 1765 founded the town of Sarepta, the most southerly of the Volga colonies. They were reinforced in 1766 by others of their brethren, of whom an official list has been preserved in the Royal Saxon State Archives in Dresden. This is the only list of emigrants to Russia found in the German archives thus far and is accounted for by the religious complexion of the colonists. Not belonging to the established churches, they lived in a compact group, and emigrating en masse, they could not avoid publicity if they desired. Hence they complied with the laws, sought permission of the government in the regular way, and were legally dismissed.[92] But these losses made Saxony all the more opposed to secret solicitation which was still going on, and April 25, 1766, a re-

---

[90]Copy of this decree is found in the Kgl. Kreisarchiv in Amberg.

[91]*Saechsischen Gesetzessammlung Codex Augusteus, Fortsetzung I,* Vol. III, Sp. 883/6 in the Kgl. Saechsisches Hauptstaatsarchiv in Dresden.

[92]For the same reasons, it is possible to trace the emigration of Mennonites whenever or wherever it occurs; while records of members of the established church can rarely be found.

script was issued "concerning means of carrying out the former rescript, and the arrest of those who go by post, and offend or commit misdemeanors."[93]

A short time previous to Saxony's first protest, July 13, 1764, the city council of Hamburg renewed an order which had been issued in 1752 to check the extensive activity of the American agents at that time. This decree forbade the "solicitation of subjects for emigration and settlement in foreign countries." The occasion for its renewal in 1764 was the establishment of a recruiting station in a suburb of Hamburg, where "various foreigners had established themselves, in order secretly to solicit and carry off all sorts of people as colonists, to which enterprise the inns and wine and beer halls frequently lent a helping hand."[94] The decree of the council had little or no effect upon the emigrant station which continued to exist as long as the campaign lasted. It was in the power of the city to remove the agents; but since the loss in its population was negligible, involving usually a class of people whom the city was glad to be rid of, and because the lodging of thousands of colonists there brought large financial benefit to the city, the order was not enforced. For example, in May, 1765, a transport of 600 to 700 persons arrived in Hamburg from Magdeburg at a time when 1,000 colonists were already quartered in the emigrant barracks. During the summers of 1765 and 1766, the baptismal records of the churches in the suburb contain the names of various children christened there "whose parents intended to make the journey to Astrakhan."[95]

The use of this suburb as a quartering place for the emigrants was continued for three years and led to much diplomatic correspondence between the municipal authorities and the Russian ambassador, Mussin-Puschkin. One of the proprietary companies made it its recruiting station also and picked up many reckless and dissolute persons who were floating around the country ready for any adventure. One of the chief characters in Zuege's narrative is the keeper of a house of

[93]*Saechsischen Gesetzessammlung Codex Augusteus, Fortsetzung I,* Vol. III, Sp. 1823/4, Kgl. Saechsisches Hauptstaatsarchiv, Dresden.

[94]Cited in a private letter of Dr. Hagedorn, Director of the Staatsarchiv der freien und Hansestadt Hamburg.

[95]One entry reads as follows: "Den 27. September, 1765: Paullus Antonius Johann Peter, ehelicher Sohn des Johann Christoffer Schnoken aus Muelhausen. Gevattern: Antonius Menonier de Precouse (Precourt) Landherr zu St. Lorett, directeur der Colonien Ihrer Majaestaet der Kaiserin aller Ruessen; Piere Deschamps; Jeanne Maria Rochee." Extract made for the writer by Dr. Hagedorn from *the baptismal records of the Church of St. Paul in Hamburger Berg.* This Precouse is undoubtedly the Proprietor Precourt. All the rest of the entries show German parentage, although one child is named for his two French godfathers, one of whom is "Seine Exzellenz, der Herr General Leonty." (The suburb formerly called Hamburger Berg is today — 1975 — the notorious St. Pauli district of Hamburg. — The editors.)

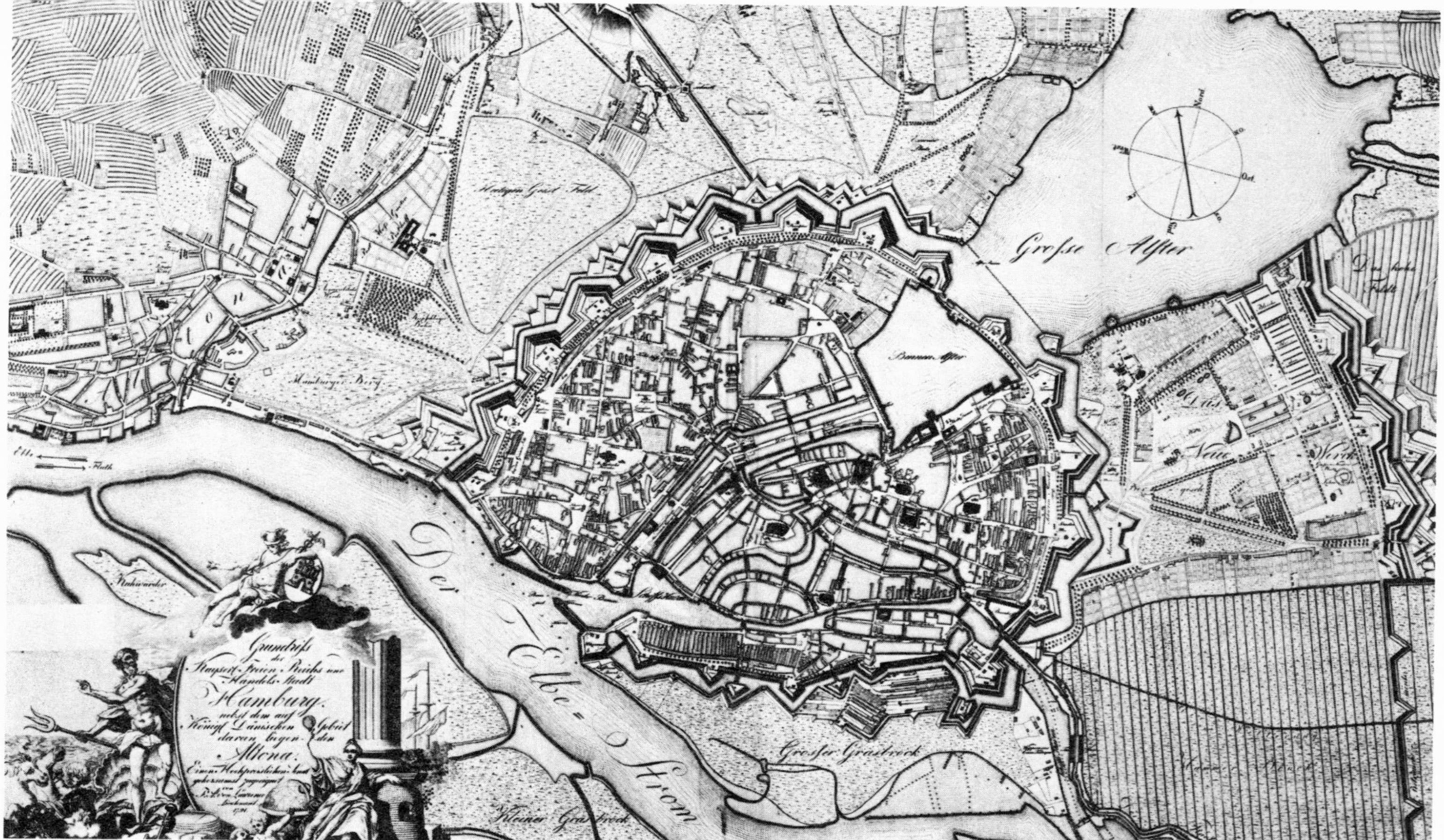

Courtesy of the Hamburg City Archives.

Plat of Hamburg in the late Eighteenth Century. Hamburger Berg where the Volga Germans gathered to go to Russia is to the left of the city walls.

prostitution from Hamburg "with his whole harem." Another representative of a somewhat different type was the *Vorsteher* of his colony, a beltmaker by the name of Kratzky. Through the encouragement of merchants, innkeepers, and shipmasters who profited financially from the traffic in emigrants and the activity of agents who brought them in from every part of the German states, the traffic via Hamburg continued in spite of decrees to the contrary.

Aside from these prohibitions in 1764, the German states seem not to have been disturbed by the activity of the Russian government until the following summer when Prussia began one of the most persistent and successful counter-campaigns waged against the movement. Decisive prohibitions, faithful cooperation of the officials, systematized and constant espionage, all prompted by Prussia's selfish interest in her own immigration campaign, brought results more satisfactory than in any other of the agent-ridden provinces.[96] Although a few of the subjects of Frederick the Great slipped through the lines and joined the crowds in Luebeck; and although he watched with jealous eye many thousands of emigrants, whom he coveted for his own vacant lands, pass through and by his domain; and although he saw some of his recent settlements practically abandoned and his borders lined with foreign immigration agents, the King persevered in his defensive campaign and secured definite results therefrom.

One of the first clashes between the Russian and the Prussian officials occurred over the transportation of the colonists. Prussia at this time practically controlled the river traffic to the north. Magdeburg, an important port on the Elbe, lay at the southern point of her kingdom while the duchy of Cleves at the mouth of the Rhine was also Prussian territory. The officers here, in line with Frederick's policy, kept a strict watch upon all emigrant transports, exacting the customary tolls and exercising the rights of search in case they suspected runaway subjects to be hidden therein. The Russian officials chafed under these restrictions and frequently complained to their ambassador.

In June, 1765, Prince Dolgoruki, the Russian minister in Berlin, insistently requested an explanation from the Prussian government concerning certain colonists bound for Russia who had been detained in their passage through Wesel and Magdeburg. The Prussian government, in asking information of the local officials concerning the incident, even at this time showed no disposition to hinder their passage and ordered that if any excessive charges had been made, the money

[96]At this time Prussia was not employing any immigration agents in South Germany although she had conducted an active and successful campaign just previous to the war and began another at the close of the Russian canvass.

should be refunded. The Magdeburg official replied that the Russian ambassador had no cause for complaint since only the regular tolls, a gulden a boat, had been exacted from the leader of the transport and that the colonists themselves had not been taxed. On the contrary, he maintained that when the people came down the river in little boats "in which they were packed like herring," the townspeople took pity on them and provided them with food, while the municipal authorities permitted their transfer to larger boats, upon which they departed unhindered.[97]

But as the number of colonists increased, the question arose as to whether Prussia should continue to allow them unhindered passage through her territories. For instance, in October, 1765, the authorities in Cleves asked instructions from the king as to whether or not they should sustain the act of one of the officials who had refused to allow a transport of Russian emigrants to pass without an official order. The document further reports that the Cleves authorities had exercised the right of search in the case of this transport of 442 colonists from Upper Germany and Switzerland which had come down the Rhine a few days previously. Four young artisans from a neighboring factory had run away and it was rumored that they were going to America by way of Amsterdam. Suspecting that they might be upon this boat, the transport was stopped and a commissioned officer searched every passenger. Not finding the runaways, the authorities allowed the transport to proceed upon the payment of the customary tolls; but, in view of the "very emphatic order during the last war" to watch for Russian commissioners, they now asked for instructions as to how to proceed. "Although the present situation had no similarity to the one of that time, since the people transported today have not been engaged out of Your Royal Majesty's lands, yet these Russian enlistments have an influence on the population of Your Royal Majesty's provinces of this place, because there is every reason to suppose that of the 442 persons who were taken to Russia a large part might easily have settled in the country here."[98]

Next to the matter of transportation came the question of the emissaries. Prussia had taken alarm at the very first steps of the Russian government; and, as has been seen, had issued strict orders to watch for the enrollers. They had been kept from openly soliciting colonists within her territory, but during the height of the campaign

[97]"Correspondence between the Cabinet Ministers, the General Directorium and the Kabinetsministerium from June 30 to August 7, 1765, in the Berlin Kgl. Geheimes Staatsarchiv, *Rep. XI, Russland, Conv. 70.*

[98]"Bericht der Clevischen Kriegs-und Domaenen Kammer, 7 October, 1765," in the Berlin Kgl. Geheimes Staatsarchiv, *Rep. XI, Russland, Conv. 70.*

in 1766 they set up numerous recruiting stations on her borders, especially in Anhalt and Saxony. To checkmate their maneuvers, Frederick ordered the local officers to renew their strict supervision over the inhabitants; and if they found any who had been persuaded to leave, they were to report to their superior officers their names, the place to which they intended to emigrate, and the amount of property they possessed. After this, they were to "make such orders that the emigrant will be dissuaded from his intention and shown how to seek an honest living at home."[99] The difficulty of carrying out these orders, however, was not slight. For instance, in May, 1766, the King was informed that 500 colonists were reported to be preparing to leave for Russia, among whom were 200 Mansfelders, Prussian subjects. The officer, after detailing the unsuccessful efforts to locate a knight who was said to be among the number, complains of the difficulty of handling the situation, as follows: "It seems that the majority of the colonists are probably very poor people who have no property and consequently can break up just as they are and go away. I do not know by what means such people could be restrained from their intentions."[100]

But the Prussian King was persistent. Even in Hamburg, through the cooperation of his ambassador, he reclaimed some subjects who had eluded his officers at home.[101] Further than this, he now assumed the offensive and demanded of the Russian government the removal of their immigration agents from his borders. How deeply he was concerned is shown in a letter which he wrote to his ambassador in St. Petersburg, Count von Solms, in June, 1766, in which he says: "The Russian enrollers are committing such excesses upon my borders that it is no longer endurable; Lieutenant N- - - has taken people out of my country from the region about Fuerstenwalde practically by force. They sent the people by boat from Magdeburg to Hamburg, and I was compelled to give orders to have any of my subjects among the colonists arrested, and to let only the foreigners pass. Such proceedings would be tolerated by no power and you may tell Panin that

---

[99]"Die Magdeburgische Kriegs-u. Domaenen-Kammer an den Landrat Carl Wilhelm V, Wulcknitz zu Volksted, 13. Feb. 1766," in the Kgl. Staatsarchiv in Magdeburg, *Rep. A 32a, Tit. XXI, No. 11.*

[100]"Oberamtmann Rennert zu Loburg an die Koeniglich Pruessische-Kriegs-u. Domaenen-Kammer zu Magdeburg, 1. Mai 1766," in the Kgl. Staatsarchiv in Magdeburg, *Rep. A 32a Tit. XXI, No. 11.*

[101]"Anlage I., Nachrichten ueber den Durchzug deutscher nach Russland auswandernder Kolonisten durch das hamburgische Gebiet 1764 bis 1766," an extract made for the writer by Dr. Hagedorn from the Staatsarchiv der freien und Hansestadt Hamburg, II., No. 1756.

I cannot endure it any longer."[102] This letter was occasioned by a report from von Brenckenhoff, who had settled 24,000 South Germans in Neumark, that the Russian agents were drawing away from Frederick's new settlements the colonists who had recently been located there. In one colony he complained that "the houses are almost entirely empty"; while a detective whom he sent to the recruiting station in Anhalt-Zerbst reported that in a few days a transport of 700 people would leave for Magdeburg, "most of whom are the very people whom Your Royal Majesty brought from the empire and established in the neighborhood of Ruedersdorff and Fuerstenwalde" (near Berlin). Besides, the agents had "presumed" to scatter their advertisements all through Pomerania and Neumark and to try to coax the new settlers away under promise of greater privileges than Prussia had given.[103] The occasion for further action on the part of Prussia was largely removed by the discontinuance of the Russian campaign, although the proprietary enrollers continued their operations in spite of the orders of the Russian government to the contrary.[104]

It has been shown that a few of the German states as Bavaria, Saxony, Hamburg, Prussia, and Wuerzburg took action in 1764 through rescripts against the Russian emigration; and that, beginning in 1765, Prussia began active measures to prevent the loss of her subjects. By the year 1766 the work of the enrollers, particularly of the proprietary agents who had concentrated their efforts largely on South Germany, began to bear such a gigantic harvest that a flood of protests and prohibitions arose from the princes of these states. One of the first persons to take action was the Bishop of Mainz and his rescript is typical of most of those following. On February 18, 1766, he issued an order reiterating his previous rules forbidding secret emigration "ausserhalb deren Reichs Laenden," and prescribed the penalties attaching to it. Any property left behind by such emigrants was to be confiscated by the state; and to keep them from selling their property for the purpose of leaving the country, all transfers and mortgages, either of personal

---

[102] "Berichte des pruessischen Gesandten in Russland an Koenig Friederich II, 1766," in the Berlin Kgl. Geheimes Staatsarchiv, *Rep. 96, (Kabinet des Koenigs) 56 K;* see also *Politischen Korrespondenz Friederichs des Grossen,* Bd. XXV, 132; and Pisarevskii, *Foreign Colonization in Russia in the Eighteenth Century* (in Russian), 133.

[103] Schreiben des Geh. Finanzrats Franz B. L. von Brenckenhoff an den Koenig, June 9, 1766, in the Berlin Kgl. Geheimes Staatsarchiv, *Rep. 96, (Kabinet des Koenigs) 56 K;* Haeberle, *Auswanderung und Koloniegruendungen der Pfaelzer,* 137.

[104] Silesia, which had come under the control of Prussia during the Seven Years' War and hence was subject to Frederick's conservation policy, was the recipient of the various prohibitory orders such as were issued in the other Prussian states. (Private letter of Dr. Minardus, Director of the Kgl. Staatsarchiv in Breslau.) Practically no emigration took place from here for the population was scant and this province itself was the goal of an extensive campaign carried on in 1772 in Hesse where numerous requests for permission to emigrate and their accompanying reports are to be found.

or real property, had to be recorded by the courts. If it could be proved that the sale had been made for the purpose of emigration, any money paid by the purchaser was forfeited and any property purchased by him was confiscated. In addition to the definite penalties attaching to property regulations, a general threat of severe punishment was made against subjects who emigrated without permission of their government, or who "cultivated suspicious relationships with the emissaries."[105]

An attempt to secure "uniform regulations against the foreign agents" among the various German states was made at this time, largely under the leadership of the Bishop of Mainz. In a letter to the Hessian government on February 7, 1766, he recited the evils which the emigration campaign was causing, both to the empire which was suffering "eine hoechst nachtheilige Entvoelkerung,"[106] and also to the people who "entweder im Ehlende zu Grund gehen, oder nach fruchtlosen Hin und Herwandern mit groesstem Nothstand Huelf- und Mittelloss zurueckkehren muessen,"[107] and he begged the administration to take some systematic and drastic measures against the agents who were to blame for the condition of affairs.[108] Partly in response to these outside appeals, and partly to checkmate a movement which they themselves had recognized as disastrous to their states, a number of princes issued severe and threatening edicts against both agents and emigrants. These edicts, in the order of their publication, were issued by the Elector of Trier on February 27, 1766;[109] the Duke of Wirtemberg on March 25;[110] the prince of Nassau-Weilburg on April 12; [111]

105*Mainz Verordnung, Rep. 85, Fasc. 2* in the Kgl. Kreisarchiv in Wuerzburg; *Historische Verein, Bamberg-Verordnungen,* in the Kgl. Kreisarchiv at Bamberg.

106Translation: "a highly disastrous depopulation" — The editors.

107Translation: "either go to ruin in misery or after fruitlessly wandering back and forth have to return home again in the greatest state of distress without help or means," — The editors.

108"Schreiben der Churfuerstl. Mainzischen Regierung an die Fuerstl. Hessische wegen gemeinschaftlicher Massregeln gegen fremde Werber," Mainz, d. 7ten Februar 1766; "Gutachten der fuerstl. hessischen Regierung betreff. die in verschiedenen Gegenden sich einfindenden Emissarien und die gegen solche zu veranstaltende Vorkehrunge, Darmstadt, 15 u. 24 Februar 1766"; "Antwort zu Mainz, Darmstadt, d. 24 Febr. 1766"; found in *Acten des Geheimen Staatsarchiv, Abtheilung XI, Bevoelkerungspolizei aus Conv. I.*, in the Grossherzoglich Hessisches Haus- und Staatsarchiv in Darmstadt. See also Learned, *Guide to the Manuscript Material relating to American History in the German State Archives, 275.* Translation: "A document of the electoral government of Mainz to the princes of Hesse with regard to common measures to be taken against foreign agents." Mainz, the 7th of February 1766; "An opinion of the princely Hessian government concerning the emissaries who are found in various places and the preventive measures which should be passed against them." Darmstadt, the 15th and 25th of February 1766; "Answer to Mainz," Darmstadt, the 24th of February 1766. — The editors.

109Letter of Dr. Domarus, Director of the Kgl. Staatsarchiv in Wiesbaden.

110Letter from the Director of the Kgl. Wuerttemburgische Archiv in Stuttgart.

111Letter of Dr. Domarus, Director of the Kgl. Staatsarchiv in Wiesbaden.

the Landgrave of Hesse on April 28;[112] the Bishop of Wuerzburg on April 29;[113] the Elector of Pfalz on May 27, reiterating the *Kreis* decree of April 21[114]; the prince of Nassau-Dillenberg on July 17;[115] and another order from the Bishop of Mainz on July 22.[116] Other states repeated the orders issued in 1764 against the Russian emigration, as Bavaria on January 3;[117] Saxony on April 25;[118] and Wuerzburg and Prussia on December 19.[119] Most of these official edicts did not mention the Russian campaign or the Russian enrollers; but accompanying letters, official documents, and advertisements used by the agents indicate, without any doubt, their object. The princes used no uncertain terms, moreover, in expressing their opinion of the matter. The immigration campaign of the Russian government was called "das verderbliche Unheil," (pernicious disaster); "einer Menschen Handel," (a slave trade); 'Menschenentfuehrer," (an abductor of human beings); and "die stille Anwerbungen und Entfuehren," (the quiet enrollment and abduction); the agents were "Emissarii," who carry on "ein ordentlicher Handel mit denen Menschen sozusagen, wie mit dem Viehe."[120]

The number of Germans emigrating to Russia at this time was so great that some of the provinces questioned whether the people should not be denied absolutely the right of emigration. In Hesse, for instance, the authorities were uncertain what action to take upon the numerous requests for permission to emigrate and discussed what ways and means could be employed to stop the dreadful disorder caused by the Russian campaign. A typical *Gesuche* read as follows:

> We, the following people are as a whole all so reduced in circumstances that we for that reason are prepared to take a beggar's staff, because even our few possessions have debts and we cannot support ourselves. For that reason we have decided to travel to the Russian Empire with others. Most esteemed landgrave, most gracious prince and master, I, Johann Hofmann, myself and family, Johannes Bechtold with

---

[112]*Idem.*

[113]Letter from Director of the Kgl. Kreisarchiv in Wuerzburg.

[114]Letter from Director of the Kgl. Kreisarchiv Pfalz in Speyer.

[115]Letter from Dr. Domarus, Director of the Kgl. Staatsarchiv in Wiesbaden.

[116]*Mainz Verordnung, Rep. 85, Fasc. 2* in the Kgl. Kreisarchiv in Wuerzburg.

[117]*Sammlung der Kurpflaz-Baierischen Landesverordnungen,* herausgegeben von Georg Karl Meyer, Muenchen, 1784, No. XXIII.

[118]Saechsisches Hauptstaatsarchiv, Dresden.

[119]"Verbot und Warnung des Bischops von Wuerzburg und des Markgrafen von Brandenburg," *Sam. II, 646, Wuerzburger Original Verordunungen* in the Kgl. Kreisarchiv in Wuerzburg.

[120]Translation: ". . . the agents were 'emissarii,' who carry on regular trade with people as though they were cattle." — The editors.

wife and children, have been arrested and put in a state of serfdom to your lordship and because of this and to be permitted to leave the country we need your gracious dispensation. We, therefore, ask your princely serene Highness that you graciously grant our most subservient, humble and prostrate request to leave your princely lands. We comfort ourselves with the thought of a most gracious favorable hearing, etc.

Johann Hofman *[sic]*	with wife and 5 children
Johannes Bechtold	with wife and 3 children
Georg Michel Mueller	with wife and 2 children
Johann Tobias Lentz	with wife and 4 children
Johannes Alten, widower	with 5 children

von Eckhardsborn — District Lissberg, Superior Bailiwick Nidda[121]

In a report of the Hessian government in Giessen to the Landgrave on March 7, 1766,[122] appeal was made concerning emigration to former legislation which regarded it both as hurtful to the state and not to be allowed. Since the chief plea made in the requests was poverty, debt, and the impossibility of making a sufficient living in their homes, the author of this report discusses at great length the reasonableness of these excuses and confesses the inability of the state to cope with the situation under existing conditions.

The futility of separate edicts by princes of the various states was early apparent. A Russian enroller, driven out of one small province, could establish his headquarters just across the border in a friendly state and do as much harm as before, but without any redress on the part of the injured party. For instance, a crown commissioner named Facius was appointed by the Russian minister Simolin to recruit colonists in Frankfurt am Main; but the authorities of the city refused to permit him to work there unless he secured a personal recommendation from the Russian Empress within three months. In spite of protests from Simolin, the municipality finally expelled the agent who was permitted to establish himself at Buedingen, in Isenburg, a few miles distant. Here he secured the support of the petty prince and was granted the use of the public buildings for emigrant houses, free access to the city, and a guarantee against high prices for supplies and pro-

121Translated from the German by the editors. *Acten des Geheimen Staatsarchiv, Abtheilung XI, Bevoelkerungspolizei aus* Conv. I, 1766, in Grossh. Hess. Haus- und Staatsarchiv in Darmstadt.

122*Idem.*

Wir Burgermeistere und Rath dieser des
Heil. Reichs Freyen Stadt Frankfurt am Mayn
fügen hiermit zu wissen: Nachdeme Wir zeithero zu Unserem grösten Misve-
gnügen vernehmen auch in der That selbsten erfahren müssen, daß in hiesige
Gegenden sich verschiedene ausländische Emissarii eingefunden, welche, durch Zusicherung und Verspre-
chung allerhand zu gewarten habender Vortheile, sowohl hier verburgerte und im Schutz stehende
Personen auch deren Kinder und Angehörige, als besonders viele hiesiger Stadt und anderer benachbarten Herrschaften Unterthanen an sich zu locken und anzuwerben auch demnächst ausser Landes un
denen Gränzen des Reichs in weit entfernte Colonien zu führen sich angemasset, Wir aber diesem, an si
Reichsgesetzwiedrigen, zu Entvölckerung derer Lande des Heil. Römischen Reichs gereichenden, höchs
strafbahren, Unternehmen in dieser Stadt und deren Gebiete auf einige Weise nachzusehen nicht g
meynet sind; Als ergehet hiermit an alle hiesige Burgere, Beysassen und Schutzangehörige w
überhaupt an die Unterthanen derer, Unserer Gerichtsbarkeit unterworfenen, Dorfschaften die erns
liche und gemessene Anweisung, Verwarnung und Befehl: nicht nur in dem Fall dergleichen frem
Emissarien sich itzo würcklich oder künftig in hiesiger Stadt oder deren Gebiete betretten lassen sollte
davon, zu Verordnung der Gebühr gegen selbige, alsofort einem derer wohlregierenden Herre
Burgermeistere oder respective Löblichem Land-Amt die geziemende Anzeige zu thun, sondern au
zu heimlicher höchstahndungswürdiger Verführ- Anwerbung und Transport dergleichen in frem
Landen ziehenden Colonisten sich weder directe noch indirecte gebrauchen zu lassen, überhaupt ab
ohne Unsere besondere Erlaubnuß nicht wegzuziehen, noch denen aus denen Landen anderer Her
schaften hier vorbey und durch die hiesige Dorfschaften und deren Bezircke passirenden dergleiche
Emigranten weder mit Vorspann, Beherbung, Atzung noch sonsten, immassen die Schulthei
gedachter Dorfschaften davor haften sollen, an Handen zu gehen oder ihnen in einige Weise Vorschu
zu thun, gestalten dann diejenige, welche sich dieser Unserer ernstlichen und wohlbedächtlichen Ve
ordnung, deren Inhalt Wir aufs genaueste befolget wissen wollen, nicht fügen oder sich dagege
das mindeste zu Schulden kommen lassen würden, mit willkührlicher nachdrücklicher Strafe beleg
und selbige an ihnen, ohne alle Nachsicht oder Entschuldigung, exequiret werden soll. Wornach si
jederman zu achten.

Geschlossen bey Rath,
den 21sten April 1766.

Courtesy of the Frankfurt am Main Archives

Decree of the mayor and town council of the Free City of Frankfurt am Main, forbidding emigration to foreign countries. (April 21, 1766)

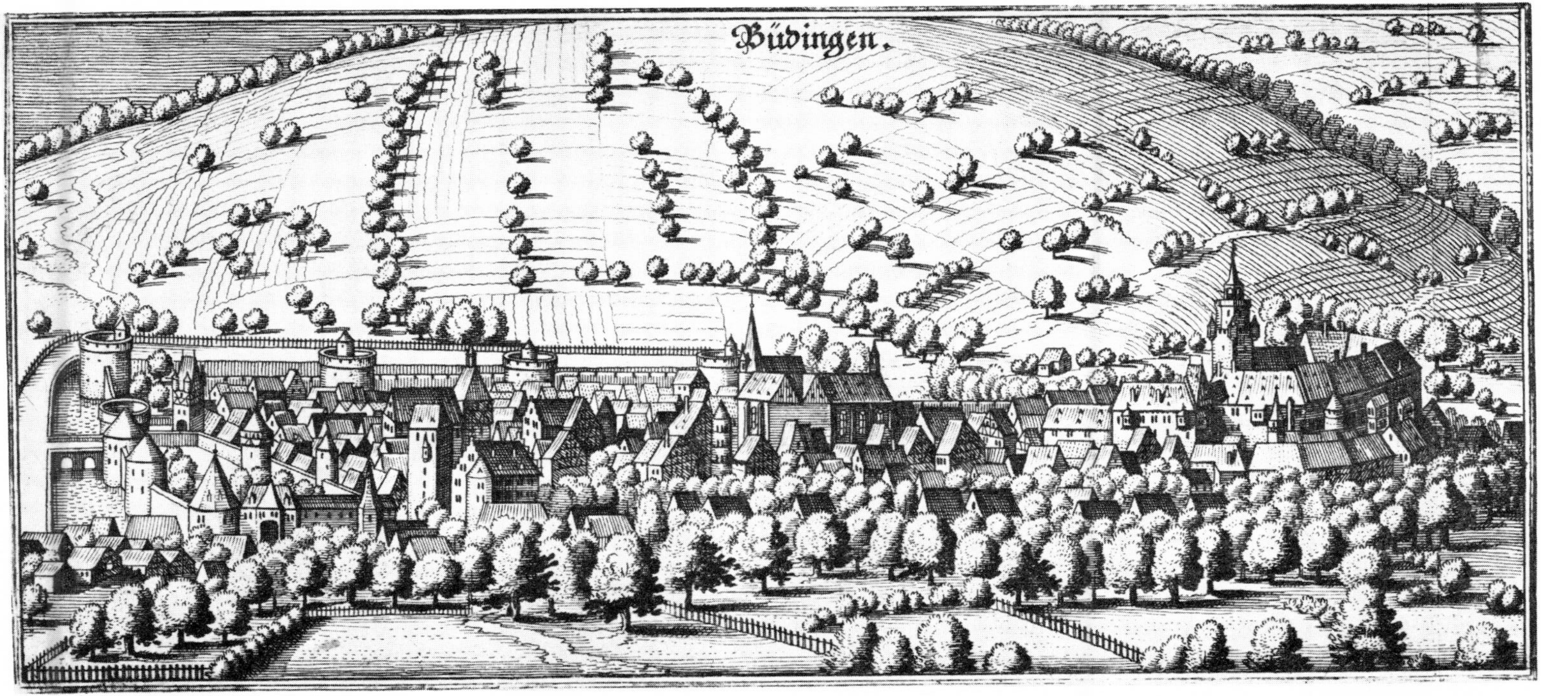

Courtesy of the Frankfurt am Main Historical Museum.

General view of Buedingen in the Seventeenth Century. Many Volga Germans were married in this town before leaving for Russia. (Artist unknown).

visions for his colonists. Safely entrenched behind the protecting care of this princeling, who had nothing to lose by his conduct and a small subsidy to gain, the Russian commissioner enrolled and shipped away to the Empress's domains thousands of subjects from the surrounding countries.[123]

The first united action was taken by the princes of the Lower Rhine, which comprises the cities of Cologne, Trier, and Mainz, and the province of the Palatinate. April 21, 1766, an edict was passed, according to the terms of which no subject, under any conditions whatever, was to be allowed to emigrate outside the Holy Roman Empire. Anyone attempting to leave secretly was to be arrested and to suffer the confiscation of his property, imprisonment, or corporal punishment or hard labor, according to the offense. The sale of personal property for the purpose of emigration was forbidden. Immigration agents were to be carefully watched for, and sentenced to corporal or capital punishment; while the greatest strictness was enjoined upon all local officials in apprehending and punishing those who disobeyed the rescript.[124]

Under the encouragement and insistence of the princes of the Lower Rhine, led chiefly by the Bishop of Mainz, other princes were led to join in similar measures. The Bavarian provinces, whose princes had early opposed the movement, took action almost simultaneously with the Lower Rhine countries and joined the latter in bringing pressure to bear upon the Frankish, Swabian and Upper Rhine districts. In addition to refusing residence to the agents, a special advantage would come from denying them transportation through their territories. This could result only from united action, and in recognition of this fact, steps were taken to make common cause between contiguous districts; as for example, the Bavarian and Frankish districts. In spite of the urgency of the situation and the prince's knowledge that almost every day many of his subjects were either leaving secretly or openly defying his orders, it was the close of the year before action could be secured in the latter district.

Meanwhile the occasion for such action was rapidly disappearing. The Russian government was experiencing great difficulties in handling its immigration campaign.[125] The complications which had arisen

---

[123]Pisarevskii, *Foreign Colonization in Russia in the Eighteenth Century* (in Russian), 142-50: also Appendix, 28.

[124]"Das Verbot der Auswanderung und die Massregeln gegen die sogenannten Werber betreffend 1709-1804," *Verwaltungs-Sachen Rubr. V,* in the Staedtisches Archiv in Mannheim. See also Learned, *Guide to the Manuscript Materials relating to American History in the German State Archives,* 319.

[125]Pisarevskii, *Foreign Colonization in Russia in the Eighteenth Century* (in Russian), 163ff

with the west European states kept the ministers busy granting requests, hearing complaints, and defending the conduct of their government. Simolin, the most enthusiastic supporter of the campaign, insisted to his superior officers that the South German states were feigning opposition simply to appease Hungary while in fact they were glad to get rid of their surplus population. The government was not easily convinced, however, and proceeded cautiously in its diplomatic relations.

A more difficult situation arose over the lack of facilities for transportation. The number of vessels at the disposal of the Russian commissioners was small and contrary winds delayed sailing so that the crowds of emigrants gathered at Luebeck became too large to handle. The city authorities feared that the lack of proper food would cause the spread of disease and that riots would break out.[126] They, therefore, forbade the Russian commissioner, Schmidt, to accept any more colonists sent by the entrepreneurs until the congestion was relieved. In April, 1766, the Russian ambassador at Luebeck wrote to his government that 24,000 colonists were expected in Luebeck that summer and that there were not enough vessels to carry them, "nor even barrels for water and beer." Not knowing what to do with the people, he begged the government to order the crown commissioners not to enroll any more colonists. As a result of this request, the College of Foreign Affairs and the Tutel-Kanzlei ordered their crown and proprietary agents respectively not to accept any more colonists for some time. The crown enrollers obeyed, but the proprietary agents went on with their work. This further complicated matters between the people solicited and the agents; and in June, 1766, word was sent direct from Panin that all enrollment must cease, the colonists already enrolled must be got rid of as diplomatically as possible and no new ones accepted. In September the Russian government decided upon an explanatory statement which it inserted in foreign newspapers, warning people against enrolling.

At first the restraints were to be only temporary "for the rest of the summer," "for a time," and then, "for a year." The government, however, was becoming more timid as a result of the storm of protests from the German states while the difficulty of transportation and the

[126]In the Staatsarchiv Luebeck is a large fascicle of documents relating to this matter "die durch die Verhandlungen mit den Kommissaren der russischen Regierung ueber die Befoerderung der Kolonisten, ueber ihre Unterbringung waehrend ihres Aufenthaltes in Luebeck, ueber ihren Gesundheitszustand, ueber Streitigkeiten, mit luebeckischen Buergern, u. a. m." Private letter from the director of the Staatsarchiv Luebeck. Translation: "discussions (took place) with the commissioners of the Russian government about the dispatching of the colonists, about their accommodations during their stay in Luebeck, about their condition of health, about quarrels with Luebeck citizens and so forth." — Translation by the editors.

WIR JOSEPH der Andere von GOttes Gnaden Erwehlter Römischer Kayser, zu allen Zeiten Mehrer des Reichs, in Germanien und zu Jerusalem König, MitRegent und Erb-Thronfolger der Königreiche Hungarn, Böheim, Dalmatien, Croatien und Slavonien, Ertz-Herzog zu Oesterreich, Herzog zu Burgund und zu Lothringen, Groß-Herzog zu Toscana, Großfürst zu Siebenbürgen, Herzog zu Mayland und Bar, gefürsteter Graf zu Habsburg, Flandern und Tyrol. rc. rc.

Entbieten N. allen und jeden Churfürsten, Fürsten Geist- und Weltlichen, Prälaten, Grafen, Freyen, Herren, Rittern, Knechten, Landvögten, Hauptleuten, Vitzdomen, Vögten, Pflegeren, Verweseren, Amtleuten, Landrichteren, Schultheissen, Burgermeisteren, Richteren, Räthen, Burgeren, Gemeinden, und sonst allen Unseren und des Reichs Unterthanen und Getreuen, in was Würden, Stand oder Weesen die seynd, denen dieses unser Kayserl. Edict fürkommet, Unseren freund- Vetter- und Oheimlichen Willen, Kayserl. Huld, Gnade und alles Gutes, und fügen Euer Liebden Liebden, Andacht Andacht, Liebden Liebden und euch hiemit zu wissen: Uns ist von denen ausschreibenden Fürsten deren vorderen Reichs Crayßen verschiedentlich angezeigt worden, was massen seither dem vor kurzen Jahren geendigten Krieg das Emigriren deren teutschen Reichs Unterthanen im Schwung gehe, und dieses bedenkliche Unweesen so zunehme, daß dadurch das teutsche werthe Vatterland einen merklichen Verlust vieler diensttauglichen Leuthen erleiden, und nicht wenig entvölkeret werde. Die von gedachten Creyß-Ausschreib-Aemteren zum Theil durch Edicten gemachte Vorkehrungen hätten aber um deswillen entgegen, diese Entvölkerung die hinlängliche Würkung nicht verschaffen können, weilen in mehreren Unseren und des Heil. Röm. Reichs Städten die Versammlungs Niederlage, und die Transportirungs-Gelegenheit, zumahlen zu Wasser gestattet, sonderlich aber denen verführerischen Anwerbern und Unterhändlern in solchen Unseren und des Reichs Städten die gröste Handbietung geleistet wird. Uns dahero dieselbe Creyß-Ausschreibende Fürsten wiederhohlt angelegentlich und bittlich ersucht haben, damit wir als Römischer Kayser durch Unser Kayserlich Obrist-Hauptliches Amt eine allgemeine Verordnung in das gesammte Reich wider die annoch täglich fürdaurende Auswanderung, besonders an unsere und des Reichs Städte wo der gemeinschädliche Unfug sothaner Werbungen am häuffigsten getrieben werde, vorzüglich und nahmentlich an die Reichs Städte, Lübeck, Bremen und Hamburg zu gänzlicher derselben Abstellung zu erlassen. Wie wir nun dieses an Uns gelangte Suchen zur Wohlfahrt des Reichs vorträglich, auch deshalb eine weitere ausgiebige Hülfe erforderlich zu seyn, ansehen, nicht weniger in alt und neueren Gesetzen mehrmahlen auch in unserer Königl. Wahl Capitulation verschiedentliche heilsame Vorsehung enthalten zu seyn, befinden, auf was Weise der Anwerbung und dem Auszug einiges Volks ausserhalb Reichs, wann dadurch, zumahlen dasselbe der Mannschafft entblösset werde, vorgekommen werden solle. So wollen Wir auch, aus wahrer dem Reich geneigter Reichs vätterlicher Liebe mit unserem Kayserl. Amt dem obgedacht- so allgemein schädlichen und unersätzlichen Uebel der Entvölkerung abzuhelfen, mithin alles Ausziehen teutscher Reichs Unterthanen in fremde mit dem Reich in keiner Verbindung stehende Länder unter allen Gattungen des Fortwanderens, welche den gänzlichen Verlust so vieler teutscher Innwohnern und dadurch dessen Entblössung und Entkommung von aller vatterländischen Beyhülffe verursachen, abzustellen nicht länger anstehen. Gesinnen und begehren dahero an Euer Liebden Liebden, Andn Andn. und Lbdn Lbdn Freund- Vetter- und Oheim und gnädiglich, anderen aber befehlen Wir hiemit gnädigst und ernstlich; besonders Euch Burgermeistern und Rath unserer und des Reichs Städten vornehmlich denen zu Lübeck, Bremen und Hamburg aus Kayserl. Macht und Unserem ernstlichen wohlbedächtlichen Willen, daß sie und ihr,

Erstlich Niemanden, wer der auch seyn möge, ohne die denen Reichs Satzungen gemässe Weeg und Mittel in andere mit dem Reich in keiner Verbindung stehende Länder ausser des Heil. Röm. Reichs Gränzen den Auszug verstatten.

Zweytens gegen jene, so sich heimlich fortzumachen unternehmen, genaue Obacht halten, solche auf Betretten, gefänglich anhalten, dieses Frevels halber nach Befund mit gemessenen Strafen belegen.

Drittens Keinem die Veräusserung seiner Güther und Habschaft in sträflicher Absicht solch verbothenen Auszugs mittels dargegen vorkehrender genugsamer Verfügung zu geben.

Viertens auf die sich irgendswo aufhaltende oder herumziehende Anwerber, Emissarien, Verführer Unterhändler, und deren Helfer allenthalben die genaueste Kundschaft ausstellen, selbe bey entstehendem Verdacht gefänglich anhalten, sohin dem Befinden nach mit Leibs oder allemfalsiger Lebens Straf ansehen.

Fünftens unter keinerley Vorwand, welchen sie einiger Orten einen Sammelplatz vorgedachter Leuthen weder heimlich noch offentlich dulten, mithin mit genauer öffterer Visitirung scharffe Obsorg tragen, die befindende Versammlungen stöhren, die darunter wissentlich Schuldige einziehen, die andere aber zu ihren Geburths oder Wohnstädten zuruck senden.

Sechstens Allen Fuhrleuthen zu Wasser und Land, Bothen, und Weegführern, Wirthen und Gastgebern, dies Unser Kayserl. öffentliches Gebott und Verbott nebst der allgemeinen Verkündung zur besonderen Wissenschafft bringen, sodann

Siebendens, Wie sie und ihr solches vollzohen, oder was für eine fernere Hülfe zu Erreichung dieses Endzwecks erforderlich seyn möge, Uns oder denen Creyß-Ausschreibenden Fürsten, welchen sie und ihr zugehören, gebührend und zeitlich anzeigen, damit bey einiger wider vorgedachte Unsere Kayserl. Verordnung erfolgender Versaumnuß Nachgiebigkeit oder Versehens nicht nöthig seye, dieserthalb gegen die Orts Obrigkeiten selbst ohnmittelbares schärfferes und ohnausbleibliches Einsehen zu gebrauchen. Wir wollen alles solches vermittels dieses Unseres Kayserl. Edicts also hiemit ins Reich öffentlich verkündigen, und zu Männiglichens Wissen bringen. An alles dessen Beförderung und genauer Beobachtung thun und vollziehen Euer Lbdn Lbdn, Andacht Andacht und Lbdn Lbdn ein gutes und annehmliches, und Uns benebens zu gnädigen Gefallen gereichendes Werk, all andere hingegen erfüllen andurch Unseren gnädigsten Willen und Meynung. Geben zu Wien den siebenden Juli Anno siebenzehen hundert acht und sechzig. Unseres Reichs im Fünfften.

Joseph m.p.

Vt R. Fürst Colloredo m.p.

L.S.

Ad Mandatum Sac. Cæs.
Majestatis proprium.
Franz Georg von Leykam m.p.

Courtesy of the Hamburg City Archives.

Final decree of Joseph II, Emperor of the Holy Roman Empire (1765-1790), forbidding emigration to foreign countries (July 7, 1768).

enforced delay in settling the colonists was causing it enormous expense. Disagreements with the entrepreneurs had arisen, and several of these had been arrested and taken to St. Petersburg for trial, while the one remaining proprietor, Beauregard, insisted that the government fulfill its three-year contract with him by allowing him to continue his solicitations. Under these circumstances, Orlov, the president of the College of Foreign Affairs, recommended to the Empress that all solicitation of colonists be stopped for an indefinite period. In November, 1766, Catherine confirmed his report by a resolution to this effect and ordered that copies of the report be printed in French and German and inserted in the foreign newspapers.

So great had been the result of the agents' work among the German people, however, that the largest number of colonies settled in any one year on the Volga was established in 1767; but thereafter, solicitation by the enrollers ceased. The *ukaz* of 1766, while forbidding the systematic invitation of foreigners, stated that it would accept those coming of their own will and on this basis some colonists were accepted from 1767 to 1773.[127] In contrast with the former carelessness about the fitness of the immigrants, these colonists were obliged to pass an examination in agriculture before the Tutel-Kanzlei.

The Russian government had not seen fit, meanwhile, to renew the immigration campaign as it had been expected to do. The German princes had finally prevailed upon Emperor Joseph II to come to their aid in stopping emigration; and on July 7, 1768, he had issued an edict aimed directly at the free cities which harbored the commissioners and their agents.[128] As a result of this order the Russian commissioner in Luebeck was informed that he could no longer assemble the colonists in that port; but the ambassador thought it "merely a formality" and that the city authorities could not afford to refuse them a rendezvous. However, the Russian government did not renew the campaign, for

---

[127]In 1767 sixty-nine families emigrated voluntarily; in 1768, twelve families; in 1769, five families; in 1771, seven families; in 1772, 25 families; and in 1773, thirty persons, a total of 604 persons.—Pisarevskii, *Foreign Colonization in Russia in the Eighteenth Century* (in Russian), 177. Some of these emigrants were settled in the colonies already founded on the Volga, while a new settlement (Pobotschnaja) was founded in 1772. *Historical Survey of Fifty Years' Activity of the Ministry of Imperial Domains* (in Russian), Pt. I, Appendix; *Volksfreund Kalender,* 1911, 60. An old manuscript, entitled "Lebensbeschreibung des Bruders Adam Friedrich Heinke," gives the experiences of a Moravian who emigrated in 1769 to join the colony at Sarepta. Cf. *idem,* 173-81.

[128]Copies of this document, entitled "Copia kayserlichen Rescripti an einige Reichsstaedte," are found in the Kgl. Kreisarchiv Bamberg, *Rep. 141, No. 55;* in the Kgl. Kreisarchiv Wuerzburg, *Sign. Sam.* II, 646; in the Kgl. Kreisarchiv Speyer, *Abtheilung, Oberrheinischer Kreis,* Akt. No. 1798; in the Staatsarchiv Luebeck; and in the Archiv der freien Hansestadt Bremen.

other matters at home were claiming Catherine's attention.[129] The Polish situation culminating in 1772, the war with Turkey (1768-1774), and the Pugachev rebellion (1771-1774) occupied the center of the stage.[130] They not merely deprived the Empress of an opportunity to continue her immigration policy, but even prevented proper attention being given to the care and management of the colonies already established on the Volga.[131]

Cessation of Russian Campaign and Later German Colonization in Russia

In spite of the enforced change in Catherine's first immigration plan, she did not soon give up her original idea. Her second experiment (1778-1779) proved, however, as barren of immediate profits as did her first. In 1778 she issued an *ukaz* inviting to a refuge in her empire the Christians who were being persecuted in Turkey. Thirty thousand Greeks, Moldavians, Serbs, and Armenians accepted her invitation and emigrated into the province of Azov. They were given the same privileges as the Volga Germans with the exception of freedom from the quartering of soldiers; but the government was just as little prepared to handle them as it had been to care for the Germans, and the colonists suffered great privations.[132] Again, in 1781-1782, a group of Swedes (935 people) from the Island of Dago in the Baltic Sea was enticed away from the Hungarian immigration agents and settled in the province of Kherson. They were given free land,

[129]After the settlement of the families which emigrated voluntarily from 1768 to 1773, as above noted, no additional colonists were ever settled in the villages on the Volga except some German prisoners taken in the invasion of Russia in 1812. In a list of the 105 family names in the colony Jagodnaja Poljana (Volkszeitung, October 6, 1913) are five prisoners of war who settled in that village in 1812, and doubtless other village registers would reveal more such settlers. Holzhausen, *Die Deutschen in Russland 1812, Leben und Leiden auf der Moskauer Heerfahrt,* 214 ff., tells how these unfortunate German soldiers were scattered over Russia, as far from its western border as possible; and that when some were brought to Saratov, the German colonists nearby pleaded with the government to allow these men to settle in their colonies.

[130]Emigration to Pennsylvania increased from 1771 to 1773. See Rupp, *A Collection of Thirty Thousand Names of German . . . Immigrants in Pennsylvania . . . from 1727 to 1776.* But Hungary seems to have been the chief goal. In 1770 over 19,000 men, besides women and children, emigrated into Hungary from the single province of Bavaria. Learned, *Guide to Manuscript Materials relating to American History in the German State Archives.* Famine contributed to the increased emigration at this time. See *Annual Register,* XIV, 84-85.

[131]Later additions to the Volga colonies were made by the Mennonites. In 1853 the Koeppenthal colony was founded east of the Volga in the province of Samara. During the next twenty years, it expanded into ten villages. The second settlement, begun in 1861, was known as Alt-Samara. It also expanded into ten villages of which Alexandertal is the best known. See *The Story of the Mennonites* by C. Henry Smith, 401-402. — The editors.

[132]Pisarevskii, *Foreign Colonization in Russia in the Eighteenth Century* (in Russian), 205-220.

but their privileges were less extensive than those granted the Volga Germans.[133] At the same period (1781) certain Greeks and Corsicans who had been driven out of the Island of Minorca upon its capture by Spain, were secured by the Russian immigration agents and settled in Kherson.[134]

The last foreign immigrants settled in Russia by Catherine were, like the original colonists, Germans. Between 1775 and 1783 huge land holdings on the Dnieper (Dnepr) River as well as the entire peninsula of Crimea had been added to Russian territory as a result of wars with Turkey. In 1785 Catherine issued a manifesto inviting foreign colonists to settle in this area. The invitation aroused immediate interest among the poorer classes about Danzig who had been reduced to poverty after the first partition of Poland. These people now appealed to the Russian ambassador in that city to be sent to Russia. Through Potemkin, governor of South Russia, approximately 750 Germans were settled in the colony of Alt Danzig (established in Kherson 1787) or scattered through the cities of South Russia.[135] The Manifesto of 1785 still further curtailed the privileges of the foreign colonists, granting but six years of freedom from taxation instead of thirty years as at first, while all special privileges given were to expire in 1797. These colonists were known in Russia as the "Danzigers" although they came from various parts of Germany. For instance, in 1786 a transport of eighteen persons from St. Gall, Switzerland, arrived in Luebeck on its way to Kherson; another party of one hundred fifty persons came from the vicinity of Aachen under the leadership of men from the province of Juelich, and a third contingent of twenty persons from Switzerland passed through that port. At this time there were assembled in Luebeck about six hundred emigrants who were on their way to Russia.[136]

Of particular interest at this time was the renewed attempt to gather colonists in southwest Germany since it furnishes one of the very few glimpses of the Volga Germans which their friends and relatives in the Fatherland ever had of them after their emigration. The Russian government in 1788 sent enrollers into the South German states, armed with letters from colonists on the Volga. One of these communications is preserved in the Herzogliches Haus- und Staats-Archiv in Zerbst and gives details of the life of the writer's family since emigrating to Russia. This letter ran as follows:

---

[133]*Idem,* 221-226.

[134]*Idem,* 227-261.

[135]*Idem,* 262-289. *Historical Survey of Fifty Years' Activity of the Ministry of Royal Domains* (in Russian), Pt. II, Appendix.

[136]Private letter from the director of the Staatsarchiv Luebeck.

Jesus be with you. Greatly beloved relatives and friends, my innermost wish is that these few lines will find you in good health. It has taken a long time, I believe, to fulfill my promise to write, but I now feel bound by this opportunity to report to you how I am getting along. My first wife with whom I had two sons and three daughters died in the year 1770. The two sons are also in eternity, the three daughters are married. I was married for the second time to our neighbor Christian Grassmann's oldest daughter, Maria Rosina, and with the same I begot two sons and five daughters of which one son and one daughter died. My father-in-law Grassmann is already six years dead, my mother-in-law still lives and is again married. The brother-in-law Christian and Hennrietta are married. With regard to my profession, I am a farmer and have, God be thanked, land, meadows, horses, cows and other animals as much—yes, more than I am able to care for. I have never had occasion to complain over scarcity. We also have churches and schools and have to travel about one hour to the district church. The place in which we live is Sunonereffba[137] on the Great Karamann River not far from the province city of Saratov on the other side of the Volga River. Our trip from Roslau to my home here lasted from March 1766 until July 1767. The weather in winter is very cold, in the summer on the contrary it is very warm. The fields are fruitful and necessities of life are cheap. As far as my house which I left behind in Oranienbaum is concerned, it is given to my brothers and sisters. Sell it and divide the money among yourselves as proof of my brotherly love which I still have for you my beloved brothers and sisters. Greetings also from my wife and children to my father and mother in case they are still living. And you beloved brothers and sisters, brothers-in-law and sisters-in-law, cousins and other good friends, I greet many thousand times. I entrust you to the protection of God. May He bless you body and soul. May He bless your going out and coming in from now until eternity. Farewell. I remain your faithful and well meaning son, brother, brother-in-law, and cousin and friend until my death.

Sunonereffba Andreas Reinefeld
the 3rd of July, 1788.

---

[137]This could be the colony of Schwed which had the Russian name of Swonarewka. — The editors.

If you write to me again, you must put an envelope around the letter. The address on the envelope should be made out to Herrn Georg Heinrich Rieger. It should be given to H. H. Emmendoerffer, innkeeper of the City of Ansbach in Frankfurt am Main.

P.S. Again I beg that you will write to me taking advantage of this opportunity and it will not be in vain because the above mentioned H. Rieger is invested with full powers and has been sent by highest authority and he lives only a quarter of an hour from here.

To David Reinefeld – Citizen and inhabitant in Oranienbaum near Dessau.[138]

Unfortunately, this letter relates to personal matters, but no criticism of existing conditions could be expected in a letter carried by a government official.

The only other German colonization which Catherine secured during her reign laid the foundation for some of the best foreign immigration Russia has ever reached, viz., the Mennonites.[139] When driven out of Holland in the sixteenth century, a group of these people had been settled by King Sigismund in Polish territory about the city of Danzig where they had enjoyed religious liberty and freedom from military duty. By the partition of Poland (1772) this part of the territory fell to Prussia which levied a heavy tax upon them in view of their refusal to perform military duty. They began to look about for some place to emigrate, and at the invitation of Prince Potemkin, sent a deputation to Russia to look into the offer of Catherine. As a result of their negotiations, eleven colonies containing 300 families were founded in Ekaterinoslav (1789-1790)[140] under practically the same privileges accorded the Volga colonists, except that freedom from taxation was granted for ten years only. The favorable reports sent back to their co-religionists at Danzig induced many to join their friends in Russia. From 1803 to 1840, under the direction of Czar Alexander I, over forty colonies of Mennonites were settled in the province of Tauria along the Sea of Azov, and the emigration of these people into Russia continued intermittently for nearly a century. Most of them were wealthy and came without aid from the government, bringing with them their own stock and farming implements.

138Waeschke, "Deutsche Familien in Russland," *Jubilaeumsschrift des Roland*, 99-100. Translated from the German by the editors.

139Friesen, *Die Alt-Evangelische Mennonitische Bruederschaft in Russland (1789-1910)*; Klaus, *Unsere Kolonien*, 156-336; Stricker, *Deutsch-russische Wechselwirkungen*, 158ff; Haxthausen, *Innere Zustaende . . . Russlands*, II, 171-202.

140Present day Dnepropetrovsk. — The editors.

Courtesy of Mr. Joseph Schnurr of the Landsmannschaft der Deutschen aus Russland, Stuttgart.

A general view of Sarepta of the early Nineteenth Century.

Aside from the Mennonites, other and smaller groups of German sectarians have from time to time settled in various parts of Russia under special privileges from the government. The first and one of the most important of these colonies is Sarepta, founded in 1765 in the province of Astrakhan on the Volga River by Moravians from Herrnhut in Saxony.[141] Complete records concerning these emigrants are to be found in the Unitaetsarchiv der Bruedergemeinde in Herrnhut, Saxony. In the Koeniglich Saechsisches Hauptstaatsarchiv in Dresden is a document relating to the emigration of Moravians in 1766 to join their brethren at Sarepta, including a list of the names of these emigrants. They were among the very first to take advantage of Catherine's manifesto of 1763, and their settlement, more prosperous and advanced than the neighboring German colonies, became widely known as the outpost of western civilization on the Asiatic border of Russia. Other sectarians are the Hutterites, who fled into the province of Chernigov from Hungary in 1770[142] and several colonies in the Caucasus formed by the "society of the children of God" in the early part of the nineteenth century. The latter were Wuerttemberg peasants who later came into South Russia in 1817 on their way to Mt. Ararat, where they believed the personal reign of Christ was soon to begin. For twenty years the Protestants in South Germany had discussed the millenium, and 1816 and 1836 had been fixed upon as the dates for its ushering in, while the place was set as "beyond the Caucasus, between the Caspian and the Black Sea." Many peasants in Wuerttemburg and Bavaria sold their lands and houses and started for the place. The difficulties and dangers on the way were frightful. Three thousand are said to have succumbed to sickness and privation. They were given shelter and help by Czar Alexander I and many settled in South Russia while others went on to Georgia and settled in seven villages not far from Tiflis. The size of the movement may be guessed from the fact that the last "swarm" contained seven thousand people.[143] The history of these various groups of German sectarians in Russia is as fascinating as the story of their brethren in Pennsylvania.

The southern provinces of Russia received a large immigration of German Evangelicals during the first quarter of the nineteenth century. Alexander I began his reign with the avowed intention of emulating the principles and spirit of his grandmother, Catherine II, and for a time continued her plan of colonization. During his reign (1801-1825) almost two hundred German colonies were established in Russia, chiefly in the provinces of Bessarabia, Kherson, Ekaterinoslav,

---

141Klaus, *Unsere Kolonien*, 92-156.
142Klaus, *Unsere Kolonien*, 46-92.
143Pinkerton, *Russia*, 143-152; Bryce, *Transcaucasia and Ararat*.

and Tauria.[144] These Germans are known, as in Hungary, by the general name of *Schwaben* (Swabians) because the first settlers were largely from the province of Swabia. However, the colonists are from many parts of Germany. For example, those in Bessarabia come from Prussia as well as from Wuerttemberg.[145] Although the bulk of these German colonists were Protestant, a substantial number of Catholic colonies were established at this time in the southern provinces.[146]

During the reign of Alexander I, sentiment in Russia turned against foreign colonization and the scheme came to be looked upon as a failure. Even flourishing colonies had had great difficulty in securing an economic foothold and the original expense to the government had been enormous. Catherine had spent five million rubles in the establishment of the Volga colonies. This sum was to have been paid back after ten years, but it was not fully returned by the colonists until almost a century later. The conditions under which the colonies of Alexander I were established were somewhat more rigid. Only such persons were eligible as could be shown to be competent as farmers or artisans; they must be married and have 300 gulden in cash or property; their transportation was paid, but tax exemption and service privileges existed for but ten years; and but two hundred families a year could be admitted. In 1810 the embassies in foreign countries, particularly in the German states, were ordered to cease giving any assistance to immigrants, and active propaganda for colonists was discontinued. In 1819 the Czar issued an *ukaz* forbidding the inviting of foreigners into Russia, and the embassies were not allowed to issue passports to persons wishing to emigrate thither.[147] From this time on, colonization took place only by special permission of the Crown.

The majority of the foreign settlements in Russia since 1830 have been merely offshoots from earlier colonies and have been occasioned by lack of land in the original grants. As a rule, the settlers in the Volga region had received thirty *dissiatines* and those in South Russia sixty *dessiatines* per family.[148] However, the fecundity of the German people, supplemented by their freedom from military duty, caused the population to increase with unusual rapidity, while the amount of land available for cultivation and pasture remained stationary and its pro-

---

[144] *Historical Sketch of Fifty Years' Activity of the Ministry of Domains, Pt. II; Learned, Guide to Manuscript Materials relating to American History in the German State Archives,* cites numerous documents relating to this emigration.

[145] Compare the custom of calling the Germans in Pennsylvania "Palatines."

[146] See Giesinger, *From Catherine to Khrushchev: The Story of Russia's Germans;* Height, *Paradise on the Steppe: A Cultural History of the Kutschurgan, Beresan, and Liebental Colonists, 1804-1944;* Stumpp, *The German-Russians: Two Centuries of Pioneering,* translated by Height. — The editors.

[147] Klaus, *Unsere Kolonien,* 44.

[148] A *dessiatine* is 2.7 acres.

ductivity decreased.[149] In 1825, 1828, and 1840 the government had made new allotments;[150] but the time came when there was no longer any vacant land in the neighborhood of the villages. The complaints of the settlers were met by grants in distant parts of the provinces of Samara and Saratov and elsewhere. Upon these lands swarmed the overflow from the original settlements. In the decade 1853-1863 more than one hundred daughter colonies were founded on the steppes in southern Russia, Siberia, Samara, and Saratov. Many of these new settlements, as has been pointed out, were designated by the name of the mother colony; e.g., Neu Norka was settled by Germans from Norka, Neu-Schilling from Schilling, etc.

German immigration to Russia during the second half of the nineteenth century assumed a still different type from the immigration of the preceding time. The immigrants did not settle in colonies to which land had been given by the government, but were scattered out by families upon lands which they themselves bought, or upon estates where they were hired as individuals.[151] Others settled in the cities where they pursued the trades or entered into commerce. In this manner, also, thousands of Germans have been scattered over the Russian empire as permanent settlers or merely as temporary residents. Because there were many of the latter, since artisans and laborers crossed the border to work during the busy season and returned to their homes in the interim, the net gain of German immigration to Russia was less than it had been in the earlier period.

---

[149]The Germans on the Volga increased sixteen times in one hundred and forty years.

[150]Stricker, *Deutsch-russische Wechselwirkungen,* 153. Haxthausen, *Studien ueber das inneren Zustaende . . . Russlands,* II, 36.

[151]It was at this time that Germans settled in the Volhynian section of Russia. — The editors.

chapter three

The Volga Germans In Russia

In many ways, the most interesting of the various groups of Germans in Russia is the one which came in such crowds at the first call of the great Catherine and settled along the Volga River in the provinces of Saratov and Samara. They are known among their countrymen in Russia as the "Volga Germans."

Like the vast majority of the German colonists in Russia, they have retained the language and customs of their ancestral home; and they, therefore, furnish a rich field of study for the linguist and folklorist. Nowhere else in the world are the dialects and customs of the Germany of the eighteenth century more faithfully preserved. Moreover, no other group of Germans so large as this has been so far removed from the progress of the world and has shared so little in the past century's onward sweep of civilization. In their lack of progressiveness they furnish a good example of arrested development, but when given the opportunity for growth they go forward as rapidly as any other people. Since this study has to do mainly with this group of people, consideration will first be given to their experiences in

Russia which furnish the background and account for many of the things which make them a "peculiar people."

It has been seen that the Empress Catherine directed her efforts mainly toward the German states for immigrants. Every nook and corner of their land had been ransacked by her agents, persuading those bent on emigration to turn their steps toward Russia, and coaxing those who were undecided about leaving their homes to migrate with their neighbors. It will be recalled that conditions in the German states were conducive to emigration, and that the decade, 1760-1770, furnished one of the most numerous emigrations of a century which saw thousands of Germans scattered over the world.

Number and Distribution of Immigrants to the Volga Region

The exact number of Germans who settled on the Volga is probably preserved in the Russian state archives since the inhospitality of that land would naturally lead to a careful record of all incoming strangers.[1] Pisarevskii, who had access to the Russian archives, nowhere gives the total number of immigrants; but states that from 1763 to 1766, 6,342 families of colonists (about 22,800 souls), not including the Sarepta Moravians, went to the Volga; 202½ families to St. Petersburg; 742 "souls" to Chernigov.[2]

One of the first computations was made in 1775 at the close of the Pugachev rebellion. As a result of this rebellion and the Kirghiz invasions, the original 8,000 families, consisting of 27,000 people, had been reduced to 5,502 families, with 23,154 inhabitants.[3]

In 1776, the *Annual Register* reported that there were twelve foreign colonies settled on the Volga, "which, altogether, make 6,091 families of different religions," or at a conservative estimate, about 24,000 people.[4] Pallas, whose accounts of the colonies are doubtless

[1]Even these records will be found to be not entirely accurate if one may judge from the following related by Zuege concerning the arrival in Russia: "I made a second discovery of this kind (of graft) when, on another day, there came upon our ship a Russian officer to whom the list of passengers was turned over. Our names were read in order, and as at a mustering of soldiers, each one called responded, "Here"; but several times this "Here" came from one mouth upon the call of two different names. Probably several persons had agreed to this in order to help the captain in the cost of transportation to the extent of several heads. Whether this deceit was afterwards discovered, I do not know. The officer appeared satisfied with the checked list and returned with it to land." *Der russische Colonist,* I, 57.

[2]Pisarevskii, *Foreign Colonization in Russia in the Eighteenth Century* (in Russian), 169.

[3]Bauer, *Geschichte der deutschen Ansiedler an der Wolga,* 76. Haxthausen, *Studien ueber die inneren Zustaende . . . Russlands,* II, 41, gives 23,184, but does not give the source of his authority.

[4]*Annual Register,* XIX, 177, 189.

as trustworthy as any in existence, says: "The number of colonists who settled on the banks of the Volga originally amounted to twenty-nine thousand persons; two thousand of these gradually emigrated to different parts of the empire; about four hundred were carried into captivity by the Kirghiz-Kazakhs during the trouble of 1773; nevertheless, the present population (1793) of the German colonies on the Volga amounts to thirty-three thousand persons of both sexes."[5] One of the most authentic sources, aside from the actual records of the Tutel-Kanzlei, is found in a letter from Catherine to Voltaire in 1769 in which she writes that the number of immigrants at that time amounted to twenty-seven thousand souls.[6]

The first census (known as the fifth revision) taken by the Russian government after the arrival of the colonists was in 1788 and gives the following statistics:[7]

Saratov	46 colonies	2678 families	9289 males	9350 females
Samara	56 "	2477 "	6318 "	6005 "

A total of 30,962

Although in her first manifestoes inviting colonization Catherine had given to immigrants a free choice of habitation, she soon modified this offer. In an *ukaz* of March 19, 1764, she set aside a tract of land in the province of Saratov, extending from Volsk to Tsaritsyn, between the Medveditza and Volga Rivers. Later in 1764, and in the following year, grants of land lying east of the Volga, in Samara, were made to the proprietors.[8] Toward this territory the vast majority of the immigrants was directed. The colonists settled for 200 verst on both sides of the Volga; the crown colonists, as a rule, in the province of Saratov, chiefly south of the city of Saratov, and the proprietary colonists in Samara, south of the Great Irghiz River. Here, along the numerous streams or beside springs they formed 104 colonies, of which there still remain forty-six on the *Bergseite*, or west bank of the Volga,

---

[5]Pallas, *Travels through the Southern Provinces of the Russian Empire in the years 1793 and 1794,* I, 58.

[6]"You say, sir, that you think like I do on the different things that I have done and that they are of interest to you. Well, sir, let me inform you that my beautiful colony at Saratov now has twenty-seven thousand souls and that, in spite of the Cologne reporter, it has nothing to fear from invasions of the Turks or the Tartars, etc.; that each district has churches of its own rite; that fields are being cultivated in peace and that for thirty years the people will not pay taxes." Voltaire, *Oeuvres Completes,* LVIII, "Correspondance avec l'Imperatrice de Russie," 37. Translated from the French by Dr. Adam Giesinger.

[7]*Historical Survey of Fifty Years' Activity of the Ministry of Imperial Domains* (in Russian), Pt. 1. Two colonies had previously been destroyed.

[8]For the contract between the Tutel-Kanzlei and Baron Beauregard, cf. Pisarevskii, *Foreign Colonization in Russia in the Eighteenth Century* (in Russian), Appendix No. 1.

and fifty-six on the *Wiesenseite*, or east bank.[9] Under the direction of the Russian government, the immigrants were to be settled in districts not less than sixty verst nor more than seventy verst in circumference, and large enough to accommodate 1,000 families.[10] Each settlement was to be made contiguous to another so that no waste land should be left between, and that better protection of the settlers against wild tribes might be secured.

Few of the colonists took up their residence in the cities of Russia through which the immigrants passed, although many of them came from cities in Germany and belonged to the non-agricultural classes. It will be recalled that the manifesto permitted free settlement and offered bonuses for newly established factories; but the actual erection of a manufacturing establishment was an enterprise which few of the colonists were competent to undertake, owing partly to their inexperience as captains of industry and partly to their ignorance of the Russian language which they were not disposed to acquire. There were only three foreign factories in Saratov, employing less than a dozen men all told, at the time the colonists arrived; so there was little opportunity for artisans to get work at their trades. Besides, the manifesto granted but five to ten years' exemption from taxation to those settling in cities instead of the thirty years' immunity promised to the rural settlers. A very few of the Germans had remained behind in St. Petersburg where they entered into service with officials or found work in different factories.[11] A larger number gathered in Saratov, particularly those who were dissatisfied with prospects in the colonies and were able to make their way back to the city. However, this number was comparatively small. In 1769 only 137 persons of German extraction were living in Saratov, and not all of these were from the recent colonists.[12]

In distributing the immigrants among the colonies, the government arranged that, so far as possible, persons of the same religion should occupy the same village, even where such grouping resulted in separating persons from the same village in the Fatherland. Hence, Moravians and Catholics occupied separate villages, and in the beginning, even Reformed and Lutherans were divided. The latter, how-

---

9So called because the west bank is steep and terraced by hills, while the east bank is level prairie land.

10A verst is .6629 of a mile.

11Zuege, *Der russische Colonist,* I, 60. Some of those who stayed behind later found their way to the colonies where they remained permanently.

12Quoted from *Saratov Learned Archives Commission* (in Russian), II, Pt. 1, 183; in *Sarataov District Historical Sketches, Recollections, and Materials* (in Russian), I, 236.

ever, became more or less mixed through intermarriage.[13] All of the original settlements, except two which were early destroyed by the Kirghiz, remain to the present day, and are inhabited by the descendants of the first colonists.[14]

Frequently settlers in a foreign land bestow upon their towns names from which can be traced their origin, but such was not the case in the Volga colonies in Russia. This was partly due to the fact that immigrants did not come in sufficiently large numbers from any one place in Germany to dominate any village, and partly because the government was more concerned about grouping the colonists according to religious beliefs than according to the localities from which they came. Originally the settlements were given Russian names by the immigration bureau, usually indicative of the stream upon which the colony stood, or of some natural feature of the landscape.[15] But the Germans, unaccustomed to the Russian tongue and not disposed to learn it, named the settlements for their respective leaders or mayors — e.g., Messer's colony, Grimm's colony, Kratzke's colony, and Balzer's colony.[16] Later these towns were known as Messer, Grimm, Kratzke, and Balzer. This nomenclature was the more natural since these leaders had been appointed in Luebeck and other ports where the immigrants gathered to await transportation and the colonists had been in their charge from the first. It was the business of each to act as *Vorsteher* or manager of a certain group of people, to pay them their regular allowances, see that they did not desert after they had once enrolled, look after their welfare on the long trip to the Volga, and oversee the formation of the colony. Furthermore, these *Vorsteher* became the first mayors of their respective colonies. The result of this double nomenclature is that most of the original colonies have a Rus-

---

[13]Dalton, *Geschichte der reformirten Kirchen in Russland,* 233-234, says that there were originally seven Reformed colonies, thirty-one Catholic colonies, and the remainder, except the one Moravian colony, were Lutheran.

[14]A list of these colonies, with their exact location, is given in Pisarevskii, *Foreign Colonization in Russia in the Eighteenth Century* (in Russian), chap. v. Cf. Muench, *Historical-geographical Encyclopediae of Saratow* (in Russian), for sketches of the colonies in that government; also, *Die Evangelisch-Lutherischen Gemeinden in Russland,* I; and Busch, *Ergaenzungen der Materialen zur Geschichte und Statisik des Kirchen-und Schulwesens der Evang.-Lutherischen Gemeinden Russlands,* I and II, for data concerning the Volga colonies. Much of the statistical information given in Busch is repeated in Matthaei, *Die deutschen Ansiedlungen in Russland,* 21-213. A list of the colonies with data concerning contemporary matters is given in the annual issues of the *Friedensboten Kalender.*

[15]An exception to this rule is the colony Norka, the largest of the German settlements on the west side of the Volga. "Norka" is the name of the dragon in a common Russian folktale. See McCulloch, *Childhood of Fiction,* 350. The ease with which this word is pronounced probably accounts for the disappearance of the distinctive German name of Weigand by which the colony was originally known. See David Schmidt, *Studien ueber die Geschichte der Wolgadeutschen,* 49. — The editors.

[16]In the latter instance, Balzer was the given name of the *Vorsteher* whose surname was Barthuli.

sian and a German name, the former being used for official business, the latter among the occupants of the villages; but both appearing whenever the place is mentioned in print.[17] An evidence of the slow but certain assimilation of the German colonists in recent years is found in the fact that the Russian name is gradually replacing the German name in common conversation.

As before mentioned, the Volga colonists came from all parts of the German territory and were composed of almost all types of people. A few, most of whom were out for exploitation or adventure, came from the cities of Germany — Hamburg, Luebeck, Berlin, Frankfurt, and Hanover. A small number of others, chiefly artisans, came from the states of northern and central Germany; while the agriculturists came chiefly from the south and southwestern provinces. An example of the scattered origin and the different trades and occupations represented among the first colonists is found in the list of the original settlers of Balzer, one of the largest of the German colonies, and originally composed only of families of the Reformed faith.[18]

August 28, 1765	9 families	16 males	18 females
Balzer Barthuli	Hesse		Husbandman
Jakob Tischler	Gladbach, Rhine Pr.		"
Phillipp Decker	Kurpfalz		"
Jakob Scheck	"		"
Heinrich Heft	"		"
(With him, 16-year old Valentine Habermann)	Isenburg		
Leonhard Volz	Earldom Hohenlohe		"
Ludwig Tebele	" "		"
Christoph Karl	Loewenstein		"
Georg Robertus	Switzerland		Tailor
November 26, 1765	2 families	7 males	8 females
Georg Merkel	Switzerland		Blacksmith
Jakob Herzog	Kurpfalz		Peasant
March 28, 1766	21 families	39 males	42 females
Jakob Borell	Baden-Baden		Peasant

[17]The new settlements made in recent years from the mother colonies have been named either after the mother colony; e.g., Neu-Messer, or for some feature of the landscape; e.g., Hoffental, Rosenfeld, and Schoendorf.

[18]This list is taken from the church records of Balzer and was reprinted in the *Dakota Freie Presse,* November 19, 1912, and April 1, 1913. It was prepared by David Merkel of Balzer. — The editors.

Jakob Klein Sr.	” ”	”
Georg Borell	” ”	”
Jakob Klein, Jr.	” ”	”
Georg Berg	Hesse-Darmstadt	”
Michael Baer	” ”	”
Johannes Moehser	Switzerland	”
Jakob Spaedt	Kurpfalz	”
Johannes Buseck	”	”
Philipp Eichner	”	”
Peter Steinpreis	”	”
Wilhelm Kolb	”	”
Jacob Gropp	”	”
Michael Heckmann	”	”
Johannes Bauer	”	”
Adam Heckmann	”	”
Paul Stoehr	”	”
Ludwig Huber	”	”
Jakob Busch	”	”
Ludwig Bauer	”	”
Valentin Hoffmann	”	”

April 26, 1766	2 families	3 males	2 females
Wilhelm Geist	Kurpfalz		Peasant
Konrad Ritter	”		”

June 28, 1766	1 family	1 male	1 female
Jacob Dorlosch	Hesse	Captain of a Hessian light-infantry (Fuesilier) regiment	

June 1, 1767	6 families	10 males	4 females
Heinrich Triol	Isenburg		
Georg Idt	”		
Johannes Heimbuch	”		
Lorenz Kalbin	”		
Jost Erth	”		
Heinrich Heimbuch	”		

Later transferred to Mueller (Krestowoi-Bujerak)

June 4, 1767

Jakob Herbel (Unmarried) Hesse

Transferred in the fall to Dreispitz (Werchnjaja-Dobrinka)

June 18, 1767	36 families	62 males	57 females

Johann Heinrich Weisheim	Isenburg
Maria Sophie Weisheim (widow)	"
Konrad Grasmueck	"
Heinrich Wuckert	"
Konrad Schneider	"
Christoph Heitzenroeder	"
Jost Lohrengel	"
Johannes Gerlach	"
Georg Blitz	"
Christian Mai	"
Johannes Georg Bund	"
Johannes Baecker	"
Konrad Lotz	"
Andreas Gruen	"
Konrad Schaefer	"
Philipp Schlegel	"
Ernst Mueller	"
Jakob Grasmueck	"
Johannes Meisinger	"
Elisabeth Dobin (widow)	"
Wilhelm Bengel	"
Heinrich Kleinfelder	"
Johannes Reuss	"
Heinrich Jackel	"
Philipp Leichner	"
Philipp Scheidt	"
Heinrich Scheidt	"
Konrad Roth	"
Philipp Kaiser	"
Karl Rutt	"
Andreas Kling	"
Adam Eurich	"
Heinrich Magel	"
Jost Bender	"
Johannes Weisheim	"
Konrad Weisheim	"

July 1, 1767	6 families	19 males	14 females

Johannes Neugard	Isenburg
Philipp Brotzmann	"
Kaspar Koehler	"

Friedrich Kraeuter	"		
Stefan Klaus (widower)	"		
Philipp Zieg	"		

July 18, 1767	5 families	10 males	9 females
Hermann Fech	Isenburg		
Heinrich Raab	"		
Markus Kaehm	"		
Lorenz Eurich	"		
Heinrich Eurich	"		

August 8, 1767	15 families	31 males	24 females
Philipp Roehrig	Isenburg		
Konrad Heil	"		
Kaspar Kaehm	"		
Johann Heinrich Keller	"		
Georg Frickel	"		
Heinrich Engel	"		
Johannes Ross	"		
Anna Margareta Weber (widow)	"		
Heinrich Schleuger	"		
Konrad Faust	"		
Johannes Schleuger	"		
Anna Maria Sinner (widow)	"		
Heinrich Baecker	"		
Johannes Stumpf (widower)	"		
Anna Maria Scheibel (widow)	"		

Aside from the records giving the localities from which the Germans emigrated to Russia, there are numerous other indices pointing to their origin.[19] In Balzer, for example, the street upon which the first *Vorsteher* lived and where his descendants still reside, was called *Hessen Strasse* as a reminder of the old home of Balzer Barthuli and of the other colonists who came from that province. The South German origin of the majority of the colonists is preserved in the dialects, the cookery, the customs, the names of the colonists, and in certain articles of dress.

[19]Haxthausen, *Studien ueber die innern Zustaende das Volksleben und insbesondere die laendlichen Einrichtungen Russlands,* II, 37: "Die Nahrungsmittel sind vorherrschend deutscher art. Des morgens Kaffee, aber meist aus geroestetem Weizen oder Gerste, Mehlsuppe, Kartoffelnsuppe, Gemuese, nur Sonntags Fleisch." Translation: "Articles of food are predominately German. In the morning coffee, but usually of roasted wheat or barley, flour soup, potato soup, vegetables, only on Sundays is there meat." — The editors.

Pioneer Experiences

The German settlers on the Volga endured pioneer hardships as severe as those experienced by the first colonists in America. Their trials began at the time they left their homes. At Hamburg and Luebeck the immigrants were sometimes obliged to wait for weeks until enough people were collected to fill a ship. The well-to-do took lodgings among the townspeople and fared very well; but the poorer ones were quartered in barracks especially erected for them, where they were subjected to the uncleanliness, vice, disease, and exploitation of the undesirables who always infest such crowds.[20] The period of waiting was very trying, especially to the adventurers who were anxious for excitement, and to the better class of colonists who were inconvenienced and embarrassed by their enforced mode of living with uncleanly and dissolute characters. The former, because unhampered by family ties and responsible only to themselves, often attempted to get away and were thereupon thrown into jail until time for the ship to sail.[21]

The voyage to Russia, contrary to the representations of the emissaries, proved as trying and hazardous as the voyage to America. The season for sailing lasted from March to October.[22] The shortest time in which the trip to St. Petersburg – a distance of 400 to 500 miles – could be accomplished was about nine days.[23] Many of the immigrant vessels, however, were delayed on the water for weeks and sometimes for months. One contingent was shipwrecked in the Baltic Sea and reached Russia only after a difficult and dangerous voyage of almost three months. Other boats were overdue four and five weeks, ostensibly because of unfavorable winds, but in reality because the captains wanted to get rid of their stores of victuals which they sold to the colonists at advanced prices.[24]

Few of the immigrants were accustomed to the sea and the terrors of those first days were no less real because they were largely imagi-

---

[20]Bauer, *Geschichte der deutschen Ansiedler an der Wolga,* 19.

[21]Cf. Zuege, *Der russische Colonist,* I, 20ff.

[22]Pisarevskii, *Foreign Colonization in Russia in the Eighteenth Century* (in Russian), Appendix, 7. Another advertisement limits the season from the middle of April to the middle of October. "Beschreibung der Vorzuege der Russischen Colonie Catharinen-Lehen," Kgl. Kreisarchiv Speyer, *Abtheilung, Oberrheinischer Kreis,* Akt. No. 1798. Translation: "Description of the advantages of the Russian colony Catharinen-Lehen." — The editors.

[23]The advertisement noted above says: "Die Reise von Luebeck bis nach St. Petersburg geschieht gemeiniglich bey guenstigem Wetter in 6. 7. a 10 Tagen . . . ." Translation: "The journey from Luebeck to St.Petersburg occurs usually with favorable weather in 6, 7, or 10 days." — The editors.

[24]Zuege, *Der russische Colonist,* I, 49ff.

nary. A colonist describes their conduct as the ship started away from the port:

> Since the majority of us had never been upon a ship, it was hard for the people to stand up because of the natural swaying of the boat. They tumbled against each other; fear and trembling mastered every mind; one cried, another swore, the majority prayed, yet in such a varied mixture that out of it all arose a strange woeful cry. Of the Catholics among us, some told their beads, one called on this saint, another on that; the Protestants uttered pious ejaculations from the Kubach, Schmolken, and other prayer books. Finally a Catholic struck up the litany; a Lutheran the song, "Befiehl du deine Wege." And now almost the whole crowd formed two choruses of which the first sang one song, the second the other.

The ship's quarters proved inadequate for the number of passengers carried and the people were packed in like herring. The portholes had to be closed for protection against the waves and all ventilation was thus shut out, but no passengers were allowed on deck because their presence interfered with the work of the sailors. Seasickness was universal, and the general unsanitary conditions on board bred other diseases so that many died through lack of proper care and medicine.

The immigrants were landed at Oranienbaum, the port of St. Petersburg, where they were kept in barracks a number of weeks, waiting for the celebration of *Pfingsten* (Pentecost). They were then called into a church, Protestant or Catholic, according to the faith of the colonists, and there a German pastor read to them in their mother tongue the oath which they were to take as Russian subjects, while the colonists repeated it after him. After this ceremony, the immigrants bound for the Volga made ready for their immediate departure. They had been divided into several parties which took their various ways to Saratov. One company went the direct route overland through Novgorod, Tver, Moscow, Ryazan, and Pensa, wintering at the country town Petrovsk in the north part of the Saratov province. Another traveled across the country to Tver and from there sailed down the Volga. About fifty miles above the city of Saratov, the river froze over and the colonists were forced to go into winter quarters in the Russian villages about Syzran.[25]

The advertisements had represented that the journey from St. Petersburg to Saratov lasted "zu Wasser auf dem Wolga-Strohm, wegen

[25] *Idem,* 41.

Courtesy of Mr. Joseph Schnurr of the Landsmannschaft der Deutschen aus Russland, Stuttgart.

View of the Volga with the *Bergseite* in the background.

der vielen Kruemmen dieses Flusses 5. à 6. Wochen fuernehmlich wenn man taeglich das Nachtlager in denen an erwehnten Flusse liegenden Staedten und Doerfern nimmt. Die Reise dahin zu Lande dauret gemeiniglich 14. Tage à 3 Wochen, doch kann man dieselbe auch in 10. â 12 Tagen ablegen."[26 & 27] It is probable that under the best conditions this schedule could be carried out, for the first settlement on the Volga is supposed to have been made on June 29, 1764.[28] But aside from those who emigrated in that year, the colonists were delayed from nine to eighteen months on the entire trip. In one instance, "the trip from Roslau to home here lasted from March 1766 to July 1767."[29] In another case, a contingent which started in the early spring of 1766 did not reach its destination until September 1767.

During this long journey of a thousand miles into the interior, the government made every effort to throw about the colonists safety and comfort. The caravans were led by Russian officers and every ten or fifteen wagons were provided with an escort. The boats on which they journeyed down the Volga were similarly manned. Provisions were supplied to the immigrants by the captains from whom they bought with their daily allowance as much or as little as they desired. They were even permitted, not without protest however, to stop at the Russian villages along the way and vary their fare from that furnished by the government official.

But in spite of the good intentions of the government, the German immigrants fared badly. The most unfortunate feature of the trip was the slowness with which it was accomplished and the enforced wintering of so many of the colonists short of their destination. Instead of reaching Saratov in the fall and being prepared the following spring to go out to their appointed settlements and put in their crops and start their dwellings, many reached Saratov in the early spring and were detained there in barracks most of the following season. At last toward the late summer they started for their final destination, only to find upon their arrival a barren waste, with the promised buildings nowhere in sight. Their first feeling was one of bitter disappointment.

26"Beschreibung der Vorzuege der Russischen Colonie der Catharinen-Lehen," Kgl. Kreisarchiv Speyer, *Abtheilung, Oberrheinischer Kreis,* Akt. No. 1798.

27Translation: "on the waters of the Volga, because of the many bends of the river, five to six weeks (are needed) if one habitually makes a night camp in the cities and villages which lie along the river. The trip by land takes usually 14 days to three weeks, but one can also do it in 10 to 12 days." — The editors.

28*Dakota Freie Presse,* April 29, 1913, gives the following dates for the first settlements in 1764: Unterdobrinka, June 29; Beideck, Schilling, and Galka, August 19; and Anton, September 7.

29Letter from a colonist, written in 1788, quoted in Waeschke, "Deutsche Familien in Russland," *Jubilaeumsshrift des Roland,* 99-100. — Translation by the editors.

A contemporary authority describes the arrival of one contingent as follows:[30]

> When we had traveled a while longer (after leaving the last trace of a road) in a barren, sober waste, we came to a brook, which, if my memory does not fail me, was called Medwe Stitz (Medveditza)[31] or "Baerenfluss" (Bear Creek).
>
> Our guides called "Halt!" at which we were very much surprised because it was too early to put up for the night; our surprise soon changed into astonishment and terror when they told us that we were at the end of our journey. We looked at each other, astonished to see ourselves here in a wilderness; as far as the eye could see, nothing was visible except a small bit of woods and grass, mostly withered and about three shoes high. Not one of us made a start to climb down from his horse or wagon, and when the first general dismay had been somewhat dissipated, you could read the desire in every face to turn back. This, however, was not possible. With a sigh, one after another climbed down, and the announcement by the lieutenant, given with a certain degree of importance, that everything we saw here was presented to us with the compliments of the Empress, did not produce in one of us the slightest pleasure. How could such a feeling have been possible, with a gift which was useless in its present condition and had not a particle of value; a gift that must first be created by us with great toil and which gave no certain assurance that it would repay the labor and time spent upon it!
>
> "This is truly the paradise which the Russian emissaries promised us in Luebeck," said one of my fellow sufferers with a sad face.
>
> "It is the 'lost paradise,' good friend," I answered.

The government had let the contract for building their houses to a Russian contractor, but days passed and he did not appear. In the meantime the people lived in their covered wagons or in improvised tents or shacks. After a short while provisions ran low and they were compelled to forage for supplies. There were a few Russian villages

[30]Zuege, *Der russische Colonist,* I, 143-144. Haxthausen found one of the original settlers surviving in 1845 and quotes part of a conversation with him concerning the trip. His testimony corroborates the statements of Zuege as to its unnecessary length. *Studien ueber die innern Zustaende . . . Russlands,* II, 39.

[31]In *Friedensboten Kalender* 1912, 122-125, Pastor J. Erbes, Wolskoje (Kukkus), makes a comparison between the difficult first years of the early colonists with the present new settlers to the Caucasus. In it he also quotes the section from Zuege about the founding of Kratzke, stating that Kratzke was located on the brook Karamysh and not on the Medveditza River. — The editors.

scattered about, and when there was prospect of finding one of these in the neighborhood, the Germans would send out a party to search the steppe for it and to contract with the native people, through signs, for food. Cold weather soon came on and still no carpenters appeared. The native Russians told the colonists that they could not hope to live through the winter in such a condition and offered to build for them *semlyanka* such as some of the wild tribes nearby lived in. These were great dwellings in the earth, large enough to hold three or four families, and in these caves the Germans spent the winter. In the spring the carpenters came; the site for the colony was laid out by the Russian officer in command, who was an engineer, and the houses were built.

Another cause for dissatisfaction among the colonists was the fact that the government assigned all alike to agriculture, although there were among them many scholars, merchants, soldiers, and artisans of every kind. There were very few places available in the colonial office at Saratov, and only one place in each colony. These were far too few to provide opportunities for the men who desired to "work with their heads only." Catherine had offered a bonus to any immigrant establishing himself in business, but opportunities for merchants and manufacturers were open only in the cities of Russia. This meant separation from one's kinsfolk and an experiment under strange conditions which did not promise much success. Any immigrant inclined to volunteer for army service was given a subsidy of thirty rubles in addition to the regular pay; but few immigrants would come from the German states as privates at a time when Russian army service stood in such bad repute. Of artisans there was need for no more than one of each trade in a colony. Yet all who came – and many of them were expecting to make a fortune without labor – were sent into the empty steppe to clear it, break up the soil, set up a farming establishment and raise crops of unfamiliar grains. It is little wonder that years passed before they became accustomed to their task and were able to earn more than a bare living.

But the greatest cause for the early failure of the colonists was the desire and expectation of a return to their former homes. The glowing terms of Catherine's *ukazes*, and the still more attractive interpretations, put upon them by her agents, could have no other effect than to pave the way for general disappointment among the colonists. Discontent began in Luebeck among some of the immigrants who vainly tried to escape from the Russian agents after enrollment, but they were thrown into jail and later were placed upon the ship under guard. This dissatisfaction again manifested itself during the stay in Oranienbaum where certain of the colonists, during the administering of the oath of allegiance, merely moved their lips without repeating the oath. They hoped thereby to avoid the only obligation which the Russian government imposed upon the immigrants and thus would be free to return at the first opportunity. The experiences of the journey culminated in a feeling of dismay when the people reached their destination and saw the lonely steppe stretching away before them for miles, uninhabited save by a few scattered settlements of persecuted *Raskolniks*.[32] These unfortunates were obliged to hide their stock and provisions in caves in the hills to prevent them from being stolen by the wild tribes of Kirghiz and Kalmucks who roamed unhindered over the country. If the government had not built houses for the colonists, many would have resided indefinitely in temporary dwellings; even as it was, they lived for years in the hope of returning to their Fatherland.

Tradition says that a civil officer, acquainted with the German language, had visited some of the settlements on the *Bergseite,* and, for some unknown reason, had encouraged them with the words that "it is quite possible that you will be taken back to your old native land, because it is thought that you cannot endure the climate and everything here is going to destruction. The news has been received in St. Petersburg that money is being raised in Germany to make possible your homecoming."[33]

This report was sent in writing by private messengers from one end of the colonies to the other and created a furor. A group of eighteen people from Katherinenstadt started for Germany, but their hired guides proved to be robbers who led them to a lonely island in the Volga and murdered them. The crime was not discovered until years afterward. Meanwhile other colonists, supposing their brethren safe in the homeland, planned to follow. A party of forty from various colonies gathered at Katherinenstadt, but failed to get far because of disagreement among their leaders. Another detachment from Mariental got as far as Kosakenstadt, opposite the city of Saratov, and were taken back to their abandoned homes by Cossacks. From this time on, the government kept its troops ready to thwart any further attempts at return. The report was kept alive, however, that the government was going to give up its effort to found colonies and the German settlers waited for their official recall, greatly to the detriment of their happiness and progress.

When several years had gone by and they had begun to be disillusioned of this hope, a terrible blow fell upon them through the

---

[32]A more common name for this sect is Old Believers. The word *Raskolniki* means heretics. — The editors.

[33]Bauer, *Geschichte der deutschen Ansiedler an der Wolga*, 26.

raids of the rebel, Pugachev.[34] In August, 1774, he entered the German colonies, bent upon their destruction. The settlers hid their stock in the woods or on islands in the Volga and sometimes succeeded in saving it, but invariably their grain was burned and the invaders set fire to the villages before leaving them. In some colonies the rebels did not set the houses on fire, but amused themselves by seeing how much they could destroy. In every place the doors were torn from their hinges, windows broken, furniture demolished, featherbeds and pillows cut open and their contents scattered, floors dug up, and dishes broken. In the factories, the tools were destroyed; in the churches draperies were torn and candlesticks and organs broken into pieces. In one colony the *Vorsteher* was hung from the doorpost of his house when he protested against the robbers driving away all the horses. In another colony, the *Vorsteher* who was a count, was sought for the purpose of execution, but he prepared a hiding place when he heard of their approach and escaped his intended fate.[37] As a result of the Pugachev rebellion, the German colonies were considerably reduced in the number of inhabitants while their monetary loss was enormous.[38]

Although the German colonies were never again subjected to systematic warfare, they were by no means free from dangers. The steppe was filled with ferocious wild animals – bears, lynx, and wolves – so that the men never went outside their villages in the early days without carrying their guns and fires had to be built at night to keep the wild beasts at bay. In addition to the real dangers from these

[34]Southern Russia, along the Don and lower Volga, was the dwelling place of many discontented classes who chafed under the yoke of the new Empress. In 1773, Emilian Pugachev, a Cossack of the Don who had served in the Seven Years' War in Germany, passed himself as Peter III, whom he was said to resemble, and announced his intention of going to St. Petersburg to punish his wife and to crown his son. He was joined by the *Raskolniks*,[35] whose religion he embraced, by the Cossacks of the Yaitsk[36] and Don, and by the Zaporozhian Cossacks of the Dnieper. The popular uprising which resulted from his leadership grew to enormous proportions. Bands of outlaws went up and down southeastern Russia, burning the villages, destroying the crops, driving away the stock, forcing the unwilling inhabitants to join their ranks on pain of death, and everywhere hanging the nobles. One of their set purposes was to wipe out the colonies which the Empress had established on the Volga and to reclaim the lands which they had usurped. For over a year Pugachev terrorized the country and, it is claimed, caused the death of 100,000 people. He was finally betrayed into the hands of the authorities by one of his own men and executed. For further details see Herrmann, *Geschichte Russlands*, V, 679-692, and Mavor, *Economic History of Russia*, II, 21-62.

[35]According to Paul Avrich in *Russian Rebels*, New York, 1972, pp. 191 and 249, it is doubtful that Pugachev was an "Old Believer." He merely exploited religious grievances as a means of drawing adherents into his camp. — The editors.

[36]After 1775 the Yaitsk was changed to the Ural. — The editors.

[37]The first man was named Nielsen. He was *Vorsteher* of Stahl on the Tarlyk. The second man was Count Doennhof, *Vorsteher* of Doennhof which was named after him. — The editors.

[38]For an account of Pugachev's raids in the German colonies, see Bauer, *Geschichte der deutschen Ansiedler an der Wolga*, chap. iii. The colony of Sarepta, which suffered the worst, is estimated to have lost property to the extent of 70,000 rubles.

Подлинное изображенїе
бунтовщика и обманщика
ЕМЕЛЬКИ ПУГАЧЕВА.
Wahre Abbildung
des Rebellen und Betrügers
IEMELKA PUGATSCEW.

A portrait of the rebel Pugachev. From a print in the British Museum, London.

animals, there were many imaginary ones. Men of that day were extremely superstitious and strange sights and sounds affected them greatly. Tradition tells of huge tracks they found in the snow, which they supposed must be the footprints of some monster, but which they later discovered were only impressions made by the enormous bark boots which the native people wore. One colony which settled temporarily on a small stream close to a thick forest was startled by a great roaring which came from the woods and which continued day and night. At last some of the braver ones, well armed, undertook a raid against the monster which they supposed inhabited the unknown depths, only to find a great group of springs bubbling out of the side hill and forming the stream which had supplied them with water, and upon which later grew one of the largest and most prosperous of the German colonies.

But the greatest dangers and losses to the German settlers came from the surrounding peoples – robber bands and Tartar tribes of Kirghiz and Kalmucks – from attacks of some of whom they were not relieved until as late as 1880. The robber bands were one of their most inveterate foes. For years this country had been the Mecca of escaped criminals and outlaws and at one time it was the "Siberia" of the Russian government where its subjects were exiled. A century before the Germans settled there, a famous bandit, Stenka Razin, the Robin Hood of Russian folklore, had his fortified cave in a mountain not far from the Volga, whence he carried on an organized system of robbery against the travelers and merchants who passed through the country.[39] His organization became the model for robber bands who infested the region for two centuries before they were finally put down. The colonists on the west side of the Volga suffered from them the worse because their country was hilly and its ravines and forests furnished good hiding places for the bandits. The robbers always had a leader to whom they gave unconditional obedience and stationed outposts which sounded the alarm by prearranged signals. They developed a system of espionage whereby their men went about in the Russian and German villages, ostensibly hunting work but in reality inspecting the stock, studying bolts and bars on windows and doors, and locating the room of the "housefather" where the strong box containing the family treasure was kept. Colonists who went into other villages or cities to collect money for work or merchandise were often fallen upon and robbed. If the bandits were not recognized, the victim was usually allowed to go his way after he had been relieved of his

[39]See Rambaud, *History of Russia,* I, 281-282; and Haxthausen, *Studien ueber die innern Zustaende . . . Russlands,* II, 47-48.

possessions; but if he betrayed the fact that he knew them, they murdered him on the spot.

For a long time after the settlement of the German colonies, the men were obliged to perform their field work in companies in order to protect themselves with their stock and implements from the roving bands. They not only went to their daily labor thoroughly armed, but stationed one of their number upon an elevated place where he could command a view of the surrounding country and warn the men of the approaching enemy. The villages were fortified with rude walls or ditches and a sentinel was maintained constantly in the church tower. Years after, when the colonies became stronger, the Germans carried on pitched battles with the robbers in their efforts to regain their stolen property.[40] At one time two colonists went to the rendezvous of the robbers, and through a clever ruse captured the leader of the band and two of his accomplices, and with the help of forty or fifty neighbors who accompanied them to the foot of the mountain, recovered much stolen property. The captured robbers were released by the government later and the settlers secured merely a respite from their depredations.

The danger from robber incidents upon a long journey led to the forming of an interesting custom among the Volga Germans. Every year merchants from the villages went to the great fair at Nizhni-Novgorod, traveling in caravans consisting of ten to twenty wagons as a matter of safety. The journey was considered an event so solemn that a special celebration was held at the departure and upon the return. The nearest relatives were invited to the farewell meal, tears were shed, good wishes extended, and prayers even were offered; then, as the travelers drove away, pistol shots announced to the inhabitants of the village that the "Nischners" had started on their way. Their return was again announced by a salute and relatives gathered to hear the story of their adventures and to congratulate them upon their safe return. Not until 1860 were the Volga Germans relieved from these robber bands, when the governor of Saratov finally broke up their hiding place and brought about their utter destruction.

Another disturbing element in the colonies during the first years but which did not continue so long as the robber bands, were the Kalmucks, a Tartar tribe who committed their depredations chiefly in the most southerly colonies. These people had lived for two centuries on the lower Volga; and a few years before the Pugachev rebellion, had

---

[40]Haxthausen, *Studien ueber die innern Zustaende . . . Russlands,* II, 55; Bauer, *Geschichte der deutschen Ansiedler an der Wolga,* chap. iv.

moved back to their original home in Mongolia.[41] It was their boast that they intended to destroy all the German colonies on the *Bergseite*. The chief of one of their bands, however, had been healed of a malignant disease by a member of the Moravian colony at Sarepta, and in his gratitude he warned the German colonists of their danger. During their migration to Asia, bands of sixty to one hundred Kalmucks camped near the villages, but they were either captured or driven away by the settlers who were on their guard and little damage was done aside from the loss of stock.

The Kirghiz, another Tartar tribe, had for years pastured their flocks undisturbed in the territory settled by the German colonies, on whose arrival they had been pushed back into the steppes beyond the Volga. They, too, seem to have entertained the purpose of completely destroying the Germans and actually succeeded in wiping two of the new settlements out of existence. The colonists on the east side of the river suffered most at their hands. In 1774 a band of Kirghiz raided seven or eight villages there and completely destroyed one of them, carrying away its men, women and children, or killing those who lagged by the way. Many of these Germans were rescued by a detachment of soldiers sent by the government, but others were carried off on the backs of wild horses to which they were bound and sold as slaves in Asia. The same year, another band of Kirghiz attacked a group of villages in this vicinity and captured a number of their inhabitants, who either became servants to the Kirghiz in their steppe, or were sold as slaves in the distant Orient.[42]

The cruel attacks to which the colonists were subject naturally led them to employ every precaution and means of safety against their enemies. The settlers fortified their villages by huge embankments and built stockades or dug deep ditches around them, while places in the nearby steppe which invited ambush were guarded day and night. The help which they received from the government was often tardy and ineffectual. Its aid consisted in sending detachments of soldiers to guard the outposts and in establishing fortified places farther to the east in the midst of the savages. It encouraged settlements of Russians and Mordvinians beyond the frontiers and assisted in pushing back the Kirghiz into the steppes. After a time the tribe was forced to discontinue its savage raids and the capture of prisoners, but numerous thefts of stock continued up to the twentieth century. In the German colonies bordering on the Kirghiz territory, almost 10,000 horses worth a third

---

[41] Herrmann, *Geschichte Russlands,* V. 665-667.

[42] Matthaei, *Die deutschen Ansiedlungen in Russland,* 127. He speaks of these times "when the pastor at Katharinenstadt had his tongue cut out by the Kirghiz, when hundreds of Germans were beheaded, speared, trampled by horses, and drowned in the swelling steppe streams."

of a million rubles were stolen within the eight years 1875-1882, besides thousands of camels, sheep, and cattle.[43]

The political and economic life of the German colonies on the Volga falls into four well-defined periods: 1) deterioration (1765-1801); 2) economic development (1801-1850); 3) changed status under the Russian government (1850-1871); 4) emigration into foreign lands, 1871 up to 1914.

Economic and Political Life of the Volga Germans

1. *Period of Deterioration, 1765-1801.* The German colonies during the first generation of their existence in Russia were clearly a failure from the standpoint both of the colonists and of the empire. Many of the settlers, not cast in the mold of pioneers, had come expecting to gain their fortunes at once while the most sober-minded of them, insured by the government as they thought against economic failure and external dangers, had not dreamed of the hardships they would encounter. The government, on the other hand, expected from the colonists prompt self-support through the rapid agricultural development of the steppe in which they had settled, a cultural influence which should be an example to surrounding people when the population spread to that section, and a political stability which should insure commercial prosperity to the settlers.[44]

In economic advancement the colonists fell far short of the expectations of the government, not only failing to repay the loan which had been made to them, but also being unable to meet the regular taxes levied at the close of their period of immunity. It will be recalled that at the end of ten years the money advanced for buildings, stock, implements, and seeds was to be repaid to the government in three equal installments without interest; and at the end of thirty years the colonists were to be put upon the same basis of taxation as the rest of the rural population.[45] The government loan, known as the crown dues, amounted to 5,119,813 rubles, 23 kopecks,[46] and the first installment was due in 1775. It has been seen, however, that during these first years the settlers were able to eke out only a bare existence and it is not surprising that they could not meet their obligation to the government. The latter still continued its annual appropriation of 200,000

---

[43]Bauer, *Geschichte der deutschen Ansiedler an der Wolga,* 73.

[44]Pisarevskii, *Interior Organization of the Volga Colonies under Catherine II,* (in Russian), 1-8, for a summary of the failures of both colonists and government.

[45]On the other hand, those people who settled in the proprietory colonies, were expected to give a tenth of their products to the proprietors. Pisarevskii, *Foreign Colonization in Russia in the Eighteenth Century* (in Russian), Appendix 2, Section 4.

[46]Bauer, *Geschichte der deutschen Ansiedler an der Wolga,* 105.

rubles as an emergency fund to assist the colonists with their crops;[47] and in view of the desperate circumstances under which the settlers were struggling, in 1782 it remitted almost one half of the original loan.[48] Yet even in 1797, which marked the close of the period of immunity from taxation for the Volga colonies, the liquidation of the crown dues had scarcely begun.

The failure of the German colonists to meet their share of the contract seems strange in view of the cost and care which the Crown expended in settling them in the empire. Many pioneers of civilization have had much less assistance than these and have fared better. The frontiers of America have been peopled by men who had to depend upon their own initiative almost entirely except insofar as the government provided them with cheap lands. Why, then, did the German colonists make so sorry a failure at first? It has sometimes been charged to the character of the people. They are described as the "scum" of Germany – a term very familiar to American ears from the time of the German exodus of 1709 up to the discharge of yesterday's boat load of Italians and Russian Jews at Ellis Island. In the case of the Volga settlers, the allegation is most often in the mouths of their own countrymen who have visited these isolated colonists and have compared them with the sleek inhabitants of their own social class in Germany. The native Russian on the other hand, even though he has resented their presence in his country, has contrasted them with their neighbors in thrift and orderliness and has confessed to their superiority in some of the essential traits of character. While there were many of the "rabble" and the "mob" among the colonists who preyed upon the better classes, they were numerically in the minority. Those who were the poorest were often of the most sterling character, possessing the simple virtues whose worth was not surpassed by those of higher social station. But the conditions against which they struggled in Russia were beyond their control, and it is a strange fact that the worst obstacles which the colonists met was the very government which so generously invited and so maternally cherished these foreign settlements.

The frontier dangers from which the Volga Germans suffered – sickness, wild animals, rebel raids, savage tribes, and robber bands –

[47]For example, in June and July, 1774, the District Commissioner Wilhelmi bought in Simbirsk 7,000 *chetvert* of grain at government expense because of crop failure. See *Saratov District Historical Sketches, Recollections and Materials* published by the Saratov Society for the Benefit of Needy Writers, I, 237.

[48]The canceled debt included the following items: the amount paid for the erection of the first houses and churches, medical aid rendered the emigrants, and sums advanced to families who died on the way from Oranienbaum to Saratov and to those captured by the Kirghiz in the first years of settlement. Bauer, *Geschichte der deutschen Ansiedler an der Wolga,* 22, 105-106.

were such as all pioneers must face and against which no government can furnish complete protection. Where the Crown manifestly failed was in the management of the financial and administrative affairs of the settlements. Since its advent into western history, Russia has had the reputation of approximating the Orient in official graft; and today no European country compares with her in the manner in which her empire is honeycombed with this vice. In the middle of the eighteenth century, it flourished to an astonishing degree and Catherine's court, filled with flatterers, schemers and seducers, offered no obstacle to its progress. The lavish sums of money which the Empress placed at the disposal of the Tutel-Kanzlei for carrying out her pet scheme of colonization, and the annual emergency fund which she created, offered a rich source of peculation for the officials in charge. Catherine's prime favorite, Gregory Orlov, who was made head of the colonization bureau, had neither the inclination to direct its affairs nor the ability to resist the squandering of such convenient sums for his own personal benefits.[49]

From the highest to the lowest officers in the colonial administration, dishonesty and waste prevailed. At the very inception of the enterprise, a contemporary magazine details the account of one General Howarth, governor of St. Elizabeth, who was empowered to give the colonists suitable encouragement, but that general, more intent upon his own interests than that of his royal mistress, has converted the sums remitted to enable him to proceed with zeal in the establishment of this new colony, to his own private use, by which the poor settlers have been miserably distressed and her Imperial Majesty's gracious intentions frustrated.[50] The officials in charge of the transportation of the colonists enriched themselves at the expense of the government. The ship's captain, who reecived a certain sum for each voyager, padded his list of passengers and the same persons responded to more than one name at the roll call. The long, useless delays of the trip, whether due to deliberate planning or to incompetent management, brought gain to the officials.

An instance of flagrant mismanagement occurred toward the end of the journey. When the colonists finally reached the city of Saratov, each one was given outright 150 rubles, the first installment of the government loan, for the purpose of providing food and transportation out to the colonies. A number of weeks intervened, however, before

[49]See Waliszewski, *Story of a Throne,* 75ff., 321 ff., for a discussion of the character of Orlov.

[50]*Gentleman's Magazine,* XXX, (1763), 197. The distinctly non-Russian sound of this man's name is suggestive of the fact that foreign officials in "barbarous Russia" readily succumbed to the customs of the country in this regard.

they left the city, and during this period of idleness some of the Germans lost practically the entire amount while many saved not more than one half of it. Much was gambled away or drunk up in the Russian *kabaks* and much was stolen from those who tried to save their apportionment. The Russians had no qualms of conscience about separating the Germans from their money for they felt that the foreigners had no right to it and that it really belonged to the subjects of the Crown. What they could not get, therefore, through legitimate channels, in excessive prices for food and other provisions in the *kabaks,* they tried to steal; and no Russian, however respectable he might be, would come to the aid of a German who was being robbed of his money.[51] On the other hand, many of the colonists, knowing that they would be cared for by the government as long as necessary and tempted by the lure of easy money, forgot the day of reckoning and threw discretion and economy to the winds. When their allowance was gone, they appealed to the authorities for more, and some even entered into collusion with them by receipting for two or three times the amount actually received, the officials pocketing the difference.[52]

The repayment of the government loan, or "crown dues," forms a "long and dreary chapter" in the history of the Volga colonies and is an example of the atrocious exploitation practiced upon the German settlers by the officials of the colonial office.[53] In 1782 the colonists began paying back the loan at the rate of three rubles for every colonist from sixteen to sixty years of age, and after 1797, one ruble; yet in 1809 the debt had been reduced but 24,000 rubles, and in the course of a half century the sum was diminished only from 2,789,418 rubles to 2,765,356 rubles. In 1833 a special officer was appointed at Saratov to superintend the collection of the crown dues, and in that one year the colonists were credited with four fifths as much as they had received credit for in the preceding quarter of a century. The officials of the colonial office employed every device imaginable to misrepre-

[51]Zuege, *Der russische Colonist,* I, 137-138, relates that one day as a colonist was carrying home his allowance, paid him in kopecks, in a sack thrown over his shoulder, a Russian slipped up behind him and cut the sack. As the kopecks rolled out, the thief gathered up all he could and ran away while some of his countrymen stood by and laughed heartily at the dilemma of the German.

[52]*Ibid.,* 213-214, in describing the government's salt monopoly which was largely worked by criminals, Zuege relates that at Saratov the salt was hauled by certain persons called *Ruskanyky.* Their teams, usually of white oxen, and their wagons of foreign make, disclosed the fact that they were not of Russian birth. On inquiry he learned that these people had come from Hungary as colonists and that they were being forced, through compulsory service, to pay the debts contracted by their ancestors, "a bit of news which aroused in me the fear that the grandchildren of the German colonists would sometime, probably, be forced to perform compulsory labor in order to pay the debt which, in my opinion, would be paid with difficulty by those who had incurred it, largely unintentionally."

[53]Klaus, *Unsere Kolonien,* 182-183.

sent the facts in their records. The receipts of the colonists were demanded for correction or inspection and never returned to them. It frequently happened that the proper official was not in the office when the payment was made and the clerk would refuse to give a receipt. When, later, he was confronted with the matter, he would deny that he had received the money. Great confusion arose by the transfer of the dues from the original debtors to their families, and the changes which occurred through the division or extinction of families caused endless misunderstandings, complaints, corrections, and investigations. A curious custom arose among the colonists of assigning a certain share of the crown dues to their daughters as a part of the bride's dowry, and it often resulted that both families had to pay the dues.[54] Not until 1846 were the crown dues finally extinguished, and it is estimated that their collection cost the colonists as much as did the original debt; in other words, the piracy of the administrators in the colonial office at Saratov was so well organized and conducted that for every ruble of taxes with which they credited the settlers, they collected a ruble which went into their own pockets. After the liquidation of this debt which proved such a prolific source of revenue to the officials, they turned their attention to other channels which offered similar opportunities for supplementing their income through the exploitation of the colonists.[55] The persistent refusal of the colonists to familiarize themselves with the Russian language made them an easy prey through the years to designing officials.

One of the early causes for dissatisfaction among the German settlers arose over the differences in privileges granted the crown and the proprietary colonies. The entrepreneurs under whose control over half the colonists were settled, had been forbidden to make demands upon them contrary to the Russian laws or to the express terms of the manifesto, but otherwise they were allowed complete freedom in the management of their enterprises. As a result, they modeled the relationship between themselves and their colonists upon that existing in France between the peasant and his nobles. They exacted, therefore, for their personal benefit an annual tax of one-tenth of all the income of the colonists, even to the increase of domestic fowls.[56] The settlers first learned of these discriminations when they met the crown colonists in Oranienbaum, and they at once made an attempt to induce the Tutel-Kanzlei to release them from the contract and to include them among

[54]Bauer, *Geschichte der deutschen Ansiedler an der Wolga,* 108; Schaab, "Die Deutschen an der Wolga," *Dakota Freie Presse,* June 24, 1913.

[55]Bauer, *Geschichte der deutschen Ansiedler an der Wolga,* 105-109.

[56]Pisarevskii, *Interior Organization of the Volga Colonies under Catherine II* (in Russian), 1-2.

the crown colonists, but the authorities did not take any steps to this end.

In response to repeated complaints, however, the Kanzlei passed a resolution in 1767 to secure from the colonists a written statement of their relationship to the proprietors and sent out a questionnaire to the *Vorsteher* for this purpose. Several of the colonies affected then petitioned the Kanzlei for a redress of their grievances, but still at a loss to know what to do, the government took no steps. Again in 1768 the colonies sent other petitions in which they charged that the entrepreneurs had not fulfilled their duty by providing houses, granaries, and barns for the settlers and in furnishing pastors, teachers, and doctors.[57] The colonists expressed a fear that they were to be made serfs and reduced to the status of the Russian peasantry and they, therefore, asked to be relieved from the jurisdiction of the proprietors and to be known henceforth as crown colonists. The entrepreneurs resisted the movement against them, and by spreading false rumors among the people, frightened some of them into obedience while others openly defied them. The proprietors refused to obey the authorities and for a number of years the colonies under their control were in a state of utter disorganization. Finally, in 1777 the Kanzlei decided to remove the entrepreneurs and a commission was appointed to this end. The Empress accepted the recommendation to reimburse the proprietors and to take over the settlements as crown colonies. This was done in 1779. The money for the transaction, however, was not taken from the state treasury, but was added to the crown dues of these settlers.[58]

The failure of the German colonists to provide for themselves an adequate system of local self government was one of the prime causes for their early demoralization. Whatever genius for governing the German may have, the eighteenth century was not a period in which he showed himself apt at initiating governmental and political institutions, whether in the Fatherland, in Pennsylvania, or in Russia. The Manifesto of 1763 had promised to the foreign settlers local self government, offering to assist them, however, with a "guardian" or "manager" in case they desired such help. It had been Catherine's original intention to suggest different plans for their local government, leaving the colonists free to accept the one they desired or to formulate one of their own. To this end, the law of 1764 had ordered various local institutions worked out;[59] and a German pastor, detained in St. Peters-

[57]See Pisarevskii, *Foreign Colonization in Russia in the Eighteenth Century* (in Russian), Appendix Nos. 28-31, for copies of several of these petitions.

[58]Pisarevskii, *Foreign Colonization in Russia in the Eighteenth Century* (in Russian), 187-203.

[59]Klaus, *Unsere Kolonien,* 183-185.

burg against his will, was set at the task of framing a legal code for the use of the German settlers. Stricker relates the episode as follows:[60]

> In 1765 the Russian minister in Danzig, von Rehbinder, made a proposal to Pastor Reinhold Forster to travel through the newly founded settlements on the Volga. Reinhold Forster accepted the proposal, and together with his son George went to Petersburg and from there to the colonies in the Saratov District. He investigated all phases of their conditions and reported what he had learned concerning the problems of the colonies, and recommendations for their remedy, in a frank and unreserved memorandum to the Empress Catherine. With this report, which could have accomplished so much good, he blocked every chance for his success at the Petersburg court. Partly due to the intrigue of the governor of Saratov whose powerful and avaricious dealings were exposed; and partly due to the conditions of the court where favorites and schemers were struggling for power and esteem, the bewildering whirl of festivities, war plans, and proposals for internal reforms of all kinds which were brought forth, all prevented Reinhold Forster's presentation from having success or his services from being rewarded. Instead of allowing him to go where his starving family called him, he was requested to prepare a statute book for the (Volga) settlements but which also was ignored. During this entire time of neglect and want, Reinhold Forster was forced to support himself and his family with literary writings, mostly translations, at which his twelve-year-old son George assisted him. Finally he was permitted to return home but without even the smallest reward or compensation since the impetuous man would not condescend to beg Gregory Orlov for his rights as if for a favor.

But with the carelessness characteristic of so much of the work of the immigration authorities the labors of the German pastor were ignored by the very powers which had authorized them.[61]

The question of formulating plans for local self government was thus left entirely to the leaders of the individual colonies. These leaders, however, had been selected as economic administrators rather than as heads of a political body, and for the latter, they proved themselves

---

[60]Stricker, *Deutsch-Russische Wechselwirkungen,* 146-147. Translated from the German by the editors.

[61]*The Gentleman's Magazine,* XI (1770), 229, mentions an account of a new map of the Volga by Mr. John Reinhold Forster. Mr. Forster constructed this map from an actual survey and there is every reason to believe it by far the most accurate of any that has been made.

highly inefficient.[62] The colonists had no political bond or tradition to unite them, coming as they did from various German provinces which differed widely in their methods of local administration, and they brought with them a political disunion typified by the conditions in the homeland. They were divided into loosely knit religious groups and this again tended to minimize political leadership and institutions. The result was a disorganization and lack of uniformity so serious as to make coordination with the central government an impossibility, and the "inner jurisdiction" with which Catherine had so magnanimously endowed the settlements became the rock upon which they suffered almost annihilation.

The first settlers being entirely without any organization or system necessary for political units, the Tutel-Kanzlei as a temporary measure, established a subordinate office at Saratov known as the Vormundschafts-Kontor (Guardianship Office). This was to act in a purely supervisory capacity until the colonists had decided upon a system of local government, and was necessitated by the distance from St. Petersburg and the consequent difficulty of communication which made it impossible for the Tutel-Kanzlei to direct the internal affairs of the settlers. The differences with the entrepreneurs also demanded that some governmental authority be on the spot to keep an eye upon local matters. The government further assisted the settlers by the appointment (in 1768) of six district commissioners, whose duty it was to distribute the allowance among the colonists and thus avoid the necessity of leaving their work to go to Saratov for it. These men were also authorized to assist the colonists in the purchase of tools and everything they needed for their work to exercise administrative and clerical functions in the colonies. The Tutel-Kanzlei particularly requested the Kontor to be careful in its selection of commissioners, choosing not only those of good character, but men who had "some knowledge of public economy and of foreign languages."[63]

This same year (1768) the Tutel-Kanzlei drew up a system of rules entitled, "The Instruction," on the basis of which all the newly settled foreigners must act, with a designation which class of crimes is to be punished by the supreme government; that is, by the Tutel-Kanzlei and its Kontor, and which class is to be examined by their local leaders. The direct purpose of these regulations was to bring to an end the revolt of the colonists against the authority of the entrepreneur by

[62]To this day, the chief official of a German colony in the Volga territory is called *Vorsteher,* literally *manager,* instead of *Schultz* or *mayor,* as in the colonies in South Russia. The chief of the Russian *mir* is called *starosta,* which, like our word *mayor,* originally meant elder.

[63]Pisarevskii, *Interior Organization of the Volga Colonies under Catherine II* (in Russian), 9-10.

definitely limiting the scope of the latter, and to discipline the restless element among the settlers, forcing them to support themselves by agriculture, and thus preparing them to repay the government loan when it should fall due. Some writers judge the character of the colonists by the rules laid down in these Instructions, concluding that "these are no rules for the aim of regulating the life of an adult free people, but a statute for an asylum or an agricultural colony of criminal minors."[64] On the same basis, similar conclusions could be drawn concerning one of the American colonies from the Blue Laws of Connecticut.

The first section related to religious conditions which the government considered the most vital factor in bringing order out of chaos. In each parish the pastor or priest was admonished to be the uniting and guiding factor among his people, was warned that he must not mix in politics, and that his only duty to the state lay in keeping a register of marriages, births, and deaths. The parishioners must attend religious services on pain of a fine for the third unexcused absence and no excuses were to be accepted aside from five which were minutely detailed. The political functions of the community were vested in a *Vorsteher* and two *Beisitzer,* who were to be elected by the people, the former for one year and the latter for six months. They were to receive no salary, but the *Vorsteher* was to receive labor for his services and to have thirty rubles subtracted from his crown dues. One of the chief functions of the *Vorsteher* was to oversee the household economy of the settlers and to enforce the sumptuary legislation therein laid down. He was particularly enjoined to oppose extravagance among his people – the constant assembling of guests and the playing of cards for money. At weddings and christenings, not more than ten guests were to be allowed and no presents might be given unless the donor had paid his crown dues. Householders were not permitted to sell or to kill any animal for a feast without permission from the local authorities. No servants were allowed except in small families or where there were sick persons and then only in case the taxes were paid. Otherwise, the neighbors were obliged to assist those in need. No taverns or boarding houses were allowed because, as the Instructions relate, "Where they have existed, the people would not make any *kvass* or bake any bread."[65]

Since fire was the most serious internal danger to be guarded against, special measures were given for its prevention. The watch-

[64]*Ibid.*, 11.

[65]To this day there are no hotels in the German colonies on the Volga. The *Gemeinde* (colony) annually lets out the contract to a householder for the lodging of the government officials on their regular rounds and the few other strangers who come to the colonies are cared for at the same place.

man whose duty it was to guard against fire and thieves and to warn the people of the appearance of either by ringing a bell or by some other understood signal, is still a part of the village officialdom. The care of the poor was provided for by each family devoting one-eighth of a *dessiatine* of its land for that purpose. Regulations for the protection of private property and enumeration of crimes and their punishments occupied much space in the Instructions. The Kanzlei, through this document, introduced the three-field system of agriculture into the colonies, although the four-field system was not forbidden. The *Vorsteher*, like the *starosta* of the Russian *mir*, was to control the time of plowing, sowing and harvesting, and to designate how much of his crop each colonist might dispose of after reserving the necessary amount for food and seed. The government demanded the introduction of flax and hemp, furnishing the seed for these crops, and recommended the raising of sheep. Special attention was given to the conservation of the forests. Each colonist was required to plant twenty trees on his marriage, six on the birth of a son, and four on the birth of a daughter. The Instructions introduced to the German colonists two innovations — the use of rods for punishment and a restricted freedom of movement such as bound the Russian peasant to the soil. According to the provisions for the latter, the colonists were allowed to absent themselves from their villages for but three days at one time, and then only by securing a passport from their *Vorsteher* if they wished to go to a neighboring colony or to a Russian village less than fifty verst away. In case they desired to go a distance greater than fifty verst, they must secure a passport from the Kontor at Saratov.[66]

This Instruction offered by the Kanzlei merely as a temporary measure until the colonists should provide their own local government, remained in force a number of years. The Kanzlei complained that it was not carried out as it should be because of the election annually of the *Vorsteher*. This official was given certain privileges for the good conduct of his office and this led him to desire re-election. If, however, he enforced the law he would naturally antagonize certain elements who would defeat him at the next election. In serving his own interests, therefore, he frustrated the purposes of the government and to

[66]Another check was placed upon internal migration in 1776. The artisans, of whom there were many more than the colonies could provide work for, began leaving the settlements and going into the cities to find employment. This increased the difficulty of collecting the government loan and was opposed to the idea prevailing in Russia that the rural population should occupy a fixed residence. To discourage this growing practice, the Kanzlei required that all domestic passports be exchanged once a year, and that the holder must show how much money he owed the government. Since no tradesman could secure work without a passport, and since the time and money involved in securing one was considerable, it practically forbade artisans to go outside their village for work and thus forced them back into agriculture for a livelihood. See *Russian Messenger* (in Russian), CC, 105.

this fact the Kanzlei laid the blame for these bad conditions among the colonies. They could not abolish election by the people, however, for this was guaranteed by the terms of the manifesto.[67]

The colonists on the other hand were satisfied with the arrangement, particularly after 1775 when the number of commissioners was increased to thirteen – one for each district. According to tradition, the people received great consideration and help from these advisers.[68] They personally visited the colonies at regular intervals, talked with the village authorities about their needs, suggested measures concerning the public health, crops, and other local matters, while questions of weightier importance were carried by them directly to the Kontor.

In spite of the fact that the colonists were gradually becoming satisfied with their lot and were setting themselves earnestly to the task of working out their local problems with a moderate promise of success, they were facing the most serious crisis of their existence. There had been many Russians who opposed Catherine's whole colonizing system because of the special privileges with which she endowed the foreign settlers, and particularly because of the large sums of money which she lavished upon them. The peasants in the provinces through which the immigrants had passed were jealous of the preference shown the newcomers and felt that *their* lands and *their* money were being given away to foreigners who were granted privileges of which they did not dare dream.[69] Hostility came from other quarters more influential than the peasants, the Senate doing everything in its power indirectly to thwart the plans of the Empress and to cause the colonies to fail.[70] Catherine, however, was not easily to be turned

---

[67]Pisarevskii, *Interior Organization of the Volga Colonies under Catherine II* (in Russian), 44-45.

[68]Bauer, *Geschichte der deutschen Ansiedler an der Wolga,* 23.

[69]There was much dissatisfaction among the peasants all over Russia at this time, preliminary to the revolts which broke out shortly thereafter.

[70]In "Comments from Diplomatic Sources," quoted in Herrmann, *Geschichte Russlands,* V, 562-563, discordant notes are struck at the very beginning of the immigration compaign: "Petersburg, August 24, 1764. The number of foreigners, particularly of Germans, who are coming to Russia this year in order to go into the colonies which are being founded in several distant parts of this Empire, has already amounted to several thousand persons. It seems that they are going to try to lug in as many people as they possibly can." "Petersburg, November 1, 1765. When the Empress insisted upon promoting the prosperity of the colonies at Saratov, in New Serbia, and in Ingermannland, the Senate did everything in its power to frustrate indirectly all these beautiful plans and to allow these new settlements to die out unnoticed. Particularly in the region of Saratov were malicious violations of the law met with. The colonies sent into these steppes were often deprived of their property by the neighboring Russians and the latter were protected by the Kanzlei installed by the Senate for that region and dependent upon it. The colonists were greatly deceived by the contracts which they had to make on their departure (from St. Petersburg) and the natives overwhelm them with curses and blows. Already the disorder has often been so great that the breaking out of a formal rebellion has been feared. But these hindrances, the causes of which the Empress knows very well, only make her all the more determined to hold fast to her decision."

Appendage to Footnote 70: Ingermannland lies in the territory conquered from Sweden in 1721. The city of Leningrad was built there. — The editors.

aside from carrying out one of her pet schemes upon which she at first lavished her personal attentions. While the colonists were gathered at Oranienbaum awaiting transportation to the colonies, she had visited them and talked with their leaders. This incident was related by Zuege:

> Several days later, I had the opportunity of seeing the great Catherine and was surprised at the unusual combination in her of great beauty and exalted majesty which numerous travelers before me have sought already to describe. With the purpose of personally meeting her countrymen through whom she thought to improve the cultivation of her domain, she came from Petersburg to the villa at Oranienbaum and there in the garden she passed down the lines which we formed under the direction of our managers. She stopped for a moment before Kratzky who stood at our head and asked about his fatherland, its business, and similar other things, but Kratzky answered only hesitatingly. When she started away, she held out her hand to him for a kiss, but Kratzky either did not understand this or he did not have courage enough to take advantage of this permission from the condescending Empress. I was disgusted over the childish conduct of the bashful man, and encouraged by the affability of the great lady, I decided to improve upon what he had spoiled and save the honor of my countrymen. When she passed by me, I made a deep bow which the Empress returned with a friendly nod without speaking to me, however; possibly because just then she was engaged in conversation with a gentleman from her numerous and brilliant train.
>
> Through her humanity and condescension, the Empress won the admiration of all the foreigners who had cherished the hope of living happily under her scepter. Toward all who came near her she conducted herself amiably, even when the circumstances were such as might easily have vexed her. This was exhibited in the case of an old trumpeter who with his two young sons was in our party. He got the idea of serenading the Empress at her castle; so he with his trumpet and each son with a bugle began an ear-splitting trio. Since the two boys blew piteously upon their instruments, I expected that the Empress would have these offenders driven away, but she sent to them a page, who in her name presented them with

an Imperial, about ten thalers, and thanked them for their good intentions of making her happy.[71]

She early planned a trip down the Volga to inspect the region set aside for colonization and to satisfy herself of the success of her plans, and in May, 1767, she actually journeyed down the river as far as Kazan.[72] Her correspondence with Voltaire, a sympathetic friend with whom "colonies, arts of all kinds, good laws, and tolerance were a passion,"[73] shows the enthusiasm with which she followed the details of her colonization plan during the first few years.[74] But as time passed, the Empress began to lose her zeal for this project as well as for most of the other philosophical and humanitarian ideas with which she had early aroused the praise of western Europe. Besides, she was becoming more and more entangled in foreign affairs, and the exclusive devotion which she had once given to internal matters was now dissipated in world politics. With a fine disregard for the promises made in her manifesto, she abolished in 1782 the colonial office at Saratov with its system of commissioners and included the government of the colonies in the general system of the empire.[75] With this annulment of the charter under which the German colonists had come to Russia, conditions among the foreign settlements again deteriorated and the period during the next fifteen years was one "of such general distress that the Pugachev rebellion seems mild in comparison with it.[76] At the death of Catherine in 1796, her "belle colonie" in Saratov was on the verge of utter extinction.

---

[71]Zuege, *Der russische Colonist,* I 70-72.

[72]For references to this journey cf. Herrmann, *Geschichte Russlands,* V, 675; and Mavor, *Economic History of Russia,* I, 305. In March, 1767, Catherine wrote Voltaire that she intended "to make a tour of the different provinces along the Volga; and, at a moment when you least expect it, you will receive a letter dated from some paltry town in Asia." Correspondence between the Empress of Russia and Monsieur Voltaire, Voltaire, *Complete Works,* LVIII, 20. May 19/29 she again wrote, "I threatened you with a letter from some place in Asia. Today I am keeping my word. . . . I am in Asia. I wanted to see it for myself. There are in this town twenty different peoples, who resemble each other hardly at all. Clothes have to be made for them to include a type appropriate to each group. General principles can be applied quite easily, but the details?" *Idem,* 22. Translated from the French by Dr. Adam Giesinger.

[73]Voltaire, *ibid.,* 33.

[74]Ibid., 42. On September 2, 1769, Voltaire wrote to Catherine: "It is a great accomplishment to make a colony as populous as that at Saratov prosper, in spite of the Turks, the Tartars, the Cologne Gazette, and the Correspondent at Avignon." Translated from the French by Dr. Adam Giesinger.

[75]It is probable that this was part of a general plan of hers for simplifying the administration of the empire since the German provinces of the Baltic suffered a similar change at this time. "In 1783 Catherine II abolished the old constitution in order to replace it by new bureaucratic institutions . . . . The sense of justice of the Emperor Paul, however, in the year 1796, restored to the loyal men of Livland and Estland 'what had been wrongfully taken from them.' " Eckardt, *Modern Russia,* 332. Cf. also Klaus, *Unsere Kolonien,* 36, and Pisarevskii, *Foreign Colonization in Russia in the Eighteenth Century* (in Russian), 203.

[76] Klaus, *Unsere Kolonien,* 185.

Paul I, who succeeded his mother on the throne, was one of the most dreaded rulers the Russian people ever had. Like his father, Peter III, he had strong German sympathies which he paraded openly and offensively before his Russian subjects; he took a savage delight in the most sudden and drastic reversals of his mother's policies. Toward the Germans in the empire he assumed an attitude of paternal guardianship which effected for them one of the very few favorable results of his short and stormy reign. One of his first acts was to annul the *ukaz* of Catherine which included the government of the German colonies in the general system of the empire, and to establish at Saratov a separate department for the administration and care of the settlements. He gave official sanction to the German language by commanding that orders relating to the German colonies be written in their mother tongue so that the people need no longer depend upon the Russian officials for its interpretation. Two commissioners were sent from the capital to investigate the causes for the impoverishment of the colonists. They spent several years (1797-1801) collecting information from the settlers themselves and reported to the government that an administration not adapted to the needs of the colonists was the cause for their decay. As a result of this report, a series of laws was promulgated (1801-1803) known as "Uniform Instructions for the Internal Organization and Administration" of the colonies, which were designed to restore their local self government but to provide the same system for all the colonies and to coordinate it with the central government.[77]

The system of local self government was based upon the Russian *mir* and gave to the German colonies practically the same village administration which prevailed among the rural population. The title to the land which had originally been granted to the immigrants in severalty was now vested in the village community, and all individual ownership, except of the house, premises, and personal property, ceased.[78] The Russian system of agriculture was introduced, by which the arable portion of the land was divided at certain stated intervals among the inhabitants according to the number of males in each family while the pasture and forest lands were held in common. For the administration of the village (*Gemeinde*), authority was vested in the representative assembly composed of one member from each family. This body elected the *Vorsteher* and two assistants who, together with the clerk (*Schreiber*), formed the *Kleingemeinde* which cared for the

---

[77]*Ibid.*, 182ff; Bauer, *Geschichte der deutschen Ansiedler an der Wolga*, 77-84; *Russian Messenger*, CC.

[78]Inequalities had arisen in the amounts of land owned by various colonists due to the fact that some shares, belonging to persons who had either died or disappeared, had been appropriated.

Courtesy of Mrs. Clarence T. Olson, Denver, Colorado.

The Norka Reformed Church. Norka was the largest of the 104 colonies at the time of its founding and sent more immigrants to Lincoln, Nebraska, than any of the other colonies.

routine matters connected with the conduct of the village government. A second administrative unit called the *Kreis* was composed of groups of villages with a corresponding set of officers.[79]

In addition to these general administrative regulations, the "Uniform Instructions" offered detailed advice as to the personal conduct of the settlers. Like the "Instructions" of 1768, they pointed out that it was the first duty of the colonists to go to church; and enjoined upon the village authorities the necessity of discouraging luxuries among the settlers, warning them against the entertaining of too many guests and against gambling.[80] Then, as now, the excise trade was a government monopoly, the income from which was very great. The wine shops in the German colonies were ordered closed or transferred to Russian villages because the government decided that the people were less industrious and home-loving where these existed. These "Instructions" ushered in a new epoch for the German colonies on the Volga, but before discussing that, it will be interesting to glance at the contemporary notices concerning these people during their period of deterioration.

The location of the German colonies has been such as to place them in the direct line of travel in Russia, for from the earliest day to the present, the majority of those who journey through the empire for pleasure or research follow the same route—from St. Petersburg to Moscow, thence to Nizhni-Novgorod and then down the Volga. Thus glimpses of the German colonists on the Volga are afforded by the writings of a number of the members of the scientific expedition to Siberia which was sent out by Catherine in 1768.[81] The territory along the middle and lower Volga first came under their observation, and

79Haxthausen, *Studien ueber die inneren Zustaende . . . Russlands,* II, 36, 43, says that the colonies voluntarily introduced the Russian system of agriculture while the local or village organization was based upon the German model.

80These German settlers in Russia were not the only people who needed "government control" exercised in their amusements and expenditures. In discussing New England marriage laws and customs, Dr. Howard in his *History of Matrimonial Institutions,* II, 141, says: "In the eighteenth century weddings were accompanied by much revelry and extravagance. Gloves, rings and scarves, as at funerals, were given away in such profusion as to call for legislation to check the abuse."

81In 1767 Catherine gave orders to the Imperial Academy of Sciences to choose a company of learned and able men to undertake this enterprise. They were to travel into the interior of her vast empire for the purpose of collecting material upon the geography, climate, flora, and fauna of the various districts, of studying the soil and its possibilities, and of observing the habits and character of the different peoples inhabiting the country. Pallas, the noted German scientist, was chosen as leader of the expedition which was composed largely of German scholars who had come to Russia at the invitation of Catherine. Georgi, Gmelin, Gueldenstaedt, and Falck were among the foreign scientists while Lepekhin and Rytschkow were Russians. Some of the explorers were absent eight years before they were recalled to St. Petersburg by Catherine, and the results of their investigations place the expedition among the most successful and important of any in the eighteenth century. One should not look here, however, for an unbiased opinion of the results of the colonization policy of Catherine. For further details of this expedition, see Tooke, *Life of Catharine II*, II, 501-510; Herrmann, *Geschichte Russlands,* VI, 69-70; also biographies of the various members of the expedition.

A crown house built by Catherine the Great for the early colonists. This particular one was located in Stahl am Tarlyk. Drawing by Phillip B. Legler from Peter Sinner's book, *Der Deutsche im Wolgalande*.

the entire party at one time or another, visited the German settlements in the province of Saratov. Among the first was the academician Falck who traveled through the colonies in 1769.[82] He details the historical events connected with the calling of the immigrants to Russia, but erroneously estimates the total German population of the empire at only 10,000. Concerning the character of his countrymen, he says that there were some with very great ability, but that the majority were lazy and good-for-nothing.

This testimony is quite in keeping with the impression of the other German scholars of the party, but is the reverse of the opinion given by Ivan Lepekhin, who, being a Russian, was struck by the comparative superiority of the German settlers. In his account of the first village which he visited, he says:[83]

> This colony (Sosnowka)[84] has many privileges above the Russian villages . . . . Their courtyard and the buildings adjacent to it are arranged very orderly . . . . all landlords have, attached to their houses, a special garden for themselves in which they raise the necessary vegetables for their tables. You can find there parsley, parsnips, various kinds of cabbage, etc., all of which are actual rarities not only in our villages but in our distant cities. Their careful industry is shown by the fact that the potato grows in our country as excellently as in other lands. Besides they are not bad farmers and understand how much and what kind of fertilization or cultivation an acre demands, what different kinds (of crops) succeed, etc. For this reason their harvests are better than those of our native people. They make use of such tools as served them in their old home, for example, the plow.

In July, 1773, the members of the expedition gathered at Tsaritsyn on the Volga and remained there during the following winter. In August of 1773, Pallas undertook a journey through the German colonies of the *Bergseite*.[85] He writes at great length concerning the

---

[82]His report was published in the *Complete Collection of Learned Travels in Russia,* VI, Reports 112-114, ed. by the Imperial Academy of Sciences (in Russian).

[83]Lepekhin, *Tagebuch der Reise durch Verschiedene Provinzen der russischen Reichs in den Jahren 1768 und 1769,* 237.

[84]This is the Russian name for Schilling. — The editors.

[85]Peter Simon Pallas was born in Berlin in 1741. He became a student of natural history and studied in both Holland and England. In 1766 he published a scientific treatise which won him great honors. In 1768 he was invited by Catherine to Russia to lead the expedition to Siberia. On his arrival in St. Petersburg, he was made a member of the Imperial Academy of Sciences, and through the collections made in his first journey through Russia, he laid the foundation for its museum. His publications covered a wide range of scientific subjects. After 1796 he lived in the Crimea where Catherine had presented him with a fine estate. In 1810 he went to Berlin where he died the following year. The results of his two journeys through Russia were published under the following titles: *Reise durch verschiedene Provinzen des russischen Reichs* (1771-1776), and *Bemerkungen aus einer Reise durch die suedlichen Statthalterschaften des russischen Reichs,* (1799 and 1805). Cf. *Allgemeine deutsche Bibliographie,* XXV, 81-98.

Courtesy of the Institut fuer Auslandsbeziehungen, Stuttgart.

Balzer in the wintertime. A bridal party assembles.

Courtesy of the Institut fuer Auslandsbeziehungen, Stuttgart.

A typical village street scene in Messer on the Volga.

Courtesy of the Institut fuer Auslandsbeziehungen, Stuttgart.

General view of Katharinenstadt (now Marxstadt), one of the largest Volga German villages.

Moravian settlement Sarepta, which he considered a valuable outpost of western civilization on the Asian border.

Twenty years later Pallas again traveled through the Volga colonies and professed to see great changes for the better in them.[86] He speaks of the growth of the town of Saratov in trade, population, and buildings since the colonization of the surrounding country and the consequent establishment of provincial governments. He comments upon the abundant products of the region bordering on the Volga. Even Astrakhan and several distant towns were partly supplied with grain from this neighborhood:

> . . . a supply to which the German colonists greatly contribute. These colonists have, during the last twenty years, considerably increased both in population and opulence, and are now almost completely assimilated or made over; as the old settlers, who were in general rather immoral characters, are dead and are succeeded by a better and more vigorous progeny . . . . They appear to be perfectly contented and happy, and to have no wish other than to be governed by magistrates acquainted with the German language as many of the colonists are unable to speak Russian . . . .

The optimism of Pallas concerning the changed character of the colonists and their economic advance is scarcely justified in view of the history which has been related. Another similar misjudgment was expressed concerning their religious future. Commenting upon the fact that two Lutheran villages had conjointly employed a pastor from the Moravians at Sarepta, he adds, "It appears in general that most of the German colonies on the banks of the Volga will gradually embrace the principles of that persuasion; and that the profits arising to the colonists at Sarepta from the spinning of cotton have contributed to effect this religious change." As a matter of fact, this change in religious teachers was not a question of choice but of necessity, and the tenacity with which even Lutherans and Reformed have clung to their respective faiths, although united in worship and marriage, belies the traveler's judgment. The value of this testimony must be measured in view of the necessarily superficial character of all travels, and the natural desire of a patron of the Empress to place the stamp of approval upon one of her early dreams.

2. *Period of Economic Progress, 1801-1850.* The second period of historical development in the Volga colonies (1801-1850) be-

[86]Shortly before, a French traveler, Chantreau, visited the Volga colonies on a journey through Russia (1788 and 1789).

gan with the change in administration effected by the "Uniform Instructions" and is characterized by economic progress. Even during the stress of the first years, the colonists were becoming acclimated and were learning things which they quickly used to good advantage when the pressure of an unfavorable government was removed. By 1808, we are told, nearly all of the temporary houses (called *Kronshaueschen*) built for them by the government had been replaced by new and better buildings, costing from 700 to 1,000 rubles each.[87] In 1809 the colonists were placed on an equal footing with the rest of the rural population in the matter of taxation, the original period of immunity having been extended fifteen years.[88]

During the first half of the nineteenth century, agriculture which has always been the mainstay of the colonies, was in its most flourishing condition. There was as yet sufficient land per "soul" for each family to make a living. The crude Russian implements which had been provided by the government to the original colonists and used during the first years because they did not seriously undertake their work, were now replaced by better German tools. The wooden hook plow of the Russian peasant gave way to the one-share plow which the Germans had used in the homeland;[89] the sickle was replaced by the cradle, and the clumsy Russian pole wagon by the German rack or shaft wagon.[90] Dutch windmills were built, especially on the *Wiesenseite* where the Hollanders lived and where there was a lack of sufficient fall in the streams to provide water power.[91]

---

[87]Velitzyn, "Foreign Colonies in Russia," *Russian Messenger* (in Russian), CC.

[88]Bauer, *Geschichte der deutschen Ansiedler an der Wolga*, 84. Velitzyn in the *Russian Messenger* gives the date as 1824. Cf. also Haxthausen, *Studien ueber die inneren Zustaende . . . Russlands,* II, 41-42.

[89]However, in a Catholic colony, as late as 1898 the wooden plow was still in common use, there being very few iron plows. Muench, *Historical Geographical Dictionary of Saratov* (in Russian).

[90]Haxthausen, *Studien ueber die innere Zustaende . . . Russlands,* II, 38: Die Ackererwerkzeuge in den Colonien sind Pfluege mit Scharen, eine Zusammensetzung aus dem Wendepfluge der Wetterau und dem maerkischen Pfluge. Zum Aufreissen, besonders der frischen Steppe bedienen sie sich der deutschen spitzigen Pflugschar. Bei Bearbeitung der Kartoffeln- und Tabaksfeldes brauchen sie meist das runde Pflugeisen. Die russische Zogga findet man ueberall, wo Sandboden ist; wo der Boden voll Quecken und sonstigem Starkem Wurzelwerk ist, taugt sie nicht. Die Kleinrussen haben den sehr unbehuelflichen Kopfpflug der an der Schar Eisen hat, und von 3 Pferden, oft auch 6-8 Ochsen gezogen wird. Nur in den deutschen Colonien findet man eiserne Eggen. Translation: The farm implements in the colonies are the ploughshare, a combination of the swivel plough of the Wetterau and the Brandenburg plough. To tear up the soil of the virgin steppe, they use the German pointed ploughshare. For working the potato and tobacco fields, the round coulter is often used. The Russian "zogga" can be found wherever there is sandy soil. Where the ground is full of couch-grass and other strong roots, it is useless. The Little Russians have a not very efficient plow which has iron on the plowshare and is pulled by three horses, often even by six to eight oxen. Only in the German colonies does one find iron harrows. — The editors.

[91]Bauer, *Geschichte der deutschen Ansiedler an der Wolga,* 27; Haxthausen, *ibid.,* 19-20.

The native crops which consisted chiefly of the small grains — wheat, barley, and oats — were soon raised more successfully by the thrifty Germans than by the native Russians; for nowhere in the world did nature offer better assistance to agriculture than in the black soil belt of Russia. In addition to the native crops, the colonists introduced two very important products which entered largely into the support and commerce of the people. The Hollanders on the *Wiesenseite* made a successful attempt to raise tobacco from American seed and this soon became a source of profit to many of the settlers.[92] Still more important was the introduction of the potato by the German colonists who brought the product with them. This became the chief household food of the settlers, but it is a somewhat curious fact that the Russian population never adopted its use until it was practically forced to do so by an imperial decree in 1840. In spite of two serious famines — 1815 and 1833 — the first half of the century saw agriculture progressively develop and flourish in the German colonies on the Volga.

The wants of the people remained very simple and household economy supplied all their demands. Only on the *Bergseite* was any attempt made to introduce manufacturing, and this came about largely from the fact that here the settlements were more crowded and much of the land was so hilly that it was unsuited to grain production. The introduction of the sugar beet led to the establishment in one of the colonies of a factory which existed for almost a half century. But through improper management by the village authorities and through lack of private capital in the colony to operate so large an undertaking, the factory was lost.[93] Attempts to start dyeing establishments usually resulted in failure, because the soil was not suited for the culture of the madder, and the water had too much mineral in it. However, in Balzer it became a rather important industry. A small industry, which, however, found a market more distant than any other, was the making of a peculiar brand of pipes, the manufacture of which originated in one of the colonies on the east side of the Volga where tobacco was extensively raised. About twenty varieties of pipes, some wooden and some braided leather, were made by the villages and sold throughout the German colonies and into the most distant parts of the empire. The establishment of tanneries developed on quite an extensive scale, especially in the more hilly regions suited to cattle raising, and along the Volga where oak trees grew in abundance. Toward the close of this

---

[92]Cf. "Tobacco industry among the foreign settlers of the Gouvernements of Samara and Saratov," *Journal of the Ministry of Imperial Domains* (in Russian), XIX, Pt. II; Pleshcheev, *The Russian Empire*, 912; Haxthausen, *The Russian Empire*, I, 351.

[93]The colony which had a sugar beet factory was Anton on the Bergseite. See Bauer, *Geschichte der deutschen Ansiedler an der Wolga*, 93-94. — The editors.

When Volga German men gathered, long German pipes were smoked. Drawing by Phillip B. Legler from Peter Sinner's book, *Der Deutsche im Wolgalande*.

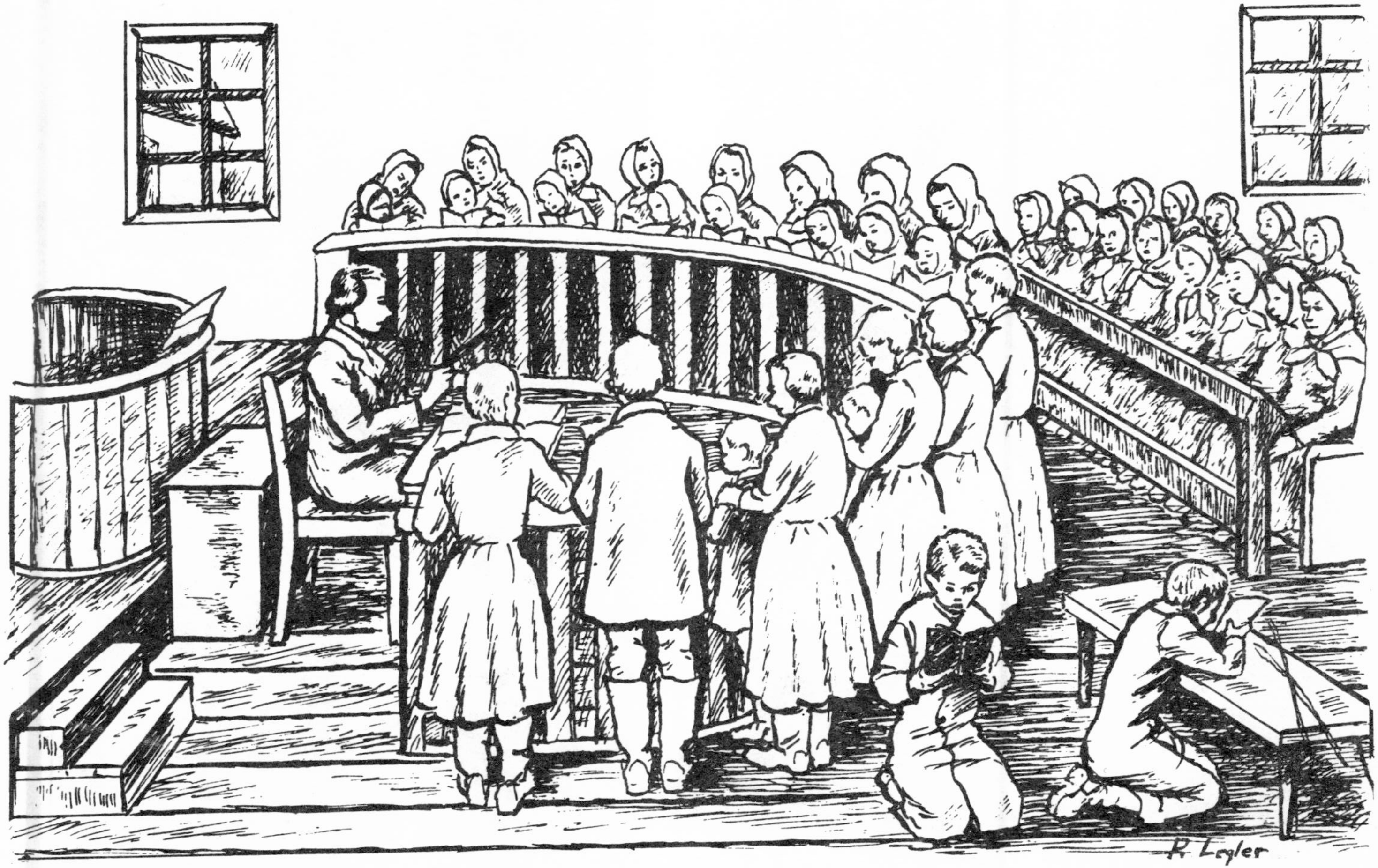

A Volga German school around 1800. Drawing by Phillip B. Legler from Peter Sinner's book, *Der Deutsche im Wolgalande*.

Courtesy of the Landsmannschaft der Deutschen aus Russland, Stuttgart.

Market scene in Grimm on the *Bergseite*.

Courtesy of the Institut fuer Auslandsbeziehungen, Stuttgart.

Granaries at Katharinenstadt on the Volga.

period, there were fifty-two of these tanning factories in one *Kreis*. Oil mills were common in the colonies, usually owned by the *Gemeinden* and rented out to the operators. The product of these mills was an oil made from the crushed seeds of the sunflower which was extensively cultivated by the Volga Germans. The manufactured product is used in place of butter and lard and the refuse from the mills is fed to the stock. The *Gemeinden* also controlled the fishing rights to the streams which they rented out to individual colonists.

The most extensive industries, however, were flour and cloth manufacture. Every *Gemeinde* owned its own mill for the grinding of flour for home comsumption, those on the *Bergseite* taking advantage of the small but rapid tributaries flowing into the Volga from the hilly west side, while those on the *Wiesenseite* secured their power from the Dutch windmills.[94] Wheat, the chief product in the colonies, soon became a purely commercial crop, since the colonists depended upon the cheaper grains and upon the vegetables – cabbage and potatoes – for family use. An excellent means of transportation was furnished by the Volga River which lay conveniently near to many of the villages. Communication was thus established with the outlying colonies. The conduct of this trade naturally fell into the hands of the Germans, who became the founders and owners of enormous flour mills situated in the city of Saratov, whose extensive commerce reached to St. Petersburg and even into foreign countries.[95]

The industry second in importance is the manufacture of *sarpinka*, a kind of cotton cloth similar to our French gingham. It was introduced into Russia by the Moravian colony of Sarepta and was taken over by the other German colonists merely as a home industry which furnished employment during the long winter months. As the land shares decreased, however, it furnished work the year around for many who were being forced out of agriculture; and year by year the number of houses in which looms were run greatly increased. The weaving process remained a home industry, but seasonal, the number of workers more than doubling during the winter months. Separate factories were established in the colonies for the manufacture and dyeing of the thread. The chief distributing center for the *sarpinka* trade outside the colonies was the annual fair at Nizhni-Novgorod from which this cloth was sent into the most distant parts of the empire.[96]

The artisan class, now forming a comparatively small part of the

---

[94]Haxthausen, *Studien ueber die inneren Zustaende . . . Russlands,* II, 19, says that he saw water mills nowhere in his whole journey until he came to the Volga.

[95]Meakin, *Russia, Travels, and Studies.*

[96]Most of the founders of the large flour mills on the Volga made their start financially through the *sarpinka* industry.

population of the colonies, also developed as regards tools and organization during this period of comparative prosperity. It will be recalled that many of the artisans were forced out of their trades in the early days of the colonies because there was not sufficient demand for their work at home and the government refused to allow them to migrate into the cities. Local conditions in the colonies forced others out of their occupations or limited their range of activity. Particularly was this true of the woodworkers because of the general lack of timber on the steppes and the profligate destruction by the early colonists of the limited amount which grew along the streams. Materials for the simple household furniture and agricultural implements had to be secured from the country up the Volga, and for the fashioning of these necessities, the artisans early improved their implements, adding the carving tools and bench to the simpler utensils of pioneer days. As agriculture improved, blacksmithing, wagon making and related trades were encouraged. Strangely enough, the German colonists, up to the time of the emancipation of the serfs, depended entirely upon Russian carpenters and sawyers for their building operations since they could secure this kind of labor at such low wages that they could not afford to do the work themselves. As a result of the development of the artisan class, guilds sprang up among them and shoemakers, blacksmiths, cabinet makers, wagon makers, and the like banded together in labor groups for the improvement and protection of their various trades.

Although the German colonies on the Volga developed in agriculture and trade during the first half of the nineteenth century, their mode of living remained very simple. In spite of this, almost before two generations had passed, they were facing a crisis because of the lack of land. When the colonists went to Russia, they were given access to practically unlimited quantities of land. Under the original plan, the government set aside a large section of territory along the Volga for foreign settlement. Each family was to receive thirty *dessiatines* of land for its individual share, but each colony was to form a district sixty to seventy *verst* in circumstance, with enough land to provide ultimately for one thousand families. One sixth of all the land of the colony was to be left vacant for the use of coming generations, and until its division among them, this "reserve land" as it was called, was to be managed by the district (*Kreis*). Another sixth of the land, called "extra lands," was to be reserved for the artisans of each colony, and was to be managed for them by the colony. But as in so many other respects, the plans of the government miscarried here. The settlers did not confine themselves to the territory mapped out

Courtesy of the Institut fuer Auslandsbeziehungen, Stuttgart.

Threshing of barley by hand along the Volga.

Courtesy of the Landsmannschaft der Deutschen aus Russland, Stuttgart.

Windmills in German villages.

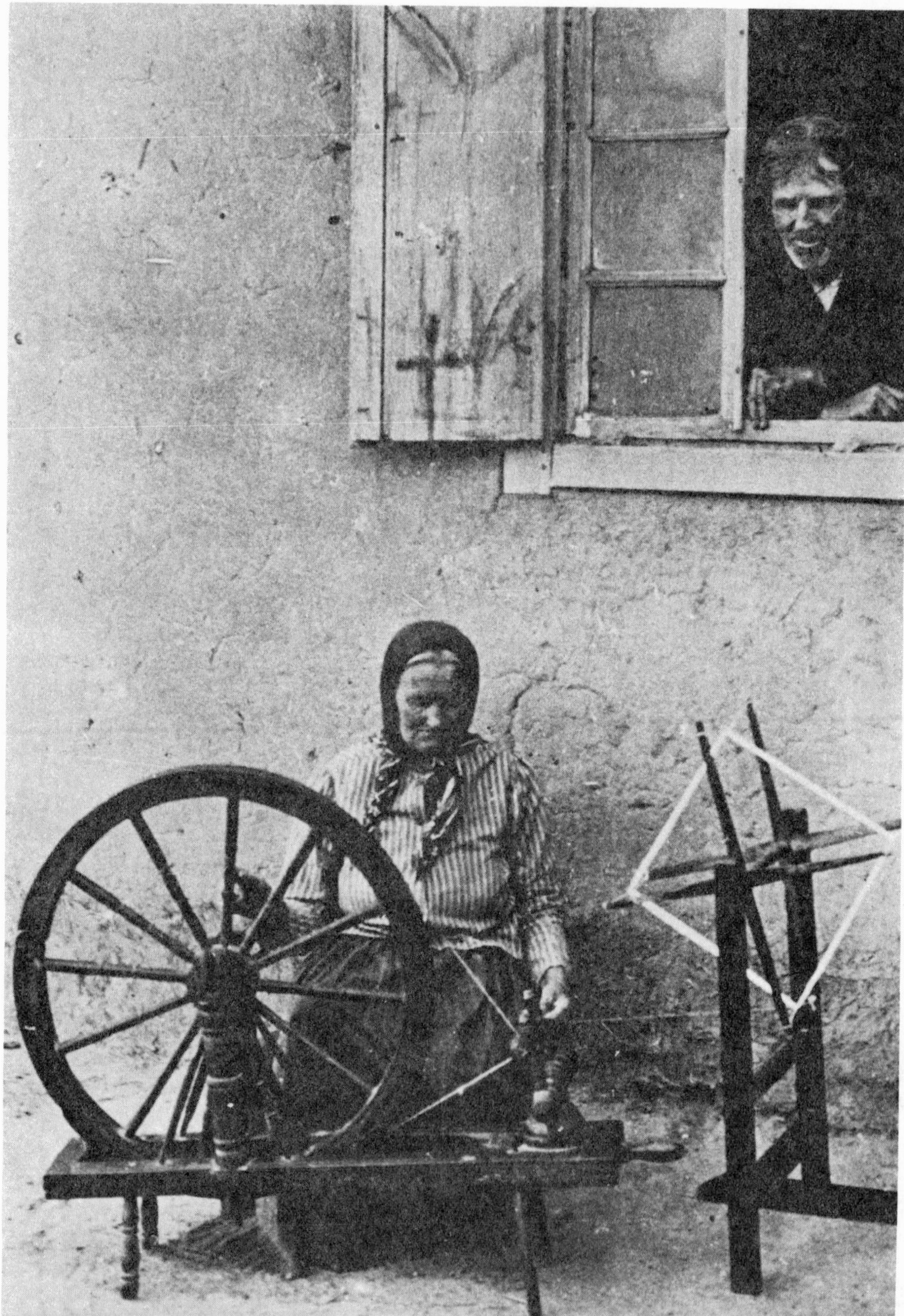

Courtesy of the Institut fuer Auslandsbeziehungen, Stuttgart.

A grandmother in Messer winds thread on a bobbin in preparation for weaving sarpinka.

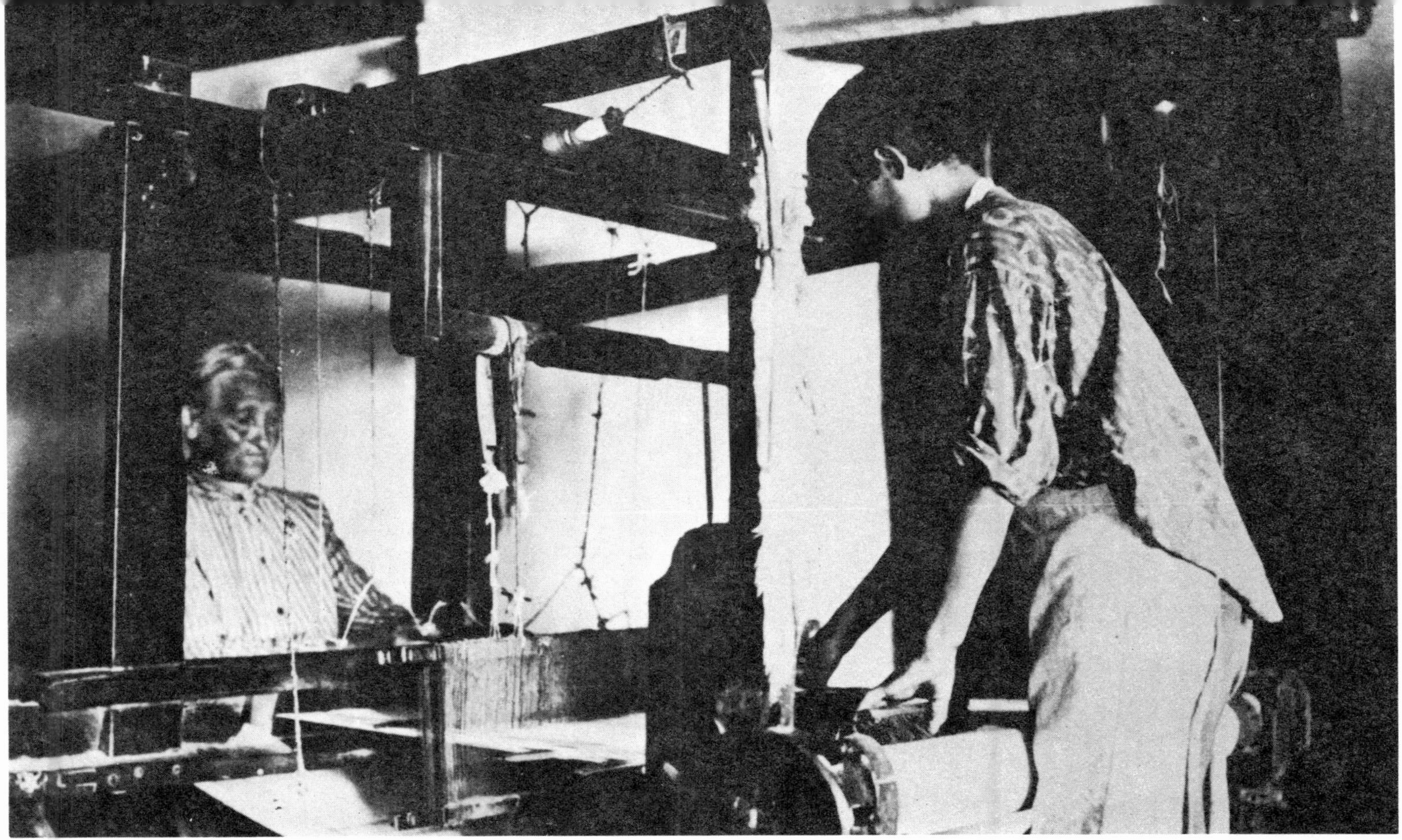

Courtesy of the Institut fuer Auslandsbeziehungen, Stuttgart.

Preparing for sarpinka weaving.

Courtesy of the Institut fuer Auslandsbeziehungen, Stuttgart.

Weaving the sarpinka cloth.

Courtesy of the Landsmannschaft der Deutschen aus Russland, Stuttgart.

The Volga River at Seelman on the *Wiesenseite*.

Courtesy of the Nebraska State Historical Society, Lincoln, Nebraska.

Mill in Frank. Mr. Eckhardt, the teacher, in foreground.

Courtesy of the Nebraska State Historical Society, Lincoln, Nebraska.

Sawing wood at Kolb.

for them, and in their desire for mutual protection and companionship, the settlements were placed too close together to permit expansion in the future. No definite amount of land was assigned to each family as had been contemplated, nor was this done until 1797 when each "soul," according to the revision of 1788 was given twenty *dessiatines*. However, by the provisions of the "Uniform Regulations" of 1801-1803, all the land belonging to the individual colonists was now made the property of the colony and the possibilities for expansion ceased. At this time, however, (1802) the government allowed the Germans to exchange their poor land for an equal amount of good land.

During the first ten years the population of the German colonies decreased by almost one third of its original number, owing to sickness, the disappearance of those who attempted to return to Germany, and to the disasters wrought by the Pugachev rebellion and the attacks of the Kirghiz. After 1775, however, the population showed a steady and constant increase. Emigration was forbidden by the government and the order strictly enforced. The tendency for large families, supplemented by the special privilege granting freedom from military service which permitted the establishment of more homes at earlier ages, resulted in a prolific increase of the inhabitants so that with every revision the amount of land upon which a family might be sustained became less. The first revision after the settlement of the colonies and the fifth revision of the government was made in 1788, according to which the colonists it will be remembered, were given twenty *dessiatines* per "soul." The increase in the population and the decrease in the amount of land per "soul" for the next seventy years were as follows:[97]

REVISION	YEAR	PERIOD	INCREASE IN POPULATION	DECREASE IN LAND
5-6	1798	10 years	26.67 per cent	15.5 dessiatines
6-7	1816	18 "	54.80 " "	10.4 "
7-8	1834	18 "	78.20 " "	5.6 "
8-9	1850	16 "	50.97 " "	3.8 "
9-10	1857	7 "	20.78 " "	3.2 "

Since these land shares included not merely the tillable land but also the forest, hay, meadow, and house plots and whatever useless soil the *Gemeinde* owned, it is evident that the people could not long exist under such conditions.[98] As early as 1840 the colonists petitioned

[97]Klaus, *Unsere Kolonien*, 151.

[98]In 1868 some of the colonies on the *Bergseite* had only 1½ *dessiatines* per male inhabitant.

the government for further grants. There was no more vacant land contiguous to the German settlements, for in the period since their formation the Russians and other nationalities had spread over the territory and occupied all the intervening spaces.[99] About 1845 a grant was made not far from the town of Kamyshin along the lower course of the Ilovlya River and within the next few years seven colonies were founded here by the inhabitants of the most crowded villages of the *Bergseite.* It is significant from the social standpoint that these first settlements were composed exclusively of people who came from the same villages so that no free interchange of the colonists took place during this first emigration. About the same time another grant was made along the source of the Great Karaman River in Samara, and there eight colonies were formed by villagers from the *Wiesenseite.* From 1855 to 1859, 250,000 *dessiatines* of land in the Novousensk *Kreis* in the province of Samara were measured off by the government to relieve the congestion among the colonies in the province of Saratov, and up to 1866, sixty-seven colonies were founded on this tract.[100]

In spite of the willingness of the Crown to furnish additional land free to the German colonists, and its desire particularly to settle the Samaran steppe, it was found to be a difficult matter to induce the Germans to migrate. The memory of the terrible sufferings of their fathers was so clearly preserved through fireside tales that they had no desire to repeat those experiences on what was a new frontier. They were alarmed by the nearness of the Kirghiz, their old enemies, who, though less savage than formerly, still made thieving raids even among the older villages and would have at their mercy the people who settled these new lands. The lack of wood and water in the steppe was another deterrent, while a still greater difficulty was found in adjusting the financial affairs in the mother *Gemeinde,* occasioned by permanent withdrawal of a part of the community. This difficulty is unknown where private instead of communal ownership exists, and each person's affairs are handled as one unit. In the colonies it was necessary to count out of the treasury in actual cash to each settler not only the value of his farm land and his house and lot, but also his share in the public buildings, the church, schoolhouse, magazine, mills, and whatever other property was owned by the *Gemeinde.* During the time in which these matters were being adjusted, some of the government grant was rented out and many of the colonists decided that they preferred to remain in their crowded villages and receive their share

[99]Haxthausen, *Studien ueber die inneren Zustaende . . . Russlands,* II, 55.

[100]Bauer, *Geschichte der deutschen Ansiedler an der Wolga,* 114; *Historical Survey of Fifty Years' Activity of the Ministry of Imperial Domains,* Pt. II; *Volksfreund Kalender,* 1911; Muench, *Historical Geographical Encyclopediae of Saratov,* 1898-1901.

of the rent from these lands rather than migrate there. However, the government was insistent upon actual settlement of the grant, and after extending the period allotted for settlement three times, in 1871 it finally withdrew the land still unoccupied and confiscated the rents which had been collected on the ground that the colonists had not fulfilled their share of the contract. In all this unfortunate transaction the colonial officials figured in an unpleasant way, discouraging the Germans from occupying the land; because through renting it, the officials were able to clear neat sums on the side and to obstruct the welfare and wishes of both the colonists and the Crown.

Three colonies were formed in 1863, not far from the mother colonies in Saratov, through division of the *Gemeinde*. It sometimes happened that a village had some of its land lying at a distance — twenty or thirty miles away — a circumstance which was probably accounted for in the exchange of its poor land for some of a better quality. In cultivating this, it was necessary for those who had drawn it to move there and remain the entire summer. As times became more settled, these people remained throughout the year and established a permanent settlement called a "chutor," which, however, remained under the government of the mother colony. In 1863 three of these settlements, which were located at a considerable distance, were permanently established and made separate colonies. The only other migration from the original colonies which occurred prior to the crisis of 1871 was into the Caucasus, where since 1840, German settlements had been founded in the province of Stavropol.[101]

During this period of economic development (1801-1850), two noted travelers visited the German colonies on the Volga—Alexander von Humboldt in 1829 and August von Haxthausen in 1844.[102] The visit of the former was very brief and admitted of only a cursory examination of the life of the people.

While von Humboldt's chief interest lay in physical geography and kindred topics, von Haxthausen was an authority on agrarian

---

[101]Matthaei, *Die deutschen Ansiedlungen in Russland,* 99-100. In this reference Matthaei mentions the colony of Michelsthal which was founded by people from Riebensdorf in the Ukraine. He does not tell who founded the other colonies. — The editors.

[102]Other travelers as well visited the German colonies in Russia. In 1816 and 1825 Erdmann published his *Reise in Innern Russland.* An encyclopedia edited by Schoberl and put out about 1825, entitled *Russia, being a description of the character, manners, customs, dress, diversions and other peculiarities of the different nations inhabiting the Russian Empire,* gives a sketch of the Volga colonies. In 1834 Dr. Fr. Goebel, Professor of chemistry at Dorpat University, made a trip with two companions down the Volga, and although his investigations and reports were purely in the interests of his science, he devotes one section of the appendix to a lengthy discussion of the German colonies on the Volga, covering every phase of their life: *Reise in die Steppen des suedlichen Russlands,* II, 277-288. About the same time, Johann Georg Kohl, a German scholar, traveled through the empire and wrote at some length of the German colonies in South Russia.

questions, and it was in view of this fact that Czar Nicholas I had invited him to make a study of these problems in Russia. Refusing any financial aid from the Russian government, he accepted the permission to make an investigation of the inner conditions of life in the empire, and in 1843 and 1844 traveled through Russia under the protection of the Czar. He took a sympathetic interest in the colonies of his countrymen on the Volga and in South Russia, and discussed them, not as isolated factors in the population, but as parts of the great problems of immigration and agrarian organization.[103] As a result of the superior privileges and prosperity of the Germans, he found among the Russians everywhere great animosity and envy of the German colonies on the Volga and comments upon the fact that the latter displayed a warm attachment to the Imperial family.[104]

Among the Volga Germans, as well as among all the inhabitants of the black soil belt along the Volga River, Baron von Haxthausen found the people suffering from lack of land. The general causes were the same, differing only in degree of intensity. The wild character of the country had forced the original settlers to form their colonies too close together and with too many people. By reason of the large size of the villages and the consequent great distance of some of their land, a sort of "nomadic" agriculture resulted, by which a part of the farmers were obliged to go long distances and practically move their villages during the sowing and reaping seasons.[105] The rapid increase of the population had decreased the number of *dessiatines* per "soul," and instead of fifteen *dessiatines* as the government legally provided, the Russian villages were now reduced to not more than eight and the German villages possessed but four or five *dessiatines* per "soul."

Further, he said, this overpopulation of a part of the Russian Empire was not necessary if the government would take steps to distribute its inhabitants better. There were thousands of *dessiatines* of unused land, much of it lying in close proximity to the overcrowded section. Some was owned by the nobles and the rest was Crown land; some of it was used for grazing land by the Tartar tribes; all was not so fertile as the occupied land, but it would afford as good a living as the over-

---

[103]Haxthausen, *Studien ueber die innern Zustaende . . . Russlands,* II, 34-59; 171-337; 391-392.

[104]*Ibid.,* 43-44: "The German colonists preserve in true German fashion a deep attachment to the Imperial House. They told with great and touching love of the visit of the crown prince who was here several years previously, who had spoken in a friendly manner with them and had carefully asked about their condition and circumstances." — Translation by the editors.

[105]Many of the villages in this part of Russia contained from 3,000 to 4,000 inhabitants, while according to the revision of 1838 the German villages contained an average over 1,200 persons. In no place else in Europe were to be found agricultural villages of a similar size: Haxthausen, *Studien ueber die innern Zustaende . . . Russlands,* II, 10.

worked soil, and if the government proceeded with a definite plan the congestion might be relieved. Hence, wrote Haxthausen, the most important question of the entire domestic policy of the empire was the colonization or settlement of the interior of the empire; for what real help was there in a million unreliable inhabitants in a conquered territory when the government might establish ten million satisfied and homogeneous subjects in the boundaries of its present confines? Only through a properly organized and thorough system of colonization could Russia become what nature and history intended it should become. For this reason it needed like England, a Colonial Ministry, although in a different sense; one which should concern itself not with colonies in foreign lands but with the settlement of the interior parts of the empire by redistributing the population in the overcrowded section and, if necessary, opening the country again to foreign immigration.

3. *Period of Changing Status in Relation to the Russian Government, 1850-1871.* With the opening of the second half of the nineteenth century, a new period in the history of the Russian Empire begins, and the two following decades witness some of the most important changes ever made in its government. In this general upheaval, practically every element of the greatly varied population of the empire was affected, including those portions which had not heretofore been subjected to the general laws. For the German colonies the period from 1850 to 1871 forms a distinct epoch in their history in Russia which is characterized by their changed status in relation to the government. Not only were they subjected to a different legal code, but their traditional position in the empire was taken from them. Hitherto, the attitude of the Crown had been one of favortism and paternalism toward them. They had been the "elder" of the two boys whose father had said, "Son, all that I have is thine." The people and the officiary, it will be recalled, looked with jealousy and growing dislike upon them; and the Crown now began to change its policy, first through passive consent and later through active measures of opposition. In order to understand the causes for this change, it is necessary to retrace some of the steps taken and to note conditions during the preceding reign when Russia was becoming ripe for the reforms of Alexander II.

The beginning of this period found Russia near the close of the long reign of suppression of Nicholas I (1825-1855). His rule had been ushered in by a Decembrist revolt which he met with the prompt and decisive measures which furnish a clue to the severity and sternness of his entire reign. In spite of repression, however, the growth of liberal ideas continued unabated and gained strength from the fact that they were rooted in slowness and secrecy; for the entire reign of Nicholas I was inimical to advanced ideas or remedial measures in government. Suppressing by force any sign of independent thought or action, he ruled people and ministry alike with an iron hand. His subjects were imprisoned or exiled if they dared express opposition or suggest progressive measures while his ministers meekly carried out his policies rather than brave his anger by questioning or remonstrating. In order to fulfill his program of martial law, he reinstated many of the despotic practices which had been discontinued by former czars, among which were capital punishment and the censorship of the press.

His policy for Russia was one of exclusion and complete withdrawal from European affairs. In his desire to shut out all western contact and influence, he not only suppressed foreign immigration to Russia, practically excluding even artists and men of learning, but he also attempted to prevent his subjects' leaving Russia for study or travel by making it more difficult to secure foreign passports. This was done by placing an annual tax of five hundred rubles upon them.[106] This anti-foreign policy began early in his reign, when the Polish rebellion of 1830 was crushed, and the Czar inaugurated a process of forcible Russification which he later planned to extend to every nationality in his empire.

In this policy he received the enthusiastic approval of the only people in Russia who dared express themselves openly at this time — the Slavophils. One of their cardinal principles was the redemption of Russia through a return to the ancient regime which existed before the introduction of western innovations by Peter the Great. They opposed the governmental and legislative institutions from occidental Europe which had been imposed upon Russia for over a century and pinned their faith upon the *mir,* which they claimed was a system peculiar to the Slavs and, if properly extended, was destined to make of the Russian people a great and unique nation. The second article of their political creed was embodied in the slogan, "Russia for the Russians." Not only would they discard all foreign institutions in the empire, but they would dispense with all foreign peoples by forcing them either to become Russians or to remain outside the country. Although the Czar did not deign to be influenced by these opinions in his policy of forcible assimilation, he at least did not disturb the Slavophils, and they alone of all the rising political parties in Russia were allowed to spread their doctrines with a certain degree of freedom.

---

[106]Tissot, *Russes et Allemands,* 181. This author speaks of Nicholas I as the "jailer" of his Empire; *idem,* 177.

Between the Czar and his Slavophil sympathizers in the ministry, the status of the foreign element in Russia was singled out for readjustment. On the western frontier were the Swedes in Finland, the Germans in the Baltic provinces, and the non-Russian Slavs in Poland and Lithuania – all foreign elements which embodied, either wholly or in part, west-European culture. Revolts and uprisings occurred in these provinces at various times, brought on by the tyrannical suppression of the Russian bureaucracy. Following these outbursts, the government naturally put restrictions upon the revolting peoples with a view to breaking down their patriotic spirit. The replacing of the native with the Russian language in educational and official circles, restrictions in religious freedom, and the introduction of Russian officials in place of the native, were the favorite means of Russification. The decade from 1840 to 1850 marked the beginning of a systematic policy against the Germans in the empire, who, more than any other foreign people, were disliked because they had always been more influential. The course of action proceeded separately against the two German elements – the nobility in the Baltic provinces and the colonists in the southern steppes of the Volga and the Black Sea. Although our interest lies only with the colonists, it is necessary to follow the fortune of both classes of Germans during the preliminary stages of their Russification.

The most important element, politically, was the Baltic provinces, two of which had been taken from the Swedish Crown in 1702 by Peter the Great. In the treaty of 1721 which ended the conflict, the Czar "became bound for him and his successors to acknowledge the predominance, throughout his new provinces of Livonia and Estonia, of the Lutheran church, of the German law, and of the hereditary constitution, and to insure for all time to come the 'augmentation' rather than the 'diminution' of the privileges of the Livlanders."[107] The small but powerful German element in these provinces was thus left free to work out its political and educational future. Although their constitution was founded upon a thoroughly aristocratic basis, its spirit was in advance of the prevailing tone of the Russian government and an educated and intelligent press led the people at various times in vigorous campaigns for reform. The University of Dorpat with its distinctively German system of education was the center of intellectual life in the Baltic provinces and took its place with equal rank among the few universities in Russia in the first half of the nineteenth century. It has been almost entirely from these provinces that the Russian government has drawn the many Germans who have served in every

[107] Eckardt, *Modern Russia,* 326-327.

official capacity in the empire — from generals and ministers of state down to clerks and subalterns in small government offices. More than anything else, this great dependence of the Crown upon a small German element aroused the jealousy of the Russian people as they became accustomed to some measure of self-expression and it became the favorite point of attack for the Slavophils.

The German colonists in South Russia and on the Volga sustained a relation to the Russian government as independent as the Baltic provinces, although of a distinctly different type. It is necessary to remember that the autocratic system of government in Russia presupposes class legislation. The very idea of autocracy is a government which gives or takes privileges in accordance with the individual judgment of the sovereign, as legislator, judge and executive, rather than a system in which all the parts are co-ordinated into a uniform whole. Hence, Catherine had felt no inconsistency in her political and social policy when she issued an *ukaz* introducing foreign colonists into the empire, set them apart from the rest of the population by superior privileges, and provided for their care and administration by a separate bureau which she placed on an equal footing with the other departments of state. Thus to the classes of clergy, nobles, townsmen and peasants, and to the Cossacks, Tartar tribes and Baltic Germans, each of which had separate laws and courts, she merely added another group — foreign colonists — who were exempt from the laws of the provinces in which they lived and subject only to legislation from the central authority.[108] The nobles of each province were obliged to furnish their quota of peasants for the army each year, but the German colonists neither served in person like the peasant, nor furnished substitutes as did the nobles. The Russian peasant owed to his lord tributes in labor and money, and the noble in turn paid certain imposts to the Czar; while the German colonists enjoyed complete immunity from taxation for many years due to the benevolence of the government in extending the original period of exemption. The Crown peasants, whose lot approached more nearly the position of the foreign colonists than any other element in the land, were obliged to furnish transportation for government officials and government stores, and to have soldiers quartered upon them, from both of which duties the German colonists were free. In the minds of the Russian people, these privileges accounted more for the superior prosperity of the foreigners than did their German thrift and economy; and while the colonists exerted little political or social influence in the empire, their military

[108]See LeRoy-Beaulieu, *The Empire of the Tsars and the Russians,* I, 305ff., for a discussion of the social classes in Russia.

freedom and their economic advantage were sufficient to make them a target for attack.

Systematic measures were directed first against the Baltic provinces. In 1840 a commission, composed largely of adherents of the Slavophil party, began making a study of municipal conditions in Livonia with a view to correcting abuses and proposing reforms.[109] They began their work obsessed with the idea of overthrowing the existing German institutions and substituting Russian methods, which would have meant a backward step for the Baltic provinces. They were supported in their policy by the head of the Russian church who desired to supplant Lutheranism with Orthodoxy, and also by the governor general of the provinces whose appointment they had secured in 1845 and who was "a declared enemy of all that was German." So drastic were the measures taken and so great was the resulting confusion and discontent that the Germans appealed directly to the Czar, who, although at first in sympathy with the work, now felt that it was being carried too far. A change of system was decided upon in 1848, the Slavophils were dismissed, and a policy of "conciliation" was inaugurated under a new and sympathetic governor general.

Less severe but no less significant were the measures adopted toward the German colonies in Russia. One of the first steps related to unifying the administration of these foreign groups, each of which was governed by a separate committee under the Tutel-Kanzlei, and managed according to the different charters or *ukazes* under which they entered Russia. When in 1837 the Ministry of Imperial Domains was created for the purpose of administering the lands belonging to the Crown, all of the foreign colonies were placed under its jurisdiction except the original Volga settlements. These were still managed by the Tutel-Kanzlei, which had previously been subordinated to the Ministry of the Interior, and which was now removed to Saratov where the actual expense of administration was taxed to the colonists themselves instead of being borne by the general government.[110]

At the head of the Ministry of Imperial Domains which now governed the foreign colonies, stood Count Kiselev, one of the brilliant men of his day, a reformer of some pretension and a man often in disagreement with the Czar. In regard to one question, however, he and the Czar agreed, and in 1840 Count Kiselev was appointed to head a commission for the purpose of studying the emancipation of the serfs in its various relations. This led him into a consideration of

---

[109]Eckardt, *Russia Before and After the War,* 248-254.

[110]Velitzyn, "Foreign Colonies in Russia," *Russian Messenger* (in Russian), CC: In 1833, a number of immigration offices had been discontinued on the ground that the colonies were now established well enough not to need aid from the government.

the status of the different elements of the rural population, which included the German colonists, and he became more impressed with the fact that the special laws under which they lived tended to isolate them from the rest of the agricultural class. This fact was emphasized in a report submitted a few years previously by the governor of the Saratov province who said that "there are only a few of the colonists who enlighten themselves as much as they should concerning the Russian language, wherefore they do not know the Russian laws, they only carelessly carry out the police orders and their own duties, and evidently take pains to avoid every intercourse with Russia."[111]

At the same time the Ministry of the Interior was busy formulating plans for readjustment and in 1840 an officer in this department prepared a "memorandum on administrative reforms in the German colonies on the Volga."[112] The most significant step was taken in 1850, probably as the result of the investigations of the commission mentioned above, when a special convention was called "to revise the laws (of the German colonies) in accordance with the needs of the times.[113] The actual changes accomplished, however, during the reign of Nicholas I, were, like so many of his efforts, inconsequential and merely laid the foundation for really constructive work a few years later.

The policy of suppression followed by Nicholas I and the disasters of the Crimean War (1854-1856) when Russia suffered defeat at the hands of England and France made the Czar's death in 1855 a relief to the country. His son and successor, Alexander II, aware of the weaknesses of his father's reign which were disclosed by the defeats of an unpopular war, took steps at once to bring the conflict to a close. This change of policy confirmed in the popular mind a belief in the liberal tendencies of the new ruler, and became the signal for a great outburst of public opinion which the Czar had neither the desire nor the power to check. The reactionary policies which had been introduced by his father were reversed, and an uncensored press, freedom of travel, the abolition of capital punishment, and similar privileges were legalized. Reforms which had lain dormant for years in the hands of the commissioners of Nicholas I were now taken up with energy and dispatch.

Before proceeding with a discussion of these reforms and their effect upon the German colonies, a few words concerning the part played by the Pan-Slavists during this period will not be out of place. The Slavophil movement which had scored its first official victory under Nicholas I, had now developed into the National Party and was

[111]Bauer, *Geschichte der deutschen Ansiedler an der Wolga,* 163.
[112]Eckardt, *Russia Before and After the War,* 26.
[113]Velitzyn, "Foreign Colonies in Russia," *Russian Messenger* (in Russian), CC.

Courtesy of the Denver Public Library, Denver, Colorado.

Alexander II (reigned 1855-1881), Emperor of Russia, under whom the serfs were freed and the Military Service Law of 1874 was passed.

the most influential power in the new Russian politics. It favored emancipation because it considered the peasant as the class most uncontaminated by western influence, and hence most amenable to its plan of restoring old Russian institutions in the empire. It almost fanatically pointed to the year 1862, which celebrated the one thousandth year since the founding of the Russian nation, as the beginning of the millenium when a new era of social and political life should dawn for Russia. It seized upon the Polish and Lithuanian revolts of 1863 as an opportunity to preach Russification of the foreigners; and, in spite of the fact that the Germans were practically the only element of the empire at that time not on the verge of rebellion, it succeeded in inaugurating against them a policy of forcible assimilation more drastic than any yet attempted. It sought to crystallize public sentiment against the German element of the population and to appeal to native patriotism through the Pan-Slavic Congress at Moscow in 1865.[114] In all these activities the Slavophils were aided by the Russian press which had sprung up everywhere in the empire at the beginning of Alexander's reign and which, though still mildly censored, exerted a tremendous influence in arousing public opinion. A corps of unusually talented and able journalists pleaded the cause of Pan-Slavism from the old Russian capital at Moscow and wielded a force in the political policies of the time previously unknown in Russian history.[115]

That the liberal-minded Czar, Alexander II, should be drawn into this course is somewhat surprising. He was not anti-German in his sentiments for he gathered about him in his ministry an unusually large number of Germans. He was on very friendly terms with his uncle, William I of Prussia, and the cordial relations between the two thrones was strengthened by the three years' residence (1859-1862) of Prince Bismarck in St. Petersburg where, as ambassador, he exerted a great influence in cementing the friendship of the two courts. During the decade from 1860 to 1870, Prussia made a very apparent effort to remain on good terms with Russia with a view to the approaching crisis with France and her plans for a united Germany. The desire for friendly relations had its reciprocal influence upon German affairs in Russia. On the one hand, it secured concessions for the colonists which the radicals would not have granted them. On the other hand, it kept Prussia from interfering in the Baltic provinces when Teutonic

---

[114]See Hodgetts, *The Court of Russia in the Nineteenth Century,* II, 86-96, for a discussion of the relations between the Germans in Russia and the Pan-Slavists. The French view is given in LeRoy-Beaulieu, *The Empire of the Tsars and the Russians,* I, 124-137; also in Tissot, *Russes et Allemands.*

[115]LeRoy-Beaulieu, *ibid.,* II, 433, expresses the opinion that the Russian press took up this subject because it was not permitted to discuss the more vital ones concerning governmental policies.

institutions and language and the Protestant faith were threatened with destruction at the hands of the Slavophils.

The National Party, as has been seen, made every effort to stir up public opinion against the Germans. It accused the Baltic Germans of being Separatist foes of the empire, and of being disloyal to the government even to the point of making overtures to Prussia for protection in case they saw fit to withdraw from the empire and join the North German Confederation. Although the wildest imaginings could conjure up no such program for the uninfluential and widely scattered colonists of the Volga and the Black Sea, the Nationalists accused them of criminal indifference to the welfare of the Russian Empire. The fact that few German troops had taken part in the Crimean War, and that a small though comparatively prosperous foreign element in the population had remained exempt from military service at a time when Russia was being crushed under a foreign foe, rankled in the minds of the Slavophils. They claimed that the government had made demands upon the German colonists for aid but that they had formally refused because of their religion; and that, meanwhile, those residing in the vicinity of the Crimea had enriched themselves at the expense of the government by providing supplies at war prices to the Russian troops.[116] It was true that the Mennonite colonists pleaded religious scruples for not responding to the distress signals of the Russian government at this time, but they were only a small part of the German colonists in Russia. Among the Lutheran and Catholic colonists of this region men were drafted and served willingly in non-combatant capacities and at the close of the war were rewarded for their services in various ways. The colonies were indemnified for the passage and quartering of troops and one village, at least, received a personal letter of approval from the Czar for the zeal and faithfulness of his German subjects in the struggle.[117] The Crimean War afforded an opportunity for the acquisition of great wealth by many of the inhabitants about the Black Sea, and the fact that the people to profit most by this were Germans was less an indictment against them than a proof of their superior thrift and industry. So far as loyalty was concerned, the Russian government had no more faithful subjects than the Germans.

The disasters of this war and the accession of a liberal-minded Czar prepared the people's minds for great and vital changes in the government. The fundamental reform upon which all others must be based was the emancipation of the serfs, and to this Alexander II first gave his attention; but so slowly did events move, so difficult was it

[116] Velitzyn, "Foreign Colonies in Russia," *Russian Messenger* (in Russian), CC.

[117] Pfeiffer, "Die Pfálz in Suedrussland," *Der Pfaelzerwald,* 14 Jahrgang, No. 1 (1913).

to adjust even the preliminary matters between the nobility and the peasants, that it was almost six years (February 19, 1861) before the *ukaz* was finally issued which freed twenty-five million peasants from the absolute will of their masters. This statute did not directly affect the Germans in Russia. In the Baltic provinces the personal freedom of the peasant had been granted by Alexander I, while in the colonies the Germans neither possessed serfs nor stood in the relation of servitude to the surrounding nobility.[118] But through the reforms which followed in every institution of the government, the Germans shared in the leveling process which was going on throughout the empire. The judicial reform, the fundamental principle of which was equality before the law of all the Czar's subjects; the political reform, which granted local self government equally to all classes through the provincial and district *zemstvos;* and the military reform, which deprived the privileged classes (the nobility and the foreign colonists) of their exemption from military service – these all affected the status of the German colonies in Russia, and took from them one after another, the rights which had been guaranteed to them and to their children.

During the decade from 1860 to 1870, while these reforms were being worked out, the German colonies became a center for investigation and study from various sources. The first was the unfriendly Slavophils who had long before become convinced of the persistent and wilful alienation of these foreigners from the rest of the rural population, and who proposed by force of laws to assimilate these "drops of oil upon the pond." A second but friendly group of investigators were those who looked to the German colonies for economic and social institutions upon which to base the pending peasant reforms. They reasoned that here, for a century, had existed a rural population directly under the patronage of the sovereigns, where regulations adapted to such conditions had been devised by experts and worked out under favorable circumstances. Hence it was here that the government itself turned for the results of legislation by former rulers and found in the "Uniform Instructions of 1800-1803" the model upon which it based its Emancipation statute.[119] Moreover, it cherished the idea that institutions and methods indigenous to the German mind but wrought out by them under Russian skies might also prove models upon which to build in the tremendous undertakings before it. Therefore, without the prejudice of the Slavophil against foreign institutions,

---

118The manifesto of Catherine II permitted the foreign immigrants to acquire serfs, but aside from an early attempt by a few of the Germans, none of the colonists ever availed themselves of this privilege. According to the manifestoes of Alexander I, which governed the colonists in South Russia, this privilege was denied.

119Velitzyn, "Foreign Colonies in Russia," *Russian Messenger* (in Russian), CC.

its officials went into the various German colonies of the empire to investigate their internal organization. Alexander Klaus, a Volga German who had risen to the position of Councillor of State at St. Petersburg, gives as a motive for his work "the possibility of utilizing the experiences of the colonies in the project of colonization and in the economic organization of peasant affairs.[120] Another volume on the same subject was a politico-economic treatise written by two Russian investigators, Kalageorgi and Borissow.

A third factor which interested itself in the German colonies in Russia during this period was their countrymen in Germany. The most important of the works they produced was occasioned by the renewed interest of Russia in colonization and the dispatch of immigration agents to the German states to secure foreign settlers. This led Friedrich Matthaei, a citizen of Saxony, to travel through Russia, visiting the colonies and making a study particularly of the economic conditions of the country. Soon after, he published in Leipzig a volume made up largely of extracts from contemporary writers, but containing a supplement in which he offered a carefully wrought out plan of his own for the colonization of Russia.[121] Whatever use, if any, was made by the Russian government of this work is not known, but its circulation within the empire was limited for it remained unknown to the German colonists themselves.

It is neither possible nor profitable to discuss here the contributions which the German colonies made through their politico-economic organizations to the great constructive measures which the Russian government inaugurated in this decade. Our attention must confine itself to the actual changes wrought in the rights and privileges guaranteed to them by their charter. It must be remembered that the reforms of Alexander II were not extended over the empire simultaneously, but that the Czar autocratically determined in which provinces they should be tried out first. The significant thing is that, when the statute was applied to the provinces in which the German colonies were located, the latter were included in the general population without special legislation to which they had always been subject previously. So gradually and unobtrusively, however, did these changes creep into local administration of the colonies that, in their isolation, they were entirely unaware of them until the military law brought them to their feet.

The first to affect the colonies was the judiciary law. Prior to this time the various functions of criminal procedure were united into one

[120]Klaus, *Unsere Kolonien,* Vorwort, vii.

[121]Matthaei, *Die Deutschen Ansiedlungen in Russland,* 1866.

organ, there being no separation between the prosecution, the inquest or examination, and the trial. Under the reform of 1864, these three branches of justice were differentiated and a new magistracy created called "judicial inquisitors,"[122] whose duty it was to conduct the criminal examination apart from the government's attorneys who were to try the case and from the police who were to testify.[123] This same year the provisions of this statute were made to cover the colonies, thereby introducing an outside element — a Russian official — into the local courts of the German colonies. "This measure was the first one to interfere with the internal administration of the colonies since it took away from the jurisdiction of the local administration all power of investigation in court matters and left it merely the police-executive part."[124]

The second change came with the establishment of local self government in Russia. The Emancipation Act which had deprived the nobility of the exclusive right of owning land necessarily led to a change in the provincial and district administration which had previously been entirely in the hands of the nobles. It was now proposed to form in each of these political units new popular assemblies, called *zemstvos*, composed of representatives of all classes, who should have charge of affairs in their particular communities. This reform, promulgated in 1864 and extended over the Volga colonies in 1866, further deprived the German colonies of their local self government, for although they were proportionately represented in the *zemstvos*, local matters formerly handled by the Germans exclusively were now transferred to the assemblies. The two chief cares of the *zemstvos* have been education and health although they were originally limited only by the needs of their communities. In the matter of sanitation and health, the German colonies have been benefited without suffering any conflict with previous work since physicians and public health appurtenances were formerly unknown. More serious, though very gradual changes have resulted in the matter of education. At first the *zemstvos* attempted merely to supplement the village schools of the Germans by the organization and support of higher institutions of learning. Gradually the wedge has entered more and more, until today, backed by the more rigid educational policy of the government, the German schools are being supplanted and the process of Russianization thereby greatly accelerated.

122This office had been established four years previous to the time when it was extended over the empire generally.

123See LeRoy-Beaulieu, *Empire of the Tsars and the Russians,* II, 345-349, for a discussion of this phase of the judicial reform.

124*Historical Survey of Fifty Years' Activity of the Ministry of Imperial Domains* (in Russian), 129.

After these two invasions of the rights of local self government in the German colonies brought about through the judiciary and the *zemstvo* reforms, the government appointed a special commission in 1867 under the chairmanship of the Ministry of Imperial Domains, assisted by representatives of the departments of Justice and the Interior, to work out the details for finally incorporating the German colonies into the rural population. In 1870 this committee reported the results of its work and in 1871 the report was officially confirmed.[125] According to its provisions, all foreign settlers, significantly denominated *foreign colonists,* were to be placed in charge of the general provincial and district offices and were released from the *Kontor* for foreign colonists which had directed the affairs of the settlers for over a century.[126] Within the next ten years, every phase of administration of the colonies was placed under its corresponding department of state — lands, taxes, churches, schools, public works, etc. — and thus the isolation of the Germans was made no longer possible.

The loss of the last of the special privileges granted by the manifesto of Catherine came with the introduction of universal military service into Russia, following an edict of the Czar on November 16, 1870, which proclaimed the liability of every Russian subject to military duty. Up to this time the army had recruited almost wholly from the peasant class under a procedure common to medieval times. The number of recruits necessary to fill the ranks was determined by the census, usually at the rate of one out of every five hundred males in times of peace and two to five in times of war. These were apportioned among the various landed proprietors of the empire, and the nobles nominated such of their serfs as they chose to furnish their quota. All peasants with few exceptions were liable to military duty if of the proper age and stature. The term of service was from twenty-two to twenty-five years, ten to fifteen of which was in active service and the remainder was spent in the reserve; i.e., upon an indefinite leave of absence. Although the urgent need of military reform had been exposed to the world in the defeats of the Crimean War, and the government had faced the necessity of reorganizing upon a modern basis its entire military system, this measure was forced to wait until the more fundamental reform of emancipation was carried through. Even then, the engrossment of the empire in internal affairs and the peace-loving disposition of the Czar delayed the matter to the last of his great reforms.

---

[125]*Code of Laws,* (in Russian), 1876, ed., IX.

[126]Bauer, *Geschichte der deutschen Ansiedler an der Wolga,* 84, states it was not until 1876 that the transfer from the *Kontor* to the various state departments was completed and the office abolished.

This edict of 1870, establishing universal military service, was followed by the appointment of a commission to devise a plan for putting the law into effect; and its report, submitted in January, 1871, was adopted to become operative the next year. The regulations decreed that all males without distinction of class were liable to military duty and that exemption by purchase or substitution was prohibited; that all who had completed their twentieth year must appear at the lot drawing, where those chosen must spend seven years in the active service and eight years in the reserve; while those not drawn were to be enrolled in the militia. Another statute covering further details was promulgated in January, 1874, and this became the basis for the revised military system of Russia.[127] In October of that same year, the initial conscription took place and for the first time since their emigration from Germany, the Czar's German subjects marched in the rank and file of the Russian army.

[127]Greene, *Sketches of Army Life in Russia,* 142.

chapter four

Immigration To The United States

By 1870 practically all the land in the United States which was then considered fit for settlement had been taken by homesteaders, although the Trans-Missouri section was as yet scarcely touched. The states of Nebraska and Kansas, and the Dakota Territory were still on the frontier; indeed, all but their eastern fringes were beyond the frontier. In spite of the fact that Nebraska had been the direct route during almost a generation for successive waves of migration to the west, her actual settlement had scarcely begun. The Mormon passage in 1846-48 and the gold rush to California in 1849 had left scarcely a trace of their existence in increasing settlements in Nebraska. A second gold rush to Colorado in 1859 and 1860, and the building of the Union Pacific Railroad from 1864 to 1869 served merely to advertise the territory rather than to add any considerable number of actual settlers. In Dakota, Indian hostilities had kept that territory practically uninhabited until 1866. The most advanced of the Trans-Missouri section was Kansas which received numbers of more or less permanent settlers beginning in 1854. Later, immigration into all these territories began and by 1870 the Federal Census gave to Nebraska 122,993 inhabitants, to Kansas 364,399, and to Dakota Territory 14,181.

Even within the limited areas of settlement lay much unoccupied land. Since the passage of the Homestead Law in 1862, most of that lying east of the sixth principal meridian had been appropriated, but much of it was in the hands of speculators who had secured it under pretense of settlement. As soon as they had secured permanent possession of it, they abandoned it, leaving it lie idle until it was made valuable by the surrounding cultivated areas. Most of this land was in small lots and its sale was correspondingly slow because it lacked organized and persistent advertising.[1] Beyond this meridian lay vast areas of land which apparently could not be given away, for there was a nation-wide opinion, born of a generation's schooling concerning the "Great American Desert," that agriculture could not flourish beyond this point.

The State Board of Immigration in Nebraska attempted to carry on an extensive advertising campaign. It published a number of pamphlets and a map or two which it distributed abroad through its agents—the first ones being in English and German for use in their respective countries; later in Norwegian, Swedish, Danish, and Czech. Another means of advertising was through the governors' messages which from 1870 on were translated into various languages and distributed by members of the legislature. Almost without exception, the governors urged immigration as Nebraska's most urgent need. A third instrument for encouraging immigration was the newspapers which were scattered broadcast through Europe to individuals and organizations. The report of 1873-75 estimated that 100,000 copies of newspapers were sent abroad in one biennium, 100 copies per week going regularly to Germany.

The most effective agents in the Trans-Missouri states for securing settlers, both native and foreign, were the railroads. Contrary to all precedent, the railroads here preceded settlement. In the Dakota Territory it was the Northwestern and Northern Pacific, in Nebraska the Burlington and Missouri, and in Kansas the Santa Fe and Kansas Pacific which carried on a competitive warfare and spent lavish sums through a comparatively long series of years in a campaign of which the motto was "Land for the Landless." Their motive was purely selfish because being in private hands their maintenance depended upon their drawing settlers to them and direct financial gain was of vital importance. Hence, the feverish interest they displayed in securing

[1] A. L. Child in an early history of Plattsmouth, Cass County (1877), calls the land speculator "the curse of Nebraska."

immigration and the great sums of money which they could well afford to turn into this channel.

In Nebraska the two leading railroads were the Union Pacific and the previously mentioned Burlington and Missouri, both of which had received liberal land grants in the state. The U.P. had completed its line from Omaha to Promontory Point (near Ogden, Utah) in 1869, and under the terms of its contract with the United States government it received almost 12 million acres of land, being each alternate section for twenty miles on either side of its track.[2] The Burlington and Missouri River Railroad was granted "every alternate section of public land . . . to the amount of ten alternate sections per mile on each side of said road" which was to be built between Plattsmouth and Ft. Kearney.[3] Just at the period when the Burlington and Missouri in Nebraska began activities, great efforts were being made by all forces to stimulate foreign immigration. It is probable that this railroad was the greatest single factor for the bringing of foreign immigrants into Nebraska during its early days of statehood[4].

The land office of the Burlington and Missouri had, like most other roads from that time to this, its Foreign Department at whose head was an agent especially adapted to that type of work.[5] His activities manifested themselves through literature and agents stationed in foreign lands. It was at first customary for direct translations of pamphlets intended for use in the eastern states to be sent abroad, merely inserting at convenient intervals references to the Germans, or Swedes, or other recipients.

But however attractive this literature, it was merely the tool in the hand of the immigration agent whose personal work was felt to be indispensable. For that reason the Burlington and Missouri maintained for a number of years one or more agents at Castle Garden, New York City, where they labored to turn the newly arrived immigrants to states containing company lands. Besides these agents, the railroad maintained permanent immigration agencies abroad.

While natives of west European states were free to emigrate when and where they pleased, subject only to the emigration laws of their country, and while no offical protests were made against American immigration agencies within their borders, there was one

---

[2]For a detailed discussion of "The Pioneer Railway of Nebraska," see Morton, *Illustrated History of Nebraska,* II, 85, Footnote 2.

[3]*U.S. Stat.,* XIII, 364.

[4]For a modern report of the role of the Burlington and Missouri River Railroad, see *The German-Russians. Those who came to Sutton* by James Ruben Griess. Hastings, Nebraska, 1968, 61-91. — The editors.

[5]Land sales were begun by the Burlington and Missouri in April, 1870.

country where it was a crime not only to emigrate without the permission of the government but also to induce one to emigrate.

That country was Russia, and thither no immigration solicitors, either public or private, had sent their literature or established their agencies.

The Universal Military Service Law of 1874 in Russia

Before 1870 emigration was not a live issue among the German colonists in Russia. In the course of three or four years, however, hundreds of families, especially among the Volga Germans and among the Black Sea Mennonites, suddenly acquired an intense desire to leave the land of the Czars. The event which brought about this relatively rapid change of attitude was the introduction of universal compulsory military service, which became final by the *ukaz* of Alexander II in January 1874.

This *ukaz* aroused consternation among the Czar's German subjects, who had come to Russia under promise of immunity from military service. With the Mennonites it was purely and simply a religious question from which there was neither withdrawal nor compromise. One of the founding articles of their faith was to be noncombatant and being forced into military duty meant the virtual loss of their religion. But with the far larger number of German colonists it was not primarily a religious scruple.

One great objection the colonists had to military service in Russia arose from the ill treatment that was meted out to the Czar's soldiers. They had themselves seen crippled soldiers begging in the streets of their colonies because the government made no provision for pensioning them after they became incompetent. In general, the conditions in the Russian army at that time were as uncivilized and brought forth as much condemnation from other countries as exile in Siberia did a few years later. The Russian soldiery, recruited largely from the peasant class, fared worse as servants of the empire than as serfs of their lords. In the army, as elsewhere in Russia, the most common punishment was flogging, except that here it was meted out for misdemeanors as well as crimes. For falling asleep at one's post, vexing an officer, or failing to answer to roll-call, the beating was administered in the form of "running the ranks," in which the culprit, stripped to the waist, was led at the point of the bayonet to the head of a line of soldiers each armed with a knout. As he ran down the line, each struck a blow as fast and furious as the excitement of the occasion warranted.

Another and very potent reason for the dislike of military service among the colonists was the feeling that "they had no country to fight for." It is interesting to note in this connection that the Germans in Russia unanimously were of the opinion that the colonists were not Russian subjects but would be forced to become such if they remained. Hence, it is explained to you, they left Russia to avoid becoming Russian subjects. As a matter of history, we know that about the only demand Catherine made in her manifesto of July 22, 1763, was that the Germans take the oath of allegiance to the Russian crown immediately upon their arrival. This *ukaz* was the model upon which later colonization was based and it is fair to assume that the same demand was made in each case. Yet the invariable answer from the most intelligent Russian Germans to the question, "Why did Russia allow you to leave?" is "Russia had nothing to say about it. We were Germans and had a right to go"; or, "Bismarck made the Czar let us go"; or, "We were under the German government until our fathers signed away our rights (1871) without knowing what they were doing." Another explained, "In 1871 when the French and Germans were at war with each other, Russia told Germany that she wanted to take control of the Germans now and that the 100 years were past (the "forever" in the *ukaz* mean 99 years), but Bismarck told Russia he must give the Germans ten years to get away if they wanted to."[6] Many of the Russian Germans who left before 1881 disavowed allegiance to the empire of Germany when they became American citizens because they believed themselves not Russian but German subjects.

While the introduction of compulsory military service was the immediate cause for the beginning of systematic emigration from Russia, it was only one factor in it. Back of it there was the almost universal feeling among the German colonists that the Russian government had broken its contract with them and that this was not the last of the changes which would occur. The clause in the manifesto relating to exemption from military duty was somewhat obscure, although by common consent it had been interpreted to mean "forever."[7] Now the rumor spread that said "forever" meant only 100 years, and since it was now 100 years since the manifesto had been promulgated, the government was at liberty to repudiate it all. Ever since the emancipation of the serfs in 1861, the local government had suffered changes and for five or six years there was talk of the removal of their special privileges. The loss of freedom from military service they felt would be followed by the loss of their freedom of religion, free local government, and free schools, and the German colonists imagined themselves

[6]There is no historical basis that Bismarck intervened for the German people of Russia. See David G. Rempel, "C. B. Schmidt, Historian: Facts and Fiction," *Mennonite Life,* Vol. 29, Nos. 1 and 2, (1974), 33-37. — The editors.

[7]See Articles 6 and 7 of Manifesto.

soon in the toils of forcible attempts at Russianization. Accordingly, in three unrelated parts of Russia the question of whether or not to emigrate was being discussed.

Immigration of Three Unrelated Groups of Germans in Russia

1. *The "Odessa" Germans.* One of these areas was in the province of Kherson in the Black Sea region, one of the most prosperous parts of Russia.[8] Here there was no lack of land, for energetic and ambitious Germans could go out from their colony, rent a tract from a lord's estate, and in a few years begin buying land, which was then permitted. The leading spirits in this movement were wealthy landowners near the colony of Worms, northeast of Odessa. One of these leaders, Heinrich Griess, when a young man had taken his share of property, which consisted of three horses, a wagon, and a plow, had left the colony and set up for himself. He rented land from a nearby estate and began raising wheat and sheep. Under his skillful management and the opportunity South Russia offered during those years in these two products, he prospered greatly until at this period, he owned 4,000 acres of land, an estate equal to many a nobleman's in that part of Russia.

At this time Russia exercised a very close censorship over emigration propaganda. However, a book fell into the hands of these Germans which gave them just the information needed to stimulate their desire for emigration. It spoke well of eastern Nebraska but not of the western part of the state. The book was written by a German pastor, Reidenbach, who had traveled through the United States twice and was very impressed with the opportunities of acquiring land here.[9]

A second factor in determining the destination of these incipient emigrants was a visit to the colonies by a former resident, then living on Kelleys Island, near Sandusky, Ohio. This man was one of a company of approximately 30-50 Germans from Rohrbach and neighboring colonies who had come to America in 1849. In 1872 he returned to Russia to visit relatives. His reports of the liberties enjoyed in the United States and the opportunities through cheap land, which corroborated the printed reports, were eagerly seized upon by his former countrymen. As he went about from one colony to another, the news

---

[8]For information concerning the emigration of the "Odessaers" as they are called, I am indebted to Mr. Peter H. Griess of Sutton, Nebraska, who, then a young man of 22 years, came with the colonists of which his father was one of the leaders. Much of his story is found in *Dakota Freie Presse,* November 18, 1909, and January 31, 1911.

[9]Reidenbach, J. A. *Amerika. Eine Kurze Beschreibung der Vereinigten Staaten, sowie ein Rathgeber fuer Auswanderer.*

of his reports spread like a contagion. Through fear of the officials he was forced to leave the country, but not before his visit bore fruit. Many Germans in the colonies of Worms, Rohrbach, and Johannesthal began selling their possessions preparatory to leaving in spite of protests from their pastor. The latter had lived several years in Philadelphia and knew the economic advantages in the United States, but he was disturbed at the promptness with which the American immigrant put aside his German language and customs, and strongly advised against the Germans leaving Russia.[10]

However, in the fall of 1872, 21 families from the colonies of Johannesthal, Worms, and Rohrbach in the province of Kherson started for America.[11]

They landed at New York and from there they went to Sandusky, Ohio, where they left their families to spend the winter with friends while the leading men of the group went out on land-exploring expeditions. They had come with the expectation of engaging in farming, and, so far as possible in the same way they had farmed in Russia; hence they desired to settle in a colony and, believing that thousands of immigrants would follow them, they were anxious to settle in a region where there was an abundance of free contiguous land. They made excursions into Michigan, Illinois, Iowa, Wisconsin, Minnesota, Kansas, and Nebraska and possibly other states to the southwest, especially Arkansas, returning without being satisfied. Spring was now coming on and they were beginning to get anxious to settle down, when they heard of Dakota, and five of them, against the advice of their Ohio friends, decided to visit the territory. They reached Yankton in the midst of a premature spell of spring weather, and after traveling over the prairie for several days, chose a location twenty miles northwest of Yankton. Claims were staked out and they started back to Ohio for their families. On their return to Yankton with their party from Sandusky, they found the country buried in snow, and had great difficulty to persuade their countrymen that they had not lied to them. Through the interest of the inhabitants of the town of Yankton the Russian Germans were persuaded to remain, and it is probably this circumstance which accounts for the fact that the first settlers in Dakota secured from 8 to 20 quarter sections of land when three was the legal maximum. The fact that this was the first of a large immigration which would probably follow them and that because of blizzards, hot winds, and Indians, Dakota was in very bad repute, led the land officials to resort to a scheme. Under their advice

[10]The man from Kelleys Island was Ludwig Bette and the pastor who had been in the United States was named Karl Bonekemper. — The editors.

[11]*Dakota Freie Presse,* July 8, 1909, and November 11, 1909.

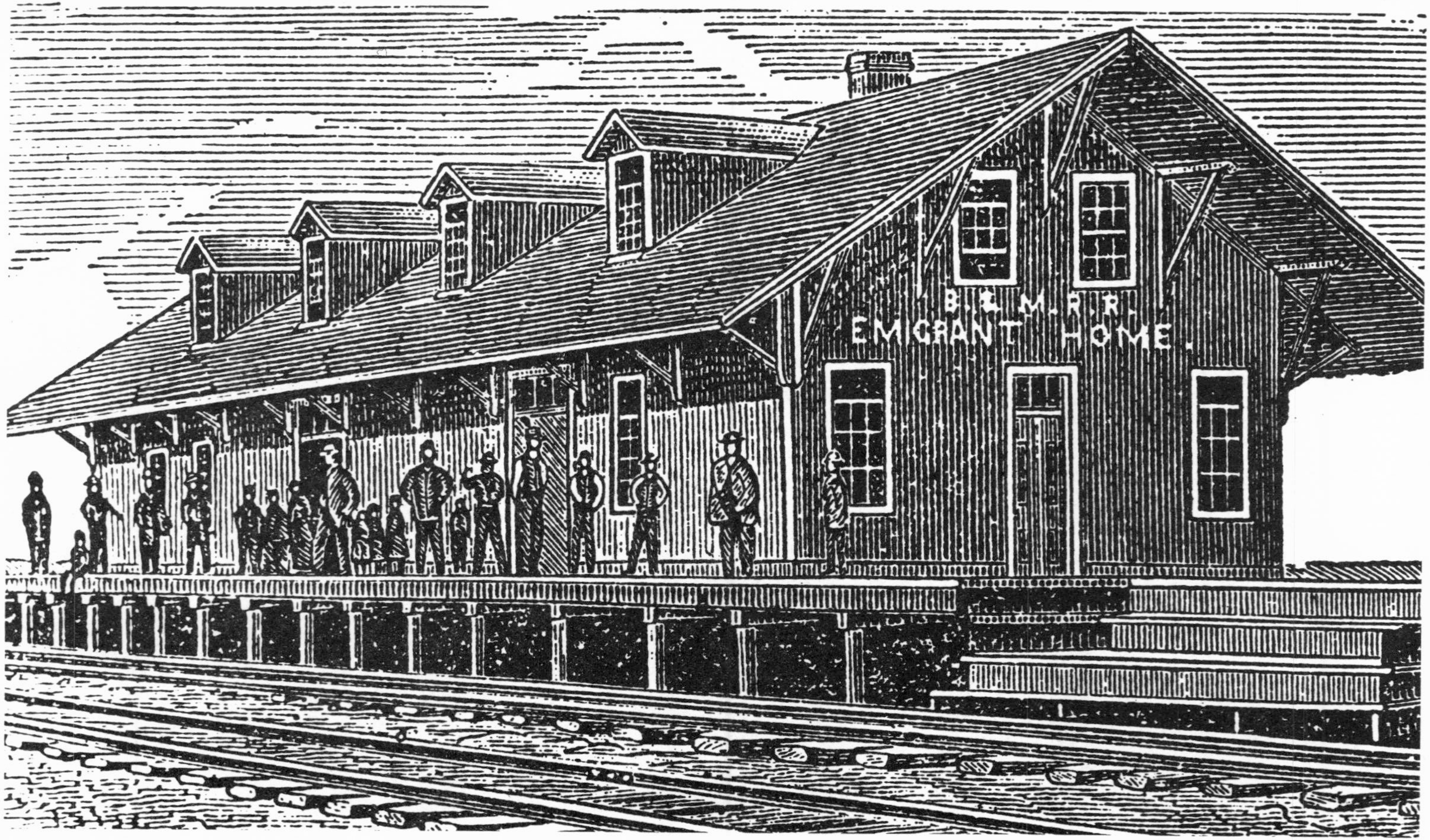

Courtesy of the Nebraska State Historical Society, Lincoln, Nebraska.

Burlington and Missouri River Railroad Emigrant Home built in 1870 at Lincoln, Nebraska. In an advertising pamphlet issued by the B&M in 1872, it was stated that this Emigrant Home was the first ever built by a railroad.

the people took out homesteads under strange names, paid out on them for six months and then bought them from the unknown owners. The Land Office advised the people to do this for a short time until the stream of immigration turned to Dakota when the practice would have to be given up.

In June 1873, 150 families comprising over 400 persons, were ready to start for America. This group was made up largely of farmers but there were also several teachers, and various kinds of artisans, besides common laborers, indicating that they would form a compact colony. At New York City the party divided, one group going to their friends who had settled in Dakota that spring, and the remainder going to Burlington, Iowa, where they found acquaintances and relatives.[12] The latter had decided before leaving Russia to locate in Nebraska. Accordingly they liberally supplied themselves with weapons and ammunition, for they had been warned that it was very "wild" out there, and after a short stay in Burlington, Iowa, proceeded to Lincoln, Nebraska. The more prosperous went to the hotels until they could rent houses for their families, while the majority of the party was sheltered in the Burlington and Missouri Emigrant Home. With their families temporarily provided for, the leaders started out on a search for land. The country about Lincoln was rapidly filling up. Much land was held by speculators and its value had been greatly enhanced by the location of the capital in 1867. Burlington and Missouri still owned considerable land in the vicinity but it was selling for $12 to $20 an acre. While the leaders were able to pay such prices, they "thought more of the poor than of themselves" and because they "had a heart for other people" they cast their lot with their poorer brethren on the frontier, for they were convinced that a large immigration would follow. Hence they desired a location which would be suitable for all, for it was originally their intention to settle together as a colony, found a town of their own, and duplicate here the manner of life in Russia.

The search for land occupied several weeks and covered large areas in central Nebraska and parts of Dakota. The lack of large adjoining areas of government land in Nebraska, except in the western half which was then all in the hands of the cattle barons, led one after

---

[12]A man named Heinrich Heil, who was a member of the party which left Russia on June 23, and arrived in New York on July 31, 1873, is the authority for the statement that the group divided in New York (*Dakota Freie Presse,* November 11, 1909).

This fact is not mentioned by Peter H. Griess in the November 18, 1909, issue. See Theodore C. Wenzlaff's translation of the Griess article in *Nebraska History,* Winter 1968, 379-399, "The Russian Germans come to the United States." — The editors.

another of the poorer families to go to join friends in Dakota where homesteads were available.

When the leaders had about decided to abandon Nebraska for Kansas, a German minister was sent to them by the Burlington and Missouri and offered his assistance in the search. Although quite discouraged about the possibility of finding good cheap land in sufficiently large adjoining quantities, they at last yielded to his importunities and accompanied him west. The result of their trip was the purchase from the Burlington and Missouri of 3,690 acres of land north of Sutton in Clay County at $4.25 an acre cash. This land ordinarily sold for $5 to $12 per acre under favorable terms but the reduction was given for cash payment.[13] Contracts were at once let with carpenters at Lincoln for the construction of dwelling houses while the men went to work at preparing for the oncoming winter by cutting hay and building barns and granaries.[14] Men who had never been accustomed to a day of manual labor in their lives dug and slaved, separated from their families, and lying about the haystacks for shelter, with the sky as their roof. By November of 1873, preparations had sufficiently advanced for them to be joined by their families, and word was sent back to Russia of the successful beginning made.[15] Another group of 30 families, consisting of about 100 persons, who had promised to come if the first party "liked it" followed in 1874 and settled beside their friends.[16] Altogether the Burlington and Missouri sold these Russian Germans at Sutton 10 sections of land at prices ranging from $4.00 to $7.00 per acre.[17]

2. *The Mennonites from South Russia.* A second unrelated group of Germans in Russia who were meditating emigration were the Mennonites in the province of Tauria, around Berdyansk on the Sea of Azov. The leading spirit in this case was Cornelius Jansen, German consul at Berdyansk. He had emigrated to South Russia from Marienberg near Danzig in 1856,[18] but repelled by the restrictions

---

[13]Ernst, C. J., Records of Land Office of Burlington and Missouri.

[14]*Dakota Freie Presse,* November 18, 1909.

[15]*Dakota Freie Presse,* November 11, 1909.

[16]*Nebraska State Journal,* July 1, 1874, says "We understand that a number of Russians direct from the old country, arrived in the city Monday, bound to join their friends and countrymen near Sutton. There were about 50 leaders of families represented, most of whom have already purchased lands in Clay County through their friends there." The issue of July 12, 1874, contains the following advertisement: "Early in the spring of 1874 nearly every wagon manufacturer in the northwest sent a sample of his work to the Rusian colony at Sutton. . . . After a six-month trial of the different wagons, the Russians have bought 60 of the celebrated Studebaker wagons, leaving Studebaker Brothers of Lincoln only 150 to retail in Lancaster County this fall."

[17]Ernst, C. J. — Records of Land Office of Burlington and Missouri.

[18]This was the second trip Jansen had made to Berdyansk. He had been there briefly from 1850 to 1852. See Reimer and Gaeddert, *Exiled by the Czar,* 8-14. — The editors.

Zweiter Teil

Dakota Freie Presse.

Seite 9–16

Trade-mark registered in U. S. Patent Office.

Herausgeber: Freie Presse Printing Co.
Post-Adresse: Dakota Freie Presse in Aberdeen, S. D., Nord-Amerika.

Erscheint jeden Donnerstag.

Gegründet im Jahre 1874. Aberdeen, Süd-Dakota, den 18. November 1909. Laufende Nummer 1851.

Weitere Beiträge zur Geschichte der deutsch-russischen Ansiedlungen in Nord-Amerika.

(Fortsetzung aus No. 1850)

In Nebraska.

Clay County.

Sutton, Neb. Im Juni 1873 schlossen sich eine größere Anzahl Familien, etwa 400 Seelen, aus Worms und Rohrbach zusammen, um ihren schon früher ausgewanderten Familien nach den Ver. Staaten zu folgen. Der Abschied von der alten Heimat und den zurückbleibenden Verwandten und Bekannten war ein schmerzlicher, ja für viele ein unvergeßlicher. Auf der Station Wradiewka bestiegen wir den Eisenbahnzug, um über Oesterreich und Berlin nach dem gepriesenen Lande der Freiheit zu fahren. Außer mir befanden sich unter anderen noch die Familien Joh. Grashaus, Lehrer Jakob Orth, Lehrer Nuß, H. Hoffmann und meine Eltern Heinrich und Margarethe Gries mit ihren Kindern und Geschwistern.

In Berlin machten wir einige Tage Halt, um mit den Dampfschiff-Gesellschaften über die Reise zu verhandeln. Wir benutzten diese Tage, um uns das schöne Berlin anzusehen. Wir besuchten den Zoologischen Garten, das Museum, das Zeughaus, den Ratskeller und das königliche Schloß. An einem Sonntag Abend ging es dann per Bahn nach Hamburg, von wo aus wir am folgenden Mittwoch auf dem Dampfer Thuringia nach Amerika abzufahren gedachten. Aber noch vor der Abfahrt des Dampfers hatten wir durch Erkrankung meines jüngeren Bruders und einiger Kinder von Hoffmann eine herbe Enttäuschung zu erleben. Wir mußten [illegible] zwei Erkrankungen teilen, der größere Teil fuhr mit dem geplanten Dampfer, wo- [illegible]

die Familie Bachmann aus Rußland angeschlossen, die auch freudig von uns allen begrüßt wurden. Unterdessen wurde der Hunger nach Land bei uns immer größer und da im Staate Nebraska außer dem äußersten Westen, der damals ganz in den Händen der großen Viehzüchter war, keine Aussichten mehr auf Regierungsland waren, so nahm eine Familie nach der anderen Abschied von Nebraska und wandte sich nach dem unbesiedelten Dakota, so daß im Ganzen nur noch ein kleines Häuflein hier verblieb. Nachdem mehrere Ländereien besichtigt waren, die sich nicht so recht zur Besiedelung eignen wollten, kam ei- [illegible]

Kirche in Sutton, Nebraska.

[illegible] Omaha nach Lincoln und durch dessen Mithilfe wurde uns dann das

unsere Frauen aus Lincoln nachkommen zu lassen. Gegen Ende Oktober waren unsere Häuser fertig und wurden auch ohne Verzug bezogen. Ehe wir aber alle in unseren Heimen eingerichtet waren, wurde es doch Mitte November. Wie viel leichter hatten es die späteren Ankömmlinge, Heinrich Grieß und Johann Grieß und andere, die im September 1874 ankamen und freundliche Aufnahme bei ihren Freunden und Verwandten fanden bis sie sich ihr eigenes Heim gegründet hatten. Bei uns war anfangs der Himmel unser Dach und der Heuschober unsere Herberge, während unsere Familien in Lincoln verbleiben mußten. Und vor wie viel Beutelschneidereien wurden sie durch Rat bewahrt, da wir nur kurze Zeit hier, doch durch bittere Erfahrungen gewitzigt worden. Im Spätherbst desselben Jahres folgten dann noch die Mennoniten-Einwanderer, die sich nördlich von Sutton in den Counties Hamilton und York ansiedelten, da aber zu jener Zeit nördlich von Sutton noch keine Eisenbahnen vorhanden waren, so gewann Sutton sehr durch diesen Zuzug, da die Mennoniten gezwungen waren, ihre Geschäfte dort zu verrichten. Die ersten Mennoniten, die sich hier ansiedelten, waren folgende Familien: H. Epp, Jakob Friesen, H. Pemier, Peter und Gerhard Abrahams, Gerhard Loews, P. Wahl, H. Pankratz und noch andere mehr. Im Sommer 1874 traf auch ein Lehrer, Emanuel Jose aus Neusatz hier ein, der unsere Jugend in ihrer Muttersprache unterrichtete und an Sonntagen in unserer Mitte die Gottes- [illegible] 500 Einwohner mit einer ganzen Reihe guter Geschäftshäuser, Aerz- [illegible]

-wo hier an, da aber viele derselben unbemittelt waren, so mußten sie meist nach den größeren Städten, wie Lincoln, Omaha, Hasting und sogar Colorado übersiedeln, um sich bessern Verdienst zu suchen. Einige blieben hier und sind jetzt im Besitze schöner Farmen; andere versuchten ihr Glück im Geschäftsleben und haben es zu schönem Wohlstand gebracht. Oft wurde unser Städtchen Russian Town genannt, aber dies kann uns nicht zur Schande gereichen, denn während andere Städte, die anfangs ebenso groß oder größer wie Sutton waren, zurück blieben, ist unser Städtchen stetig aufgeblüht und gilt heute als das beste längs der Burlington-Bahn zwischen Lincoln und Hastings.

P. H. Grieß.

In Washington.

Hicksville. Als ich mit meiner Frau im Jahre 1902 von Süd-Rußland nach Washington auswanderte und auf der Station [illegible]creek ausstieg, wußte ich nicht, wohin ich mich wenden sollte. Da ich aber wußte, daß schon einige Familien aus der Kolonie Neusatz hier wohnten, so erkundigte ich mich und erfuhr auch, daß sie 16 Meilen südlich von der Station wohnten, aber Niemand konnte den Ort genau angeben, da damals hier noch alles wild war. Wege gab es noch nicht und nur selten traf man eine Bretterbude auf der Prärie. Endlich jedoch gelang es unserem Freund Johann und Jakob Ottmar zu finden, aber wie betrübt schauten wir die Wildnis ohne Gras und Wasser an. Das Wasser mußte oft vier bis sechs Meilen weit an einer Quelle in den Niederungen geholt werden. Heute sieht es ganz anders aus. Johann und Jakob Ottmar haben jeder ein prächtiges Haus, große Stallungen und Nebengebäude, Windmühle, Obst- [illegible] Johannes Wiging, Jakob und Johannes Schmauder und Ludwig und Johan- [illegible]

Portland und Seattle, sowie die Chicago, Milwaukee und St. Paulbahn sind bekanntlich schon fertig und die North Coast Bahn ist ebenfalls im Bau begriffen und wird die kürzeste Verbindung zwischen Spokane und Portland bilden. Ohne Uebertreibung können wir sagen, daß dies der bevorzugteste Teil des Staates ist, sofern Klima, Fruchtbarkeit und Verkehrswege in Betracht kommen. Wer also von den vielen Lesern der Freien Presse in diesem Sommer von der Wanderlust oder dem Auswanderungsfieber ergriffen werden sollte, wird es nicht bereuen, wenn er dieser Gegend einen Besuch abstattet. Die Landpreise sind noch verhältnißmäßig gering. Ich sage gering, weil der Preis von $25 bis $30 nicht mit den Preisen im Osten verglichen werden kann, wo nur die halbe Buschelzahl an Getreide eingeerntet wird.

Da ich fürchte, daß mein Bericht mit der großen Scheere des Redakteurs in Berührung kommen möchte, wenn ich ihn noch weiter ausdehne, will ich für diesmal schließen, in der Hoffnung, daß ich hiermit manchem Leser der Freien Presse die gewünschte Auskunft über die hiesigen Verhältnisse gegeben haben möchte.

Mit Gruß. Samuel Pflugrath.

Neb. Aber auch dort bleib ich nicht lange und ging wieder nach Süd-Dakota zurück. Eine Zeit lang war ich in Eureka und ging von dort nach Medina, N. D.

Wir siedelten uns etwa 15 Meilen südlich von Medina an. Dort war damals noch alles öde Prärie. Wir waren alle arme Schlucker und hatten nicht einmal Geld genug, um uns Land aufzunehmen. Aber wir vertrauten auf den lieben Gott, unseren einzigen Trost und Helfer, und unser Vertrauen war nicht vergebens. In den 12 Jahren, welche ich in Nord-Dakota lebte, habe ich mir ein hübsches Vermögen zusammengespart. Im März 1907 bin ich nach Colorado gezogen, da der Gesundheitszustand meiner Frau einen Klimawechsel notwendig machte. Ich will aber wieder auf die Ansiedelung in Nord-Dakota zurückkommen und die Namen der ersten Ansiedler nennen. Es waren Ernst Rembold, Jakob Rembold, der jetzt in Medina einen Laden besitzt, Konrad Rembold, David, Peter und John Kerner, F. Fischer sen., F. Fischer jr., Jakob Fischer, Gottlieb Wolf und mein Nachbar Peter Seidel. Alle diese haben es durch Fleiß zu Wohlstand gebracht. Aber auch alle, die sich später ansiedelten, sind

Ch. Dobler's Farm bei Burlington, Colorado.

In Colorado.

Burlington, Colorado.

Am 12. Oktober 1889 wanderten wir, im Ganzen vier Familien, Chri- [illegible]

wohlhabend geworden. Von den späteren Nachzüglern will ich noch Gottlieb Blaskowsky, F. Lehr, J. Neumann und J. R[illegible] [illegible] jedes Claim dort aufgenommen.

Ueber Colorado will ich auch noch [illegible]

Einwanderung nach Texas kam aus Deutschland. Diese ersten Ansiedler mußten das Land hier für $1.25 vom Staate kaufen. Im Anfang wurde hier fast nur Vieh gezogen. Die meisten Leute hatten große Ranches, da das Land damals noch nicht viel wert war, und wenig Ackerbau getrieben wurde. Die ersten Ansiedler hatten auch hier sehr schwere Zeiten durchzumachen und ich kenne verschiedene, die vor 25 Jahren in großer Armut sich hier durchkämpfen mußten, und die heute hunderttausend Dollar wert sind.

Von diesen möchte ich nur einige nennen. John Forth besitzt jetzt 4,700 Acres Land und 900 Stück Rindvieh. Jakob Hirsche kam vor 28 Jahren vollkommen ohne Mittel hierher und besitzt heute 3000 Acres Land und 500 Stück Rindvieh. Daraus kann man sehen, wie ein Mann in Texas vorwärtskommen kann.

Hier sind noch Millionen von Acres guten fruchtbaren Landes und ich möchte den Einwanderern empfehlen, hierher zu kommen, vor allem, da den Einwanderern bei der Landung in Galveston bei weitem nicht so viele Schwierigkeiten in den Weg gelegt werden wie in New York.

Karl Wildermuth.

Die Freunde der Dakota Freien Presse werden gebeten, weitere Berichte zu dieser Ansiedlungsgeschichte einzusenden. Alles wird mit Dank angenommen. D. R.

Die diesjährige Maisernte.

Das Ackerbau-Departement schätzt die Gesamternte an Mais für 1909 auf 2,767,316,000 Bushels, gegen 2,668,651,000 als Schlußabschätzung im Vorjahr. Die Qualität beträgt 84.2 Prozent gegen 86.9 im Vorjahr. Eine vorläufige Schätzung des Durchschnittsertrages der Acker [illegible] auf 25.4 Bushel, gegen die endgültige Schätzung von 26.2 Bushel per Acker letztes Jahr. Der Ertrag und die Qualität wird [illegible]

Dakota Freie Presse (November 18, 1909) mentioning the arrival of Germans from Russia in North America.

upon liberty and by the graft which he saw everywhere in Russian official life, he had never become a Russian subject. Being a man of education, influence and lofty character, he had been appointed by Prussia and Mecklenburg as their consular representative, which post he held for nine years.

One of his principles was that every patriot should in some way serve his country without remuneration and so he refused to accept pay for his services. During his official career, he came into touch with American affairs through the British consul who lived next door and who gave lessons to his family in the English language. Through him, *The London Times* was regularly read in the Jansen home, and when one day *The Times* came and reported the death of Abraham Lincoln he cried like a child.

Even before 1870 a rumor became current that a universal military service law was to be passed. Early in 1870, Jansen went to Odessa to consult the governor-general there. The report was confirmed and Mr. Jansen immediately began looking about for a refuge for his co-religionists. His thoughts turned toward America. In October 1867 two Quaker missionaries from England, Isaac Robson and Thomas Harvey, had come to Berdyansk, and for three weeks Mr. Jansen accompanied them on a tour of the Mennonite colonies, acting as their interpreter and translator. In the intervening years he had corresponded with them, and had followed a visit which Isaac Robson made to America with much interest. Mr. Robson had reported on the condition of things in the United States and had also given him the addresses of prominent Mennonites whom he had met.

However, among other Mennonites of South Russia, a certain prejudice prevailed against the United States. It was said that America was a refuge for criminals and that its "only important officer was a sheriff whose duty it was to go around in the morning and gather up the dead bodies." Its famous freedom had degenerated into unrestrained license. Consequently, Palestine was discussed and from a sentimental point of view presented great attraction. Australia, Canada, eastern Siberia, and the Amur Valley also had adherents.[19]

Nevertheless, on February 1870 Mr. Jansen addressed a letter to a German Mennonite in Missouri which was partly reproduced in a religious journal of that sect in Danzig. This letter served not only to

---

[19]Dr. Williams fails to mention that throughout the years 1871 to 1873, repeated delegations were sent to St. Petersburg in an attempt to protect the privileges which had been promised to the Mennonites. C. Henry Smith, *The Story of the Mennonites* (Fourth Edition), 440-443. — The editors.

*Courtesy of the **Mennonite Library and Archives**, North Newton, Kansas.*

The Cornelius Jansen family at their home in Berdyansk, South Russia, about 1870. Tante Anna (sister of Mrs. Jansen), Mrs. Jansen, and Cornelius Jansen are shown above, center.

stir the Prussian Mennonites to a similar concerted movement,[20] but also to arouse the interests of their American and English brethren in the plight of their Prussian and Russian friends. Extracts from the correspondence which resulted were made by Mr. Jansen and printed in 1872 in the form of a small book for distribution among the Mennonites "in order to counteract the almost universal prejudice among us against America."[21] The book was printed in Danzig and distributed from there, because neither would have been allowed to occur in Russia. It contained letters from brethren in Ohio, Pennsylvania, Missouri, Indiana, and Illinois, all assuring them of perfect security from enforced military service for non-combatants even in time of war, explaining the system of agriculture carried on in the United States, the kind of labor available and the prices paid for it, the localities where Mennonite colonies were located, and the prices and supply of raw and improved lands in those communities. The question of sending a deputation to spy out the land was affirmatively urged. Extracts were also quoted from the American Immigration Agent at London and the American consul at Odessa.

In spite of the care exercised, Mr. Jansen was ordered on March 27, 1873, to leave Russia within 7 days "for causing unrest among the people and inciting them to emigrate." If he had been a Russian subject, he would have been sent to Siberia; being a German he was simply ordered from the country. Because of his unselfish services to his country, the German ambassador through Prince Bismarck secured an extension of the time to two months (in order to give him more time for closing up his affairs) and in May 1873 he left Russia with his family for America. His exile was a signal for general alarm among the Mennonites, and some people left before he could get away, while arrangements for the general emigration were accelerated.

An element which tended to advertise "Russian" immigration in the early 70's and give it a picturesque aspect came about through the public negotiations carried on with our government by the Mennonite leaders of both Russia and Prussia, but particularly of the former. In Russia there were about 45,000 of the sect, who it was expected would emigrate in a body, and who would be joined by many, if not all (25,000), of their brethren in Prussia.

---

[20]*Foreign Relations,* 1872, 190. Mr. George Bancroft, writing to Secretary of State Hamilton Fish May 14, 1872, says ". . . .communities of a sect called Mennoniten, now settled in West Prussia, and numbering some 25,000 souls, are seriously contemplating emigrating to America. Their principal motive is the avoidance of military service, which their creed forbids. They are reputed to be thrifty, temperate, and industrious people. and I am assured that they are among the best agriculturists in Germany."

[21]Preface to *Sammlung von Notizen Ueber Amerika,* Danzig, 1872, 56. A copy of this book was kindly loaned for examination by Miss Helena Jansen of Beatrice, Nebraska.

Three questions concerned them primarily, which were formulated in a petition presented to the American consul at Odessa and to the ambassador at Berlin as follows:[22]

1. May our community obtain in the United States for ourselves and our posterity entire exemption from military service, *direct or indirect*, according to our principles and belief in the word of God?

2. May immigrants to the United States hope to receive a piece of land either as a gift or at a low price, and, in case of need, reckon on an advance or loan of money from the Government?

3. For the sake of obtaining satisfactory encouragement and assurances on the foregoing points, and also for agreeing upon their place and terms of settlement, would it be advisable to send (in advance of emigrating) a delegation to Washington to confer directly with the Government?

The request for aid in obtaining land was due to the fact that Russia was expected to confiscate the lands originally granted the Mennonites and permit them only the possession of the improvements they had made. This, and the enforced sale which must take place at more or less of a disadvantage to them, would greatly reduce the amount of property owned by the well-to-do and make them unable to care for the poor of their community whom they were unwilling to leave behind. The question of military service of course received a favorable answer from the American representatives. As to the land, the homestead and preemption laws were explained; and it was suggested that the Northern Pacific Railroad (among others) assists immigrants by favorable terms on land purchases, by furnishing them work, and also by assisting colonies to emigrate at reduced rates. In view of the size of the group desiring to emigrate, the possibility of Congressional aid was suggested, or of assistance from some of the western states.[23]

The suggestion of a delegation to America was approved, and in the summer of 1873, an exploring party of 12 "elders" was sent at common expense to Canada and the United States to choose a location for them.[24] When three of the party returned to New York, they were met by Jansen, who had temporarily located among Mennonites at Berlin, Ontario. They commissioned him to go to Washington and use his influence with the government in securing the desired tract of

---

[22]*Foreign Relations of the United States,* 1872, 488.

[23]*Ibid.,* 489.

[24]Fast, M. B., *Reisebericht und Kurze Geschichte der Mennoniten,* 1909.

Dr. Williams does not give adequate attention to the role played by the twelve "elders" in the Mennonite immigration to America. Perhaps in her day the information we now have about these men was not available. — The editors.

land. The mission was undertaken and with the help of the Germantown Mennonites and Philadelphia Quakers, an audience was secured with President Grant who was so greatly interested in the project as to devote a paragraph in his annual message of December 1, 1873, to the subject.[25]

Mr. Jansen returned to Washington on November 21, 1873, and came again on March 26, 1874, trying to gain government aid for the emigrants. The help of the national legislators of Pennsylvania was secured. On December 8, 1873, in the House[26] and on January 12, 1874, in the Senate,[27] a memorial was introduced from the Mennonites asking for permission to secure through homesteading or purchase a large compact tract of land. This was to be reserved for them until 1881, the limit given by the Russian government for free emigration. A bill followed in each instance, on February 24 in the House[28] and on April 2 in the Senate,[29] but neither got beyond second reading. This bill was opposed on the score that it was against the policy of the government to present its public lands to a religious sect, although everyone recognized the value of these prospective citizens to the country and desired to further them, insofar as it could be done consistently in view of Russia's attitude toward the matter.

Although nothing came of negotiating with the United States government, the Mennonites had gone on with their preparations for leaving Russia, encouraged by the letters sent back by Cornelius Jansen, which had to be mailed in England or Germany in order to avoid being confiscated. The summer of 1874, 300 families from Berdyansk and 100 from Melitopol arrived at Castle Garden.[30] So much had been said in the newspapers of their contemplated action that their arrival created great excitement among the agents who fairly swarmed about them. There were railroad agents, desiring their transportation, land agents for railroads who wished to settle the colony on their lands, and state immigration agents. Leaving their families at a Mennonite settlement near Buffalo, New York, the heads of the families, now that the colony idea had to be given up, accompanied the agents to various parts of Canada and the United States.

During the year of 1874, Cornelius Jansen had moved his family to Mt. Pleasant, Iowa, in order to place his children in the seminary there. Accompanied by his son Peter, he had previously set out on an exploring expedition. Various parts of Canada were visited, par-

---

[25]*Messages and Papers of the Presidents*, VII, 253.
[26]*Congressional Record,* 43rd Congress, 1st Session, II, 100.
[27]*Congressional Record,* 43rd Congress, 1st Session, II, 570.
[28]*Congressional Record,* 43rd Congress, 1st Session, II, 1731.
[29]*Congressional Record,* 43rd Congress, 1st Session, II, 2718.
[30]*Nebraska State Journal,* May 17, 1874.

ticularly the wheat growing sections in Manitoba, but they were passed up as too cold and too wild for settlement. The Dakota Territory which offered an abundance of homestead land was considered too stony. In Kansas, which was the most densely populated of the Trans-Missouri Territory, it was necessary to go farther west to get land than in Nebraska. In the latter they visited the Russian German colony at Sutton and, after a short journey throughout the state, they decided upon Nebraska because "it more nearly resembled South Russia in the open character of its land, than any other place they had visited."

Often in 1874, the Jansens also met the Mennonites at Castle Garden. A veritable war among land agents and transportation companies had set in. The Northern Pacific had as its representative a Jew who got the leaders of one group of Mennonites to sign a contract binding them to settle upon their lands, and then virtually made prisoners of them until released through the efforts of Mr. Jansen. Later a number were taken to the southern part of Dakota and, joined by some who had been taken to Lincoln, Nebraska, were induced to settle in Dakota about 40 miles north of Yankton, forming a settlement of Mennonites. The Burlington and Missouri offered Mr. Jansen, whom it recognized as very influential among his brethren, a section of land as a reward if he would turn the immigration toward that railroad's lands in Nebraska. Mr. Jansen's reply was that all he had done had been done by him without thought of profit and that if such a gift were made he would turn it over to the poor people who were not able to buy, and this was done. Through the influence of the Jansens, about 100 families joined them in the purchase from the Burlington and Missouri of 19,000 acres in Gage and Jefferson Counties, and another group bought the same amount in Hamilton and York Counties, the average price paid being $3.50 to $5.00.[31] The Santa Fe Railroad at the same time secured for Kansas the nucleus of what later became one of the largest Russian German settlements in the United States, centering about Newton in Harvey County.

For three years there was a steady stream of Mennonites from South Russia, with 18,000 coming to the New World. Of these the province of Manitoba, in Canada, received 8,000.[32] The remainder

---

[31]*Nebraska State Journal,* July 21, 1874. "More Immigrants: Three hundred and fifty immigrants under the charge of the Burlington and Missouri Land Company will arrive here this afternoon and encamp on the Fair Grounds. They will select lands upon the line of the Burlington and Missouri River Railroad west of here. They come 'well healed' ". Many issues of the *Nebraska State Journal* from July 23 to November 29, 1874, refer to the coming of the Mennonites and the first days in Nebraska.

[32]*Report of Chief of Bureau of Statistics, 1875-1878.* In 1875, 1505 passengers on way to Manitoba from Russia passed through United States ports; in 1876, 2293; in 1877, 1540; in 1878, 125.

settled primarily in Kansas but with a minority going to such places as Dakota Territory and Nebraska. Although the government had not felt inclined to encourage immigration from Russia, private enterprise undertook the task. Mr. C. B. Schmidt, of Lawrence, Kansas, now became head of the land office of the Atchison, Topeka and Santa Fe Railroad in Kansas. The foreign immigration department which he organized turned its attention at once to the Mennonites in South Russia and decided to send him for a tour through the colonies.[33] He set out in February 1875, and armed with letters from Mennonites in Kansas, spent more than a month visiting among the German colonies, explaining the opportunities in America and answering the questions which most concerned them. They reminded him of the presence and restlessness of the Indians in Kansas which would demand soldiers and asked what was to prevent the men from being forced to do army service. He explained the law exempting Mennonites from military duty which became of exceptional importance just at the time and which satisfied them on that most important issue.[34] He estimated the results of his trip at 15,000 Mennonites, mostly from South Russia but many also from West Prussia where he stopped for a time. This number was greatly exaggerated, but it is a fact that Kansas secured the bulk of the Mennonite emigration. They settled in McPherson, Reno, Harvey, and Marion Counties where they purchased 60,000 acres of railroad land.

By 1878, the mass movement had practically ceased. Although at first it was felt in Russia that it was better to let the Mennonites leave than to exempt them in any way from the general law,[35] the government later was inclined to make concessions. In 1875, it substituted forestry service for those Mennonites called into the army by the conscription; and sent General Todtleben, a prominent official in the army, into the settlements to try to influence them against emigration. All manner of impediments were placed in the way of the emigration. Those living in the colonies must forfeit their land, while those who had attained to individual ownership must suffer considerable loss in disposing of their estates. It was difficult to secure passports without which they dared not leave. As the ten-year limit for emigration drew near, the wealthier Mennonites made efforts to

---

[33]*Kansas Historical Collection,* IX, 485-497. "Reminiscences of Foreign Immigration Work for Kansas," by C. B. Schmidt.

[34]*Wilder's Annals,* Second Edition, gives the following interesting facts to show how promptly Kansas through legislation responded to conditions to promote emigration.

August 5, 1873. Five Mennonite leaders visit Harvey, Sedgwick, Reno, Marion, and McPherson Counties to select land for a colony from Russia.

March 19, 1874. An act exempting Mennonites and Friends from military service.

[35]*Foreign Relations,* 1872, 490. Extract from Russian World (St. Petersburg) of March 24, 1872.

change their citizenship and still remain in Russia, but all such attempts failed.

The emigration since 1878 has consisted only of individual families, or at most of small groups of families, many of whom have been brought to the United States through the fund which the Mennonites keep for the purpose of assisting needy brethren to emigrate. One of the most interesting instances is a group of about 20 families[36] from the province of Khiva in Central Asia who were brought to Nebraska at an expense of approximately $10,000 in 1884. They belonged to a colony of 365 persons who had lived in the Volga province of Samara, but in 1880 had formed a caravan and traveled overland by wagons and camels to Khiva where they formed a settlement.[37] A member of this group has given the motive for settlement as a promise from the Russian government to be unmolested by demands for military service. Tradition relates that they were influenced by a minister who counseled them that the millenium was at hand, and who led them toward a mountain in that vicinity to meet the Lord at his second coming. Dissatisfaction with the country because of the robberies by the Tartars and the final murder of one of the colonists, led them to appeal to their American brethren for aid and they were brought to their friends in Nebraska.

From Dakota, Kansas, and Nebraska the Russian German Mennonites have spread chiefly into Oklahoma, Texas, and California.[38]

3. *The Volga Germans.* The third and last area of Russia to be touched by the emigration fever in the early seventies were the German colonies on the Volga. In contrast to the Odessa and Mennonite emigration, this movement was less compactly organized with less pronounced leadership, and hence was a trifle slower in its beginning. The Volga Germans were more secluded in their manner of living, and largely due to their ignorance of the Russian language, the significance of changes in their legal status only slowly dawned upon

[36]Originally there was talk of twenty families (See *Brothers in Deed to Brothers in Need,* edited by C. Hiebert), but F. R. Belk in *The Great Trek of the Russian Mennonites to Central Asia, 1880-1884,* pp. 365-366, says fifteen families arrived in September 1884, eleven families in October 1884, and fifteen families in August 1885. Furthermore, as far as their original homes were concerned, they were evenly divided between the Volga (Samara Trakt) settlement and the Black Sea region. Claas Epp, from the Volga, was their best known leader. He is the minister referred to above. — The editors.

[37]An interesting account of this expedition by a member of it is found in *Das Evangelische Magazin,* XLII, "Erlebnisse auf Reisen nach Zentral-Asien und Amerika" by G. U. Fast.

[38]One of the most romantic and picturesque chapters of immigration is the history of the Mennonite settlements in the United States. Those in the east have received attention but those in the west have thus far been neglected. The rough sketch here given is all that this study will allow but the earnest hope is expressed that before the original settlers and the original improvements have disappeared someone will adequately picture the movement.

them. Gradually they began to appreciate that "their rights had been signed away" and that "for ten years they would be free to leave the country if they desired"; but the first draft of soldiers in 1874 was the event which precipitated emigration. There are two distinct streams of emigration from the Volga, the Catholic and the Protestant; the former a mass movement like the Mennonites, the latter a steadily increasing stream from that day to the present.

The Catholic colonies, containing 28 per cent of the Germans on the Volga, in the spring of 1874 called a meeting at Herzog on the *Wiesenseite* for the purpose of discussing the question of emigration. It was attended by 3,000 colonists and addresses were made by those who had learned of foreign lands. Brazil and Nebraska being mentioned as desirable places for new homes, five delegates from as many colonies were elected to make an exploring tour to the latter place. A hasty trip was made in the summer of 1874, the party remaining only ten days in America and spending one day of that time among the Russian German settlers at Sutton. They returned with samples of soil, prairie grass, and paper money, and with advertising literature describing the land, reporting favorably upon what they had seen. In December 1874, two other explorers spent a week along the Santa Fe in Kansas and returned with an unfavorable report which deterred a number from emigrating. Another delegate had accompanied the first group to New York and then went to Arkansas from which he brought a favorable report upon the land but criticized the custom of isolated farming. His report was confirmed in a letter written by a Russian German who with his family and four others had gone to Arkansas in the fall of 1874.[39]

The result of these investigations was manifested when in October 1875, 261 Volga Germans, mostly from the colonies on the *Wiesenseite*, under the guidance of one of the original explorers, set out for the United States. At Baltimore, they were taken in charge by the agent of the Atchison, Topeka and Santa Fe who sent them to Topeka where they were lodged in a vacant building (which later became the Santa Fe shops) until they could find suitable locations. They were not satisfied with their exploration over the Santa Fe because of the high price of the land ($5.00 per acre) and the lack of homesteads. They were then induced by the agent of the Kansas Pacific to visit Ellis County where land was cheap ($2.00 to $2.50 per acre) and adapted to forming colonies. They decided upon this as their new home. Five colonies were formed in Ellis County and one across the line in Rush

[39]The Volga German who had gone to Arkansas and written of his experiences was a Mr. Schwabauer of Doennhof. His letter was repeatedly read in public; for example, at a meeting of the citizens of Kamenka and Pfeifer which was held in Pfeifer, September, 1875. — The editors.

Courtesy of Father Blaine Burkey, Historian of the Ellis County Historical Museum, and Lawrence A. Weigel of Hays, Kansas

First church and belfry constructed in 1877 by Catholic Volga Germans in Munjor, Ellis County, Kansas. Munjor was founded in 1876.

County. Between the years 1875 and 1878, 1,387 persons are reported to have come here.

The Catholic Volga Germans more than any other have carried out the idea of living in colonies. This is first noticeable in the names – Catharine, Munjor, Herzog, Pfeifer, Schoenchen, and Liebenthal – none of which is located directly upon the railroad. Each is composed largely of or dominated by people from the same village in Russia and their loyalty to their home village is strong. Not only are the old social customs retained as at weddings and church festivals, but even remnants of political organization from the colonial life in Russia are still found. For example, some of the land homesteaded was divided into 40-acre strips running through the whole section and one individual or several took one of these. Conservative as all the Russian Germans are, the Catholic settlements have proved to be the most conservative, partly because of their religion and partly as a result of their living in colonies.[40]

Although the emigration movement from the Protestant colonies on the Volga proceeded independently of that of the Catholics, it began about the same time. No Germans in Russia lived more shut off from the outside world than did these colonists. Even their knowledge of the course of events in their own country was very limited and hazy. A newspaper was a luxury beyond the reach or desire of any but one or two of the richest persons in the village at whose house a group of the more intelligent in the community would gather to listen to its reading. Not infrequently lines or columns of black ink showed the work of the censor, and only government news such as the Czar desired became public. Their own German officials should have been aware of what was coming, for they had received, as early as 1871, the Czar's decree which changed the legal status of the colonists. Unfortunately they did not understand the significance of this and accepted it without protest. Later as rumors spread of the changed order of things, this mysterious paper was recalled and the colonists came to the conclusion that their rights had been "signed away" and that "after ten years they must become Russian subjects." Rumor can stampede the uninformed masses, as easily as strong leaders can influence independent minds; and it was largely rumor which caused the emigration fever to spread with the rapidity of contagion at this time. The largest and most prosperous of the colonies were first affected, because they were more in touch with outside affairs and they were more competent to take some action. The feelings of the German

[40]Dr. Williams obtained her information on the Volga German Catholics from Laing, Francis S., "German Russian Settlements in Ellis County, Kansas," *Kansas Historical Collections,* XI, 489-528. — The editors.

people were aroused to rebellious anger at what they considered the breaking of a sacred promise; and the statue of their beloved Catherine, which they had erected out of their poverty at Katharinenstadt, had to have a guard placed about it to keep the countrymen from "sticking out her eyes." The following song, composed by a local minstrel, was sung up and down the streets of the villages to express their sentiment on the occasion.

Das Manifest

1. Das Manifest der Kaiserin,
   Es dachte nach den Deutschen hin;
   Sie sollten pflanzen Brot und Wein
   Und sollten auch Kolonisten sein.

2. Wir verliessen unser Vaterland
   Und zogen in das Russenland.
   Die Russen warn uns sehr beneidt,
   Und weil wir warn so lang befreit.

3. So brachten sie's dahin mit List,
   Das wir nicht mehr sollten sein Kolonist.
   Ei keine Kolonisten sind wir mehr
   Und muessen tragen das Gewehr.

4. Ja, was doch durch den Neid geschicht!
   Hat man das Manifest vernicht!
   Wir stammen aus dem Deutschen Reich,
   Und jetzt sind wir den Russen gleich.[41]

---

[41]Erbes and Sinner, *Volkslieder und Kinderreime aus den Wolgakolonien,* 177. Translation by the editors:

1. The Manifesto of the Empress
   Was directed at the Germans;
   They were to grow bread and wine
   And were also to be colonists.

2. We left our Fatherland
   And journeyed into Russia.
   The Russians were very jealous of us
   Because we were free so long.

3. They accomplished it with cunning
   That we should not be colonists any more.
   No, we are not colonists any more
   And must now bear arms.

4. To think what happens through envy!
   They destroyed the Manifesto!
   We come from the German Reich
   And now we're the equals of the Russians.

The first concerted movement came in the sending of a deputation to America in 1874 to explore the land in search of a new home. Five villages, Balzer, Norka, Dietel, Messer, and Kolb, all on the *Bergseite* joined in sending the exploring party, which consisted of men in various walks of life who were willing to emigrate if conditions proved satisfactory — several farmers, a cloth dyer, and a school teacher.[42] The difficulty and danger, fancied if not real, of leaving Russia at that time is illustrated in the efforts of two of this party to secure their passports. They were evidently of the impression that in order to get the necessary documents they would have to pay an extra fee, and whether they offered their bribe clumsily or at the wrong time, it resulted in their being chased out of the building. The whole expedition was in a fair way to fall through when it was rescued by a young German colonist who had several months before secured a pass for America but was detained by the unwillingness of his father to let him leave. Being more versed in diplomacy than they, he appealed directly to the governor and secured for them the necessary "passeportes." The party journeyed together to New York City where they met the German Lutheran missionary stationed in Castle Garden who took a great interest in them and secured their confidence. From Castle Garden they proceeded to Ohio and Iowa where they visited friends,[43] then upon the advice of the harbor missionary, they traveled to Kansas City to search for land, since that was their primary object.

On their return to the colonies, their report was not unanimous. The farmers upon whose judgment most depended were least enthusiastic. The soil, they declared, was sandy and the country unpopulated; their ignorance of the language made them fearful of their ability to get along, and their failure to consult with any government officials left them without assurance against the future. The school teacher on the other hand saw in the new land great opportunities for his countrymen and advised emigration. The personal experiences of these men were not entirely pleasant. They came to the United States in the summer dressed in their heavy Russian caps, boots, and coats. The latter were made with a close fitting waist and full skirt reaching to the ankles and were lined with sheepskin. They no doubt presented a curious appearance which did not escape the eye of the passing city

[42]In AHSGR Work Paper No. 15 for September 1974, 4-20, Mrs. Haynes supplied the names of the deputies from shipping lists as follows: Johannes Kreiger and Johannes Nolde from Norka, Georg Kaehm and Heinrich Schwabauer from Balzer, Christoph Meisinger from Messer, and Johann Benzel and Franz Scheibel from Kolb. That would leave Georg Stieben as coming from Dietel. — The editors.

[43]It would be interesting to know who these friends were. Most historians had previously believed that the scouts were the first Volga Germans to come to the United States. — The editors.

crowd, nor the personal attention of the street gamin, who followed a couple of them along the streets with shouts of laughter and even clutched at their great sheepskin coats. By the time the commissioners had returned, the story of this ill-treatment had assumed more serious proportions, and the current rumor in the colonies that "the Americans had followed them down the streets of New York City and thrown stones at them" had no small effect upon the minds of intending emigrants. Some took it with a grain of salt and concluded that was the fault of bad company into which the participating commissioners had fallen here. Others accepted it as an evidence of "barbarous America" and it became one of the factors which changed their minds and kept them from leaving Russia.

But other forces were at work inspiring faith in the enterprise. In 1875 a small party of Germans from Norka, 7 families and 2 single men, had come to the United States and settled in Ohio where they worked for two years at ditch digging and other similar tasks among the farmers of the community. Meanwhile they were on the lookout for land which two years later they decided upon in Sutton, Nebraska. All of these people wrote encouragingly of their prospects to relatives in the colonies, and even the same year in which the deputation came to United States, single immigrants began coming this way. One of these was a young tailor from Balzer who had first found employment in his trade at Burlington, Iowa, while another from the Volga had gone to Ft. Smith, Arkansas, where he stayed 11 months before returning to Russia to bring his family. These favorable letters, augmented by the good words spoken for the country by some of the delegates assured the people's faith and preparations for emigration began.

Among the acquaintances made by the delegates on the exploring trip to the United States was an agent for a Trans-Atlantic steamship company who wrote to them after their return home "an alluring letter in the English language encouraging immigration."[44] They were of course unable to read this and had it translated by a Prof. Ascher of Heidelberg University who had resided for several years in the colonies for the purpose of securing materials for a history of them.[45] A copy of this translation in the handwriting of the German professor was given to the people, and this fell into the hands of the *Kreis* Secretary whom Ascher had hauled into court on the charge of misappropriating public funds. Partly for revenge and partly because stimulation of emigration was a crime in Russia, Ascher was accused by the Secretary

---

[44]Bauer, *Geschichte der deutschen Ansiedler an der Wolga,* 173.

[45]This is undobutedly the Ascher referred to by D. Mackenzie Wallace, *Russia,* New York, 1881, 609, footnote in recognition of services rendered Wallace while collecting material.

before the authorities as being "a secret agent in the service of American companies who would ruin the colonists through the enticement to emigration." The translation in his own handwriting was offered as proof of the charge, and upon order of the Ministry, Ascher was driven out of the country in a very short time.

On June 11, 1875, the first organized group of Volga German Protestants left Saratov for the United States under the leadership of one of the delegates who had made the trip to the United States the year before.[46] The company was composed of 12 families and 18 to 20 single young men, making in all between fifty to seventy-five persons, chiefly from the colony of Balzer, with several families from Dietel and Moor. The company reached New York City in August where they were met and cared for by the harbor missionary who had befriended the delegates. He was now working in the interests of the Burlington and Missouri Railroad and was authorized to allow the leader of the group a rebate of $2.00 on each immigrant sent to Burlington and Missouri territory.[47] Largely through the influence of this harbor missionary, the company was sent to Red Oak, Iowa, which was a district point for immigration on the Burlington and Missouri system. Small quantities of railroad land were still for sale in this area. But the land was too high priced and too hilly to suit the immigrants and they wanted to look farther. Meanwhile several families went to Kansas for land; some secured work on the railroad and remained in Red Oak, while many of the single men scattered out through the nearby country hunting for work. After almost a week's stay in the depot at Red Oak, they received a visit from Cornelius Jansen who told them about the Russian German settlement at Sutton. Through the good offices of the road superintendent of the Burlington, they were brought to Lincoln and sheltered in the Emigrant Home[48], from which those who were prepared to buy land could go to Sutton to investigate. Here they were kindly received by their countrymen who assisted them with advice and aid, found work for them, which was not the least factor in causing them to decide upon that location. After purchasing land from the railroad company the group left Lincoln for Sutton, arriving in September, 1875.

This beginning of emigration from Russia from the Volga called for action on the part of the forces in America encouraging immigration, and in 1875 the Burlington and Missouri Railroad sent

---

[46]This was Heinrich Schwabauer. — The editors.

[47]This sum of money was voluntarily applied to pay the fare of the poorer members of the party instead of being retained by the leader.

[48]In April 1870 an Emigrant Home (not Immigrant Home) was built in Lincoln, Nebraska. — The editors.

Courtesy of the Nebraska State Historical Society, Lincoln, Nebraska.

Volga German women and children along the tracks of the Burlington Railroad before World War I.

Robert Neumann, the harbor missionary at Castle Garden, upon a mission to the Protestant colonies on the Volga. Rev. Neumann was not allowed to speak from the pulpits because the pastors disliked letting other ministers occupy their places, but he preached and held meetings in the homes of the people and under cover talked emigration to Nebraska. The officials decided to arrest him and it was necessary to escape hidden in a load of hay. Chiefly as the result of his mission, one of the largest body of Volga Protestants which has ever come at one time emigrated in 1876.

Eighty-five families, mostly from the colony of Norka, but including some from Balzer, gathered at Saratov and journeyed to Bremen, from which port they sailed for the United States, landing at New York July 7, 1876. Here they were set upon by all manner of land agents, chiefly in the employ of railroad companies, who held out to them every possible inducement. Some of them were persuaded to go to Milwaukee, Wisconsin, on the ground that there were many Germans there, but they did not stay long, coming to Sutton the following spring. Another group of thirty families was taken to Kansas free of charge by the Santa Fe Railroad and while waiting at Atchison, one carload of these were stolen by the Burlington and Missouri immigration agent and sent to Sutton, Nebraska. The remainder were taken to the immigration house at Pawnee Rock in Barton County, Kansas, but were not satisfied with the surrounding country. They got in touch with the Burlington and Missouri land agent in Lincoln where they purchased land along Turkey Creek not far from Friend. Another group was brought to Red Oak, Iowa, and many of these settled at Harvard, Nebraska. But before long, Lincoln became the center of Protestant Volga Germans because of its greater opportunities for employment. From this city many people moved on to new homes in Portland, Oregon, Denver, Colorado, and other points in the west.

As time went on economic motives became a controlling factor. This was due to a peculiar combination of circumstances which occurred in Russia and the United States about 1890 — the great famine in Russia and the rise of the beetfield in the western states of America.

Of the thirteen provinces which the famine covered, the province of Samara was one of the most terribly afflicted and Saratov was scarcely less destitute.[49] In the former more than half of the inhabitants were reported utterly destitute, and the government and private charity were unable by their most heroic efforts at relief to care for the needy. The United States responded with great liberality, the movement being led by those western states in which Russian

[49] *Foreign Relations,* 1892, 366.

Germans had largely settled. Five steamers laden with flour and other breadstuffs were sent to Russia, besides large sums of money, collected mainly in the eastern cities of the United States. A comparatively large proportion of both grain and money was expended in the Volga provinces partly because they were in the most destitute district and partly because the donors in the western states were espcially interested in the German colonists in those provinces.[50] The American in charge of the first relief ship personally supervised the distribution of food in Samara and his reports to various Philadelphia papers preserve the record of his visits among the German colonies of the *Wiesenseite*.[51] He found about half the houses closed, the families having moved together to save fuel. Many of the thatch-roofed houses had been uncovered and the straw fed to the stock, yet one-third of the horses had died and the rest sold at very low prices. Sickness was everywhere and no medicine available within fifty miles. Each colonist is required to contribute a certain amount of grain annually to the village storehouse as an insurance against crop failures, but now there was no seed for next year's crop, the granaries having been emptied the previous year. The government had opened soup kitchens in some of the villages where the people got barely enough to sustain life.

For the native Russian of these districts the famine was merely a darker shade in the somber tinted landscape of his existence. He did not dream of escape from it and reacted with patient endurance. But to the German colonist it was otherwise. Hundreds of his friends and relatives were in the land of plenty whence relief had come, and many of them had joined in sending help, either directly or through the collected funds. The letters from America told of prosperous people with plenty to eat and wear, and prepaid tickets were offered to those who wanted to come to the United States. These encouragements were enhanced by rate wars among the transportation companies which forced the steamship fares down while railroads carried passengers from the seaboard to Lincoln for $8.00. The result of this combination of circumstances was a tremendous influx of Russian Germans to America during the three years of 1891-92-93. By this time the worst of the famine was over in Russia and the emigration of large numbers of colonists had relieved the situation for those remaining. Meanwhile the panic had struck America and it was in the midst of hard times itself.

But an industry was in process of development at this juncture which was to have an important bearing upon Russian German im-

[50]*Ibid.*, 382.

[51]Blankenberg, *The Russian Famine of 1891 and 1892*. He visited Wolskoje (Kukkus) from which many Russian Germans in Lincoln, Nebraska, came.

migration. This was the sugar beet industry which had been started on a large scale in New England and Delaware from 1879 to 1882 and which had failed chiefly because the labor demanded by these crops was not congenial to American farmers. To be assured of a uniform stand of beets, the farmer generally plants four or five times as much seed as is actually needed. Consequently seventy-five percent of the original stand must be removed to give the beets room for proper growth. This is accomplished by blocking and thinning the beets, generally a month after planting, when four true leaves appear on the plant. At that time the more mature workers remove blocks of plants from the solidly planted rows by use of long-handled hoes and space the hills about ten inches apart. Younger workers follow, crawling on their knees, to finish the task by removing with their fingers all but one plant, as well as all weeds, from each blocked bunch. The nature of this back-breaking process in beet culture was such that the American farmer would not perform it and only when foreigners willing to do it lived in the vicinity of the beet field, was it possible for the industry to succeed.

The government had been conducting investigations since 1885 concerning the sugar beet industry, one of its experiment stations being located in Nebraska. The main thing needed was labor, and this the Russian Germans were found willing to perform. Large families whose men, women, and children could be employed at such a task were especially adapted to the situation, and many families had settled in Lincoln in 1891-93. It was possible for them to go out into the beet fields without expense to themselves and earn from $500 to $1,200 a summer, returning in the fall and finding work in the city during a large part of the winter. This insured the new immigrant laborer of good pay, and since the opportunity to secure homesteads or to buy land from the railroads was now a thing of the past, it was a necessary complement to the immigration. Since the early 90's, few Volga Germans have come to Lincoln without planning to spend the first few years in the beet fields.

The Ebb and Flow of Immigration

It is not our purpose to follow further the history of Russian German immigration in detail, but causes controlling its ebb and flow to the United States now claim our attention.

When the colonists were deprived of their special status in 1871, they were granted a period of ten years in which they were free to emigrate. This was a great concession because Russia has never recognized the right of free movement either within or without the empire.

Courtesy of the Great Western Sugar Company Library, Denver, Colorado.

Topping sugar beets before World War I.

Courtesy of the Great Western Sugar Company Library, Denver, Colorado.

Hauling sugar beets to the beet dump.

Courtesy of the Great Western Sugar Company Library, Denver, Colorado.

Picking potatoes, one of the many forms of stoop labor performed by Germans from Russia.

Courtesy of the Nebraska State Historical Society, Lincoln, Nebraska.

Wheat harvest scene. Shocking bundled grain.

Emigration from the empire can occur only on a passport issued by the government of the province, in the absence of which one can only steal out of the country. Moreover, if one attempts to return to Russia without this passport, he is liable to punishment. This passport is only a five years' leave of absence and is subject to the following dues: fifteen rubles for the first six months or fraction thereof, with an additional fine of fifteen rubles if the holder overstays the five-year limit.[52]

War or mere rumors of war are the signal for a great rush of emigrants from the German colonies and these waves have surged up ever since the immigration began. The first soldiers drawn under the universal military service law (October 1874) took part in the war between Russia and Turkey in 1877-1878 and this active service sent many of the younger German boys to America. In 1885 threatened hostilities between England and Russia led to the greatest emigration since the close of the "free emigration" period. In 1892 a rumor became current in the colonies of a threatened war with Turkey and a number of families, many of whose heads had participated in the former Russo-Turkish War, sold out their belongings precipitately and left without taking time to communicate with relatives in America. The Russo-Japanese War in 1904-1905 was the occasion for another large emigration. First came young men who were eligible to appear at the next drawing; then families whose heads were enrolled in the reserve or the militia and who feared they might be called upon to serve if the war continued for any length of time.

The Balkan trouble in 1912-1913 was peculiar in its effect on Russian Germans emigrating. The numbers leaving were unusually large, but during this period many married men from the reserve came without their families, expecting to stay in America only so long as the disturbances continued and then to return to their homes. This marked a new departure because the Russian German is essentially a family man and consents to a separation from his wife and children for only a few months and then under necessity. That he should deliberately plan to leave home alone for two years suggests a strong impelling force, which though chiefly military, was augmented by hard times in Russia.

Government "pressure" upon Germans as a cause for emigration has been more of a fear than a reality. In decided contrast with the Russian Jew, the Russian German has been a privileged character in his adopted land, far surpassing the native Russian in the rights and immunities he enjoyed. The first conscious withdrawal of his priv-

---

[52]For the Russian law concerning passports, I am indebted to a personal letter from Baron E. Schilling, Imperial Russian Consul at Chicago, Illinois.

ileges started the emigration as we have seen, scarcely less from the dislike of military service than from the fear that other privileges of language and religion would be denied him. So twenty years later, when in the 90's Jewish disturbances swept over western Russia, the Germans were also seized with the fear that the hand of the government would be laid upon them, and they would be denied the peculiar privileges remaining to them.

In March 1891, an immigration commission was appointed by Congress to investigate European conditions causing emigration. Two members of this commission visited western Russia and presented a lengthy report chiefly concerned with the Russian Jews, although several references are made to the emigration of the Russian Germans.[53] At immigration stations in Hamburg the commissioners interviewed Russian German emigrants, some destined for the Middle West of the United States and others for the Argentine Republic.

> All of these parties stated that one of the reasons for their emigration was the failure of the crops, which threw upon the communities the support of the poorer ones, and this made their taxes extremely burdensome. They cited as an additional reason the pressure brought to bear upon them by the authorities. German is now forbidden to be taught in their schools; their churches must be built according to plans approved by the Russian officials, and, while there has been as yet no edict issued by the Emperor further restricting their privileges, it was the common talk and belief among their people that such edict or edicts would be issued, and that the best way out of their troubles was to either join the Greek Church or emigrate. They stated to us that all will go who can, as they fear that the same measures will be inaugurated against them as had been directed against the Jews. The increased movement of this class of immigrant is already apparent at the port of New York, and from information derived from various sources the coming spring will probably show a large volume of such immigration.[54]

This "pressure" was felt more keenly by the Germans in South Russia than by those on the Volga because the former were nearer the scene of the Jewish persecutions. In Bessarabia, Kherson, and Tauria

[53]Letter from the Secretary of the Treasury transmitting a "Report of the Commission of Immigration upon the Causes which Incite Immigration to the United States," 2 vol., Executive Document 235, Pt. 1 and 2, 52nd Congress, 1st Session (Washington, 1892), Pt. 1, 54.

[54]Foreign Relations, 1892, Pt. 1, 111. Jewish Exodus from Russia.

Courtesy of the Free Evangelical Lutheran Cross Church (80th Anniversary Edition), Fresno, Calif.

Mr. John Bitter (left) from Laube and Mr. Michael Leisle in soldier uniforms in Russian army in 1907.

particularly, the Germans were in close touch with the affected Jewish settlements.

The causes hindering immigration are quite as interesting and significant as those promoting it, though much less discussed. But the negative side shows the power of the effective administration of the exclusion laws far better than any other feature. The section of law relating to the exclusion of immigrants suffering with trachoma, and its rigid enforcement, has had a marked effect upon Russian German immigration.

In February 1909, the *Dakota Freie Presse* undertook to champion the cause of Russian German immigrants who were being excluded at Ellis Island because of trachoma. Their attention had been called to the matter by a Texas physician who had spent nine months in Russia and had met many would-be immigrants who had been turned back from America. On examination of their eyes, he became convinced that they did not have trachoma but were merely suffering from inflamation due to wind, dust, and bad air in the steerage. The *Dakota Freie Presse* prepared a circular which it asked Russian Germans to clip from its columns, sign, and send to their senators in Washington. The matter was presented to the Bureau of Immigration and Naturalization and the letter from Commissioner General Daniel J. Keefe concerning the question, together with one of the circulars, was made of record. The government took the position that it must enforce the law, which required an examination at the port of entry by a United States official, and that reported cases of trachoma be deported or detained till cured. This decision of the government to stand firm in its enforcement of the law led to more care being exercised among intending emigrants. Warned by the fate of returned Volga Germans, the German colonists began the practice of going to Saratov and having their eyes examined before taking any steps toward emigrating. If they were at all infected, they gave up their plans and fell back into their place in the colony; if they were pronounced free from the disease, they began selling out and preparing to leave. Few have been turned back either by the ship's physician or by the United States government if they have been passed by the physician at Saratov. But during 1909 there was a marked decrease of Russian German immigration directly traceable to the fear of not being able to pass the immigration authorities because of trachoma.

Since 1902 the annual reports of the Commissioner of Immigration show the various races coming from each country and it is now pos-

---

[55]*Senate Document No. 729,* 60th Congress, 2nd Session, Washington, D.C., February 18, 1909.

sible to know exactly the proportion of immigration from Russia who are Germans.[56]

	TOTAL IMMIGRANTS FROM RUSSIA	GERMANS	RUSSIANS	HEBREWS
June 1901-June 1902	107,347	8,542	1,536	37,846
June 1902-June 1903	136,093	10,485	3,565	47,689
June 1903-June 1904	145,141	7,128	3,907	77,544
June 1904-June 1905	184,897	6,722	3,278	92,388
June 1905-June 1906	215,663	10,279	3,269	(not given)
June 1906-June 1907	258,943	13,480	16,085	114,932
June 1907-June 1908	156,711	10,009	16,324	71,978
June 1908-June 1909	120,460	7,781	9,099	39,150
June 1909-June 1910	186,792	10,016	14,768	59,824
June 1910-June 1911	158,721	8,779	17,581	65,472
June 1911-June 1912	162,395	11,031	21,101	58,389[57]
June 1912-June 1913	291,040	17,857	48,472	74,033

The return movement among the Russian Germans has been an almost negligible quantity until very recently. When the Russian German came, he usually brought his family and cut loose entirely from the old home. Often the head of the family came first and worked and saved until he had amassed a sufficient amount of money to send for his wife and children. Later a home was purchased and they settled down to stay. Sometimes after a short residence here, a young man becomes homesick and against the advice of friends and usually against the protests of his wife, he scrapes together his last cent and goes back. But almost without exception he returns, poorer but wiser. There are also people who save their money with the intention of spending their old age in "the land in which their cradle stood," and they have made a return trip. With one or two thousand dollars they will be considered independent. They can buy out any villager or build the best house in the *Gemeinde*, barring the minister's residence, and probably will rent the village mill, which is the aristocratic industry in most of the colonies. But they are not happy. The changes time had wrought in the old surroundings, and especially the differences between life in Russia and in America, send them back satisfied with their adopted home. Few ever remain in Russia after once living in America.

---

[56]*Annual Reports of Commissioner of Immigration,* 1903-1913.

[57]Compare statistics on German emigration as given by Georg Rath, "Die Russlanddeutschen in den Vereinigten Staaten von Nord-Amerika," *Heimatbuch 1963 der Landsmannschaft der Deutschen aus Russland,* 22-55. — The editors.

Courtesy of the Nebraska State Historical Society, Lincoln, Nebraska.

House of Henry Baum in Frank on the *Bergseite*. He had been in America, worked as a section hand, and returned to his native village as a wealthy man.

Conclusion – Character of Russian German Immigration

The Russian German immigration has been like the Scandinavian and Czech, primarily a movement to the rural communities. This is due to two factors. It began at a period when tremendous efforts were being made to settle vacant lands which rested under suspicion and doubt of their ever being inhabitable. Probably no force except the great railroads which were fighting for their very life would have been able to draw settlers to these "deserts" at this time. The foreigners who came pre-empted certain localities and all later comers have joined their friends in these. All the other nationalities coming during that period have decreased to almost a negligible quantity while the Russian Germans have steadily increased. In spite of the general cityward trend of population even in the western states, the Russian German has remained a rural factor. The census of 1910 shows the following distribution in the states having a number of Russian Germans: Nebraska had 8,172 and South Dakota 27,662 Russian Germans in towns of less than 2,500. In towns with a population of 2,500 to 25,000 inhabitants, Nebraska had 2,264 and South Dakota 721 Russian Germans. The two cities of Lincoln and South Omaha had a combined population of 4,677 Russian Germans. Omaha had a population of 119 Russian Germans.[58]

The opportunity to obtain cheap land in the 70's but half accounts for the rural character of Russian German immigrants. This must be supplemented by the native "land hunger" which is an instinct of the Russian German. It is true he left Russia to avoid certain changes in his relationship to the government which he felt were being forced upon him through a breach of faith, but he would not have gone to any country where he could not have duplicated his manner of living in Russia. His primary desire was land; and land in such available quantities that not only he but all his countrymen, rich and poor, who should come after him, might settle nearby. He had been accustomed to unusual privileges in regard to land ownership in Russia. In the southern provinces, individual ownership such as was accorded only to the nobility was vouchsafed to some of the Germans, while in all the Volga German colonies, the land was the actual possession of the villagers, and although held in common, gave them the feeling that the

[58]It is surprising that Dr. Williams never mentioned North Dakota and its role in the history of the Black Sea Germans. According to Richard Sallet in *Russian-German Settlements in the United States* (translated by LaVern J. Rippley and Armand Bauer), North Dakota had more Germans from Russia than any other state in the union. See chart on pages 110-111 of the Sallet book. — The editors.

Courtesy of Reuben Goertz of Freeman, South Dakota.

Sod house in South Dakota, formerly built and owned by Germans from Russia.

land belonged to them instead of the Russian peasants' idea that they belonged to the land. This land hunger then was not merely the possession of those who had money with which to satisfy their desire, but has extended to the poorest and humblest of the Russian German immigrants down to the present day.

A second characteristic of the Russian German immigration to America is that it began in a pioneer environment. The people settled in America, as they had in Russia, upon the frontier and the first immigrants were subjected to all the hardships of that existence. Many of them were unaccustomed to manual labor, but like other pioneers they were forced to do all kinds of tasks themselves. Young men and women from well-to-do families in Russia worked side by side in the building of their first homes. They introduced into the timberless region in which they settled a kind of home-made brick which was an improvement over the sod houses of the region. This building material was made from a clay secured along the creek banks and mixed to the proper consistency by treading it out with the bare feet, then shaping it into large bricks and letting it dry in the sun after which it was cemented together by a crude mortar. Many of the first homes were made in this way, and even the American and other settlers of the region adopted it for their homes and barns and employed the Russian Germans in its making.

In Dakota and Kansas while waiting for crops to mature, the first settlers earned their living by gathering buffalo bones on the prairies and hauling them to market, sometimes a three-day journey. The young unmarried men, of whom there were very many among the first immigrants, went from place to place hunting work, either upon the railroad, or on the farms. Their ignorance of the language and of the customs of the country sometimes brought them to grief. One of the young men in the first group of Volga Germans was taken up into central Iowa as a farm laborer, where he was the only German in a neighborhood of "bluebelled Yankees." He worked here for three years without a cent of pay; when, on receiving a letter from his father that the family were on their way to Nebraska and that he should meet them there, he was given $25 by his employer who evidently thought he was in this way well rid of him. However the young Russian German returned in a couple of months for his wages, which the Yankee refused to pay, and after another month of fruitless waiting the foreigner left for Nebraska with $5 in his pocket as the result of his first three years of work in America. Had it not been for the fact that he had been liberally supplied with clothing by his family on leaving Russia, he could not have existed.

This abuse of the native honesty of the Russian Germans occurred more than once during the first few years of their life in America, and the wonder is that they were not robbed of more than they were. Absolutely honest in their financial dealings, it was unthinkable to them that every other man in America was not the same. It was not uncommon for a wealthy Russian German to go to a neighbor and buy a large number of cattle or other stock telling the man that he would send for them some days later and count out the cash then and there and pay for them. The neighbor, if he was a kindly man, would warn him against such faith in Americans, while another would use his "Yankee wits" to cheat the confiding foreigner. Sums of money loaned out to Americans were never returned; the contractors who built the first houses for some of them drew them into a lawsuit which was decided in their favor only through the good offices of a friendly attorney. A turn at grain speculation caused further financial loss, and the drought of the 90's brought the wealthier Russian Germans to the verge of bankruptcy. Such financial reverses were the result of mutual misunderstandings between native and foreigner based upon different business ideals and customs, and of actual attempts by unprincipled natives to gain an unfair advantage over the "green" foreigner. The experiences of the first and wealthiest men undoubtedly lie at the bottom of the general opinion among Russian Germans that America is no place to come for those who have money, though it is the poor man's paradise. On the other hand, these experiences shielded later comers from similar hardships. They were sheltered and fed by their bretheren until they could get their families settled in homes of their own, and then provided with work until their crops or a permanent job set them on their feet, while in all their financial dealings they received the advice of their "experienced" countrymen.

Of all the foreign immigrants who came to the Middle West in the 70's, none attracted more attention than the Russian Germans. In the towns where they were housed in immigrant stations until they decided upon a location – as in Yankton, Dakota Territory; Lincoln, Nebraska; and Topeka, Kansas – they were the center of interest. Many nationalities, and many classes and types of native immigrants found shelter in the same places, but none of them received the attention by the newspapers which was bestowed upon the Russian Germans. Lincoln was at that time a town of less than 5,000 inhabitants and a group of 150 to 200 persons coming into its midst at one time was very noticeable. The fact that during the first years the Russian Germans came in large companies was of itself a conspicuous feature. Then their peculiar style of dress attracted attention. The immigrant house had sheltered Germans, Irish, English, Swedes, and Czechs; but

A typical Russian German grandmother whose life was devoted to her family, her home, and to God. Drawing by Phillip B. Legler.

none of their men wore sheepskin coats tanned with the wool worn on the inside, felt boots, and big billed caps, nor did their women wear little black shawls tied beneath the chin. This was the distinctive garb of the majority of Russian Germans who came through Lincoln.

The final thing which attracted attention was the source of emigration. Everyone who came into contact with the people knew they were Germans for no one could converse with them unless he spoke the German language. Yet the fact that they came from Russia was the striking thing for up to 1870 there had been as little movement of population from Russia as there had been commerce from Japan before 1854. The total number of alien passengers from Russia to America from 1820 to 1870 had been only 3,279,[59] many of whom were tourists or officials whose stay was temporary. But in the decade 1870-1880, immigration from Russia increased greatly. It was in this decade that the Germans began coming. Russia, as usual, was considered almost outside the pale of Europe and an emigrant from the Czar's country was a novelty. Hence newspapers and citizens seized upon the name "Russian" with avidity since it represented the unusual and striking. The "Russian" immigrant became a marked man both to land agents who entered into violent competition for his settlement, to townspeople who watched his entrance into their community, to merchants who secured his trade, and to reporters who eagerly wrote up all the details which they could secure through their limited knowledge of his mother tongue. He has ceased to be a novelty now, not because he dresses differently nor because he has stopped coming, for hundreds still enter the community. But the town is ten times its former size, and the Russian German slips in unnoticed with his family and is met by relatives who take him to the settlement where he is swallowed up.

Not all of the Russian Germans have been an equally steady factor in immigration to the United States. The first to be eliminated were the Mennonites who, as we have seen, came in a mass movement between the years 1874 and 1878. Since then only a few families have come at irregular intervals as they have been sent for by relatives.

The Volga German Catholics most of whom came from the *Wiesenseite* also emigrated en masse during the years 1875 to 1879, later comers being a negligible quantity. The reason for the discontinuance of emigrants among them is given by their historian as follows: ". . . military service was disliked but was not regarded as a violence

---

[59]Executive Document No. 1, 1st Session, 42nd Congress, p. XII-XIX.
1820-1830 — 86
1830-1840 — 280
1840-1850 — 520
1850-1860 — 423
1860-1870 — 1970

to conscience, as in the case of the Mennonites. With the lapse of years the colonists on the Volga had come to look upon conscription as a matter of course and letters relating the hardships in the New World had given military service the appearance of a lesser evil."[60]

The Odessa Germans[61] have been a more constant factor in American immigration and in actual numbers probably stand second only to the Volga Germans.[62]

The most steady immigrants of all the Russian Germans were the Volga Protestants. This is primarily due to the fact that economic conditions in that part of Russia have been gradually growing worse and that invaribly those who have come to America have prospered. Hence when any one has felt his lot no longer endurable there, he has appealed to a relative in America who has sent him a ticket to the "poor man's paradise."

Religion has always played a dominant role in the lives of Germans from Russia. It was an outstanding motive in the coming of the Mennonites and was also an incentive in the case of many other Germans. All of these people sought a land of liberty, and no Pilgrim at Plymouth Rock ever showed greater piety and higher moral purpose than did those Russian Germans who first settled on the western prairies.

---

[60]Laing, "German Russian Settlements in Ellis County, Kansas," *Kansas Historical Collections,* XI, 502. However, Catholics from the *Bergseite* continued to come to America until the outbreak of World War I. — The editors.

[61]By "Odessa Germans" Dr. Williams means Black Sea Germans other than Mennonites. They included Lutherans, Catholics, Reformed, Baptists, and independent Pietists and came to America from the whole Black Sea region, from Bessarabia in the west to the Don River in the east, including the Crimea. Dr. Williams was not nearly so well informed about them as she was about the Volga Germans. — The editors.

[62]Sallet, *Russian-German Settlements in the United States,* 112, gives 118,493 Volga Germans of the first and second generation as living in the United States in 1920 and 116,540 Black Sea Germans. — The editors.

BIBLIOGRAPHICAL NOTES

There is much material on the German emigration in the eighteenth century which has been exploited, particularly with reference to the Pennsylvania Germans. An especially valuable contribution is Marion Dexter Learned, *A Guide of the Manuscript Material Relating to American History in the German Archives*, Carnegie Institution of Washington, D.C., 1912.

Chapter II, German Colonization in Russia, is based almost exclusively on material found in the Russian and the German state archives. Access to the former is had through Gregorii Pisarevskii, *Foreign Colonization in Russia in the Eighteenth Century from Unpublished Sources* (in Russian), Moscow, 1909, in which much original material is quoted. A second source is the *Yudin Collection* of 80,000 Russian books in the Library of Congress, Washington, D.C., containing among other things, government reports, codes of laws, and complete sets of annals.[1] Especially valuable for this chapter is *Orders of the Most Illustrious, Most Powerful Great Empress Ekaterina Aleksieevna*—from June 28, 1762, to 1763 (in Russian), St. Petersburg, 1763.

For the German sources, material consisting only of state papers, was found in the following German state archives:

1. Koenigliches Kreisarchiv, Amberg.
2. Koenigliches Kreisarchiv, Bamberg.
3. Koenigliches Geheimes Staatsarchiv, Berlin.
4. Archiv der freien Hansestadt, Bremen.
5. Koenigliches Staatsarchiv, Breslau.
6. Koenigliches Staatsarchiv, Coblenz.
7. Koenigliches Staatsarchiv, Danzig.
8. Grossherzoglich Hessisches Haus- und Staatsarchiv, Darmstadt.
9. Saechsisches Hauptstaatsarchiv, Dresden.
10. Koenigliches Staatsarchiv, Duesseldorf.
11. Stadtarchiv, Frankfurt am Main.
12. Staatsarchiv der freien und Hansestadt, Hamburg.
13. Staatsarchiv Luebeck.
14. Koenigliches Staats-Archiv, Magdeburg.

[1]The *Yudin Collection* no longer exists in the Library of Congress as a separate unit, having mostly been absorbed into the Library's general collection. Cards on the *Yudin Collection* are included in the Cyrillic Union Catalog, which, contains cards for about 625,000 entries for publication in the Cyrillic alphabet in the collections of the Library of Congress and 184 other American libraries. This catalog, presently available in the Slavic Room of the Library of Congress, is divided into author, title, and subject categories. — The editors.

15. Staedtisches Archiv, Mannheim.
16. Koenigliches Staats-Archiv, Muenster.
17. Koenigliches Allgemeines Reichsarchiv, Munich.
18. Koenigliches bayerisch Kreisarchiv fuer Schwaben und Neuburg, Neuburg.
19. Koenigliches bayerisch Kreisarchiv, Nuernberg.
20. Koenigliches Kreisarchiv der Pfalz, Speyer.
21. Koenigliches Wuerttembergische Archivdirection, Stuttgart.
22. Koenigliches Staatsarchiv, Wiesbaden.
23. Koenigliches Kreis-Archiv, Wuerzberg.
24. Herzogliches Haus- und Staats-Archiv, Zerbst.

Until the outbreak of World War I, there was promise of a quantity of new material being brought out by the Volga Germans who were planning to celebrate in 1915 the 150th anniversary of the founding of their colonies. Among the original documents which it was hoped would be published at this time is a two-volume manuscript written in Russian, containing a complete register with personal information concerning the original settlers. This manuscript is owned by J. E. Dietz of Kamyshin, an attorney and a former member of the Duma.

The manners and customs of the Volga Germans are best shown through the *Dakota Freie Presse,*[2] Aberdeen, South Dakota, 1874-1915, in which letters of a more or less personal nature are published from Volga Germans all over the world. Many valuable historical abstracts have been reprinted in this paper of late, although care must be taken to avoid errors due to careless printing. The *Volkszeitung,* Saratov, 1909-1914, also reflects the social and educational problems. Cf. also August Lonsinger, *Nor net lopper g'gewa! Eine Erzaehlung aus den deutschen Wolga Kolonien,* Saratov, 1911.

The history of the Volga Germans has been gleaned from the following sources:

Allgemeine deutsche Biographie, XXV. Leipzig: Duncker and Humblot, 1875-1912.

Annual Register of World Events; a review of the history, politics, and literature, for the year 1758 to the present, V-XXIII. London: Longmans, Green, & Co., 1758-1780.

Annual Report of the Commissioner General of Immigration to the Secretary of

[2]*Dakota Freie Presse,* a weekly newspaper. Place of publication: Yankton, South Dakota, 1874-1909; Aberdeen, South Dakota, 1909-. The paper was published in Aberdeen until 1920. It was moved to New Ulm, Minnesota, 1920-1932. From 1932 until it ceased publication on February 24, 1954, it was printed in Winona, Minnesota, but the editorial duties were performed in Bismarck, North Dakota, from 1932-1948, and in Kulm, North Dakota, from 1948-1954. — The editors.

Labor and Commerce (for fiscal years ending June 30, 1903, through June 30, 1913.) Washington, D.C.: Government Printing Office.

Barker, J. Ellis. *Modern Germany; her political and economic problems, her foreign and domestic policy, her ambitions, and the causes of her success.* 3d ed. London: Smith, Elder, & Co., 1909.

Bauer, Gottlieb, ed. *Geschichte der deutschen Ansiedler an der Wolga seit ihrer Einwanderung nach Russland bis zur Einfuehrung der allgemeinen Wehrpflicht (1766-1874).* 2d. ed. Saratov: Buchdruckerei "Energie," 1908.

Biedermann, Karl. *Deutschland im achtzehnten Jahrhundert.* 4 vols. Leipzig: J. J. Weber, 1854-1880.

Bittinger, Lucy Forney. *The Germans in Colonial Times.* Philadelphia and London: J. B. Lippincott Co., 1901.

Bosse, Georg von. *Das deutsche Element in den Vereinigten Staaten unter besonderer beruecksichtigung seines politischen, ethischen, sozialen, und erzieherischen Einflusses.* Stuttgart: Chr. Belsersche Verlagsbuchhandlung, 1908.

Bryce, James. *The Holy Roman Empire.* Rev. ed. New York: The Macmillan Co., 1886.

______ *Transcaucasia and Ararat: being notes of a vacation tour in the autumn of 1876.* 4th ed. New York: The Macmillan Co., 1896.

Busch, E. H., ed. *Ergaenzungen der Materialen zur Geschichte und Statistik des Kirchen- und Schulwesens der Ev. Luth. Gemeinden in Russland.* 2 vols. St. Petersburg: Commissionsverlag von G. Hassel, 1862 and 1867.

Chantreau, Pierre Nicolas. *Russland aus philosophischem, historisch-statistischem und literarischem Gesichtspunct betrachtet auf einer Reise durch dies Land in 1788 und 1789.* Aus dem Fronzoesischen (uebersetzt von M.C.S. Mylius). Berlin, 1794-95.

Child, Albert Lyman, compiler. *Centennial History of Plattsmouth City and Cass County, Nebraska.* Omaha: Herald Book and Job Printing House, 1877.

Cobb, Sanford Hoadley. *The Story of the Palatines. An Episode in Colonial History.* New York and London: G. P. Putnam's sons, 1897.

Code of Laws (in Russian), 1876 ed. Vol. IX.

Congressional Record. 42nd Congress, 1st Session, Executive Document No. 1. Washington, D.C.: Government Printing Office, 1871-1873.

______ 43rd Congress, 1st Session, II. Washington, D.C.: Government Printing Office, 1873-1875.

Cronau, Rudolf. *Drei Jahrhunderte deutschen Lebens in Amerika; Ruhmesblaetter der Deutschen in den Vereinigten Staaten.* 2d ed., Rev. Berlin: D. Reimer (Ernst Vohsen) A-G, 1924.

Note: Mrs. Haynes, who tried to check all references, was forced to use the later edition of this book. Dr. Williams used the 1909 edition.

Dalton, Herman. *Geschichte der Reformierten Kirche in Russland.* Gotha: R. Besser, 1865.

______ *Lutherische Kirche in Russland.* 2 vols. Gotha: R. Besser, 1887-1889.

Die Evangelisch-Lutherischen Gemeinden in Russland. Eine historisch-statistische Darstellung. Ed. by Zentral Komitee der Unterstuetzungen-Kasse fuer Evangelisch-Lutherischen Gemeinden in Russland. St. Petersburg, 1909.

Eckardt, Julius Wilhelm Albert von. *Russia before and after the War.* Translated from the German (with later additions by the author) by Edward Fairfax Taylor. 2d ed. London: Longmans, Green, & Co., 1880.

______ *Modern Russia: Comprising Russia under Alexander II, Russian Communism. The Greek Orthodox Church and its Sects. The Baltic Provinces of Russia.* London: Smith, Elder, & Co., 1870.

Eddis, William. "The Wretchedness of White Servants," *American History told by Contemporaries,* II, pp. 308-370. Hart, Albert Bushnell, ed. New York and London: The Macmillan Co., 1899.

Erbes, Johannes and Sinner, Peter, eds. *Volkslieder und Kinderreime aus den Wolgakolonien.* Saratov: Verlag "Energie," 1914.

Erdmann, Johann Friedrich. *Reisen in innern Russlands.* Leipzig: Kummer, 1825.

______ *Beitraege zur Kenntniss des Innern von Russland.* Leipzig: Kummer, 1825.

Erdmannsdoerffer, Bernhard. *Deutsche Geschichte von westpfaelischen Frieden bis zum Regierungsantritt Friedrichs des Grossen, 1648-1740.* Berlin: G. Grote, 1892-1893.

Fast, G. U. "Erlebnisse auf Reisen nach Zentral-Asien und Amerika," *Des Evangelische Magazine,* XLII.

Fast, Martin B. *Reisebericht und Kurze Geschichte der Mennoniten.* Scottdale, Pennsylvania: Herald Press, 1909.

Faust, Albert Bernhardt. *The German Element in the United States, with special reference to its political, moral, social and educational influence.* 2 vols. Boston and New York: The Steuben Society of America, 1927.

Note: Mrs. Haynes was forced to use this edition. The 1909 edition was used by Dr. Williams.

Fisher, Sydney George. *The Making of Pennsylvania; an analysis of the elements of the population and the formative influences that created one of the greatest of the American states.* Philadelphia: J. B. Lippincott Co., 1896.

Friesen, P. M. *Die Alt-Evangelische Mennonitische Bruederschaft in Russland (1789-1910).* Halbstadt, Taurien, Verlag Raduga, 1911.

Geiser, Karl Frederick. *Redemptioners and Indentured Servants Colony and Commonwealth of Pennsylvania.* New Haven: The Tuttle, Morehouse & Taylor Co., 1901.

Gentleman's Magazine and Historical Chronicle, XXXII-L. London, 1762-1780.

Goebel, Friedmann. *Reise in die Steppen des suedlichen Russlands.* 2 vols. Dorpat: C. A. Kluge, 1838.

Gordon, Thomas Francis. *The History of Pennsylvania, from its discovery by Europeans to the Declaration of Independence in 1776.* Philadelphia: Carey, Lea & Carey, 1829.

Grand-Ducal Hessian House and State Archives. *Acten des Geheimen Staats-Archivs,* XI, Abtheilung, Convolut I. Darmstadt.

Greene, F. Vinton. *Sketches of Army Life in Russia.* New York: C. Scribner's sons, 1880.

Guenther, P. H., ed. *Friedensboten-Kalender.* Talowka, (Beideck) Russia: Eben-Ezer, 1873-1915.

Haeberle, Daniel. *Auswanderung und Koloniegruendungen der Pfaelzer im 18. Jahrhundert.* Kaiserslautern: H. Kayser, 1909.

Haeusser, Ludwig. *Geschichte der rheinischen Pfalz nach ihren politischen, kirchlichen und literarischen Verhaeltnissen,* 2 vols. Heidelberg, 1856.

Hart, Albert Bushnell, ed. *American History told by Contemporaries,* II. New York and London: The Macmillan Co., 1899.

Haxthausen, August von. *The Russian Empire, its people, institutions and resources.* 2 vols. Translated by Robert Farie, Esq. London: Chapman and Hall, 1856.
______ *Studien ueber die innern Zustaende, das Volksleben und insbesondere die laendlichen, Einrichtungen Russlands.* 3 vols. Berlin: B. Behr, 1847-1853.
______ *Die laendliche Verfassung Russlands.* Leipzig: F. A. Brockhaus, 1866.
Henderson, Ernest Flagg. *A Short History of Germany.* 2 vols. New York and London: The Macmillan & Co., Ltd., 1902.
Herrmann, Ernst. *Geschichte des russischen Staates.* Gotha: F. A. Perthes, 1860.
Heuser, Emil. *Pennsylvanien im 17. Jahrhundert und die ausgewanderten Pfaelzer in England.* Neustadt a. d. Hardt: Witter, 1910.
Hodgetts, E. Arthur Brayley. *The Court of Russia in the Nineteenth Century.* 2 vols. London: C. Scribner's sons, 1908.
Holzhausen, Paul. *Die Deutschen in Russland, 1812. Leben und Leiden auf der Moskauer Heerfahrt.* Berlin: Morawe & Scheffelt Verlag, 1912.
Howard, George. *A History of Matrimonial Institutions.* Chicago: The University of Chicago Press (Callaghan and Co.), 1904.
Imperial Academy of Sciences, eds. *Complete Collection of Learned Travels in Russia,* VI, 1824. An article by Johan Peter Falck can be found on pages 112-114 (in Russian).
Jacobs, Henry Eyster. *A History of the Evangelical Lutheran Church in the United States.* 3d ed. New York: C. Scribner's sons, 1900.
Jansen, Cornelius. *Sammlung von Notizen ueber Amerika.* Danzig, 1872.
Klaus, Aleksandr Augustovich. *Unsere Kolonien. Studien und Materialen zur Geschichte und Statistik der auslaendischen Kolonisation in Russland.* Aus dem Russischen uebersetzt von J. Toews. Odessa: Verlag der "Odessaer Zeitung," 1887.
Kletke, Hermann, ed. *Alexander von Humboldt's Reisen im europaeischen und asiatischen Russland.* Zweite Auflage. Berlin: Hasselberg, 1856.
Kohl, Johann Georg. *Russia.* New ed. London: Chapman and Hall, 1848.
Laing, Rev. Francis S. "German-Russian Settlements in Ellis County, Kansas," *Kansas Historical Collections,* Vol. XI, pp. 489-528. Topeka, Kansas, 1909-1910.
Learned, Marion Dexter, ed. *German American Annals,* XII. Philadelphia: German American Historical Society, 1910.
Lepekhin, Ivan Ivanovich. *Tagebuch der Reise durch verschiedene Provinzen des russischen Reiches in den Jahren 1768 und 1769.* 2 parts. Translated from the Russian by M. C. H. Hase. Altenburg: Richter, 1774.
LeRoy-Beaulieu, Anatole. *The Empire of the Tsars and the Russians.* 3 vols. Translated by Zénaide Ragozin. New York: G. P. Putnam's sons, 1893-1896.
Macaulay, Thomas Babington. *Life of Frederick the Great.* New York: J. B. Alden, 1885.
Matthaei, Friedrich. *Die deutschen Ansiedlungen in Russland. Ihre Geschichte und ihre volkswirtschaftliche Bedeutung fuer die Vergangenheit und Zukunft.* Leipzig: H. Fries, 1866.
Mavor, James. *An Economic History of Russia.* 2 vols. London and Toronto: J. M. Dent & sons, Ltd., 1914.
McCulloch, J. *Childhood of Fiction, a study of folk tales and primitive thought.* London, 1905.
Meakin, Annette M. *Russia, Travels and Studies.* Philadelphia and London: J. B. Lippincott Co., 1906.

Milyoukov, Paul Nicolas. *Russia and its Crisis*. Chicago and London: The University of Chicago Press, 1905.

______ *Essais sur l'Histoire de la Civilization Russe*. Translated from the Russian by P. Dramas and D. Soskice. Paris: V. Giard and E. Brière, 1901.

Morton, Julius Sterling, ed. "The Pioneer Railway of Nebraska," *Illustrated History of Nebraska*. Vol. II. Lincoln: Western Publishing and Engraving Co., 1918.

Muench, A. H. *Historical and Geographical Encyclopediae of Saratov* (in Russian). 2 vols. Saratov, 1898-1901.

Nebraska State Journal, from May 17 through November 29, 1874. Lincoln, 1874.

Pallas, Peter Simon. *Bemerkungen aus einer Reise durch die suedlichen Statthalterschaften des Russischen Reichs in den Jahren 1793 und 1794*. Leipzig: G. Martini, 1799-1801.

______ *Travels through the Southern Provinces of the Russian Empire in the years 1793 and 1794*. London: T. N. Longman & O. Rees, 1802-1803.

______ *Reise durch verschiedene Provinzen des russischen Reichs*. 3 vols. St. Petersburg: Gedruckt bey der Kayserlichen Academie der Wissenschaften, 1771-1776.

Pennypacker, Samuel Whitaker. "The Settlement of Germantown, Pennsylvania, and the beginning of German Immigration to North America." Pennsylvania German Society. *Proceedings and Addresses*, IX, pp. 1-300. Lancaster, Penn.: Published by the Society, 1899.

Pfeiffer, Georg. "Die Pfalz in Suedrussland." *Der Pfaelzerwald*. 14 Jahrgang, No. 1. Speyer, 1913.

Pinkerton, Robert. *Russia: or, Miscellaneous Observations on the Past and Present State of that Country and its Inhabitants*. London: Seeley & Sons, 1833.

Pisarevskii, Gregorii. *Foreign Colonization in Russia in the Eighteenth Century from unpublished sources* (in Russian). Moscow, 1909.

______ *Interior Organization of the German Volga Colonies in the time of Catherine II*. Warsaw, 1914.

Pleshcheev, Sergeiei Ivanovich. *Survey of the Russian Empire, according to its present newly regulated state, divided into different governments*. Translated from the Russian, with considerable additions, by James Smirnov. 3d ed. Dublin: J. Moore, 1792.

Rambaud, Alfred. *The History of Russia from the Earliest Times*. Translated by Leonora B. Lang. 2 vols. Standard ed. New York: A. L. Burt & Co., 1904.

Reidenbach, J. A. *Amerika. Eine Kurze Beschreibung der Vereinigten Staaten sowie ein Rathgeber fuer Auswanderer.*

Report of the Chief of the Bureau of Statistics, 1875-1878, Vol. X. Treasury Department, Washington, D.C.

Richard, Ernst. *History of German Civilization; a general survey*. New York: The Macmillan Co., 1911.

Richardson, James D., ed. *A Compilation of the Messages and Papers of the Presidents 1789-1897*. Vol. VII. Washington, D.C.: Government Printing Office, 1898.

Rupp, I. Daniel. *A Collection of Thirty Thousand Names of German, Swiss, Dutch, French, Portuguese and other Immigrants in Pennsylvania, chronologically arranged from 1727 to 1776*. Harrisburg: Wingert & Co., 1856.

Russia. "Historical Survey of Fifty Years' Activity of the Ministry of Imperial Domains" (in Russian). Ministry of Imperial Domains. *Journal*, XIX, Part II. St. Petersburg, 1887.

______ "Tobacco Industry Among the Foreign Settlers of the Governments of Samara and Saratow" (in Russian). Ministry of Imperial Domains. *Journal,* XIX, Part II. St. Petersburg, 1887.

Sachse, Julius Friedrich. "Daniel Falckner's Curieuse Nachricht von Pennsylvanien." Pennsylvania German Society. *Proceedings and Addresses,* XIV, pp. 17-256. Lancaster, Penn.: Published by the Society, 1904.

Sanger, George P., ed. *Statutes at Large, Treaties, and Proclamations of the United States of America from December 1863, to December 1865.* Boston: Little, Brown & Co., 1866.

Saratov Historical Sketches, Recollections and Materials, I. Saratov: Saratov Society for the Benefit of Needy Writers, 1893.

Schloezer, August Ludwig von. *Neuveraendertes Russland, oder das Leben Catharina der Zweyten, Kayserinn von Russland.* 2 vols. Riga and Leipzig: J. F. Hartknoch, 1767.

Schmidt, C. B. "Reminiscences of Foreign Immigration Work for Kansas," *Kansas State Historical Collection,* Vol. IX, p. 124. Topeka, Kansas.

Schoberl, Frederic, ed. *Russia, being a description of the character, manners, customs, dress, diversions and other peculiarities of the different nationalities inhabiting the Russian Empire.* 4 vols. London: H. Colburn, 1842-1843.

Storch, Heinrich F. von. *Historisch-statistisches Gemaelde des russischen Reichs am Ende des 18. Jahrhunderts und unter der Regierung Katharina der Zweyten.* 7 vols. Riga and Leipzig: J. F. Hartknoch, 1797-1803.

Stricker, Wilhelm. *Deutsch- russische Wechselwirkungen oder die Deutschen in Russland und die Russen in Deutschland.* Leipzig, 1849.

Tissot, Victor. *Russes et Allemands.* New ed. Paris, 1884.

Tooke, William. *The Life of Catharine II, Empress of Russia.* 4th ed., with great additions, and a copious index. London: A. Strahan for T. N. Longman and O. Rees, 1800.

Velitzyn, A. A. "Foreign Colonies in Russia" (in Russian). *The Russian Messenger,* CC, Parts 1, 2, 3, and 6. St. Petersburg, 1889-1890.

Volksfreund - Kalender der deutschen Wolgakolonien. Saratov, 1911.

Volkszeitung. Saratov, 1909-1914.

Voltaire, Francois M. "Correspondence between the Empress of Russia and Monsieu Voltaire," *Complete Works,* LVIII. Paris, 1821.

Waeschke, Dr. H. "Deutsche Familien in Russland." *Jubilaeumsschrift des Roland,* Vol. 1, pp. 68-104. Dresden, 1912.

Waliszewski, Kasimierz. *The Romance of an Empress, Catherine II of Russia.* Translated from the French. New York: D. Appleton & Co., 1894.

______ *The Story of a Throne (Catherine II of Russia).* Translated from the French. London: W. Heinemann, 1895.

Wallace, D. Mackenzie. *Russia.* New York: H. Holt and Company, 1877.

Washington, George. "Desire of Importing Palatines." *American History told by Contemporaries,* II, pp. 310-311. Hart, Albert Bushnell, ed. New York and London: The Macmillan Co., 1899.

Wilder, Daniel W. *The Annals of Kansas.* Topeka, Kansas: G. W. Martin, 1875.

Zuege, Christian Gottlob. *Der russische Colonist, oder Christian Gottlob Zueges Leben in Russland,* Vol. I. Zeit und Naumburg, 1802.

BOOKS AND ARTICLES CITED IN FOOTNOTES BY EDITORS

Avrich, Paul. *Russian Rebels 1600 to 1800.* New York: Schocken Books, 1972.

Belk, Fred R. *The Great Trek of the Russian Mennonites to Central Asia, 1880-1884.* Unpublished Doctoral Dissertation. Stillwater: Oklahoma State University, May 1973.

Beratz, Gottlieb. *Die deutschen Kolonien an der unteren Wolga in ihrer Entstehung und ersten Entwickelung.* Saratov: H. Schellhorn u. Co., 1915.

Bonwetsch, Gerhard. *Geschichte der deutschen Kolonien an der Wolga.* Stuttgart: Verlag von J. Engelhorns Nachf., 1919.

Giesinger, Adam. *From Catherine to Khrushchev: The Story of Russia's Germans.* Battleford, Sask.: Marian Press, 1974.

Griess, James Ruben. *The German-Russians. Those who came to Sutton.* Hastings, Nebraska, 1968.

Haynes, Emma Schwabenland. "Germans from Russia in American History and Literature," *American Historical Society of Germans from Russia, Work Paper No. 15,* September 1974, pp. 4-20, Lincoln, 1974.

Height, Joseph S. *Paradise on the Steppe.* Tuebingen, Germany: Christian Gulde, 1972.

Hiebert, Clarence, ed. *Brothers in Deed to Brothers in Need.* Newton, Kansas: Faith and Life Press, 1974.

Hostetler, John A. *Hutterite Society.* Baltimore: The John Hopkins University Press, 1974.

Rath, Georg. "Die Russlanddeutschen in den Vereinigten Staaten von Nord-Amerika," *Heimatbuch 1963,* pp. 22-55. Stuttgart: Landsmannschaft der Deutschen aus Russland, 1963.

Reimer, Gustav E. and Gaeddert, G. R. *Exiled by the Czar.* Newton, Kansas: Mennonite Publications Office, 1956.

Rempel, David G. "C. B. Schmidt, Historian: Facts and Fiction," *Mennonite Life.* Centennial Double Issue. Mid-year 1974. Vol. 29, Nos. 1 and 2, pp. 33-37. Newton, Kansas: Herald Publishing Co., 1974.

——— "From Danzig to Russia. The First Mennonite Migration," *Mennonite Life.* Vol. 24, No. 1, pp. 8-29. North Newton, Kansas: Bethel College, January 1969.

Sallet, Richard. *Russian-German Settlements in the United States.* Translated from the German by Lavern J. Rippley and Armand Bauer. Fargo: North Dakota Institute for Regional Studies, 1974.

Schmidt, David. *Studien ueber die Geschichte der Wolgadeutschen.* Pokrowsk-Moskau-Charkow: Zentral-Voelkerverlag, Abteilung (modern spelling of Abtheilung) in Pokrowsk, ASSR der Wolgadeutschen, 1930.

Sinner, Peter. *Der Deutsche im Wolgalande.* Berlin-Leipzig, 1927.

Smith, C. Henry. *The Story of the Mennonites.* 4th ed. Newton, Kansas: Mennonite Publications Office, 1957.

Stumpp, Karl. *The German-Russians. Two Centuries of Pioneering.* Translated from the German by Joseph S. Height. Edition Atlantic Forum. Bonn-Brussels-New York, 1967.

Wagner, Ernst. *Auswanderung aus Hessen.* Jahrbuch fuer das evangelische Auslandsdeutschtum. Bensheim, Germany, 1938.

Wenzlaff, Theodore C. "The Russian Germans Come to the United States," *Nebraska History,* Vol. 49, No. 4, Winter 1968, pp. 379-399.

Urbach, William F. *Our Parents were Russian-Germans.* Hamden, Conn., mimeographed bound volume published by the author, June, 1963.

INDEX[1]

[1]The index includes footnotes indicated by the use of "n". — The editors.